Fixing Men

Fixing Men

SEX, BIRTH CONTROL,
AND AIDS IN MEXICO

Matthew Gutmann

UNIVERSITY OF CALIFORNIA PRESS
Berkeley   Los Angeles   London

University of California Press, one of the most distinguished university presses in the United States, enriches lives around the world by advancing scholarship in the humanities, social sciences, and natural sciences. Its activities are supported by the UC Press Foundation and by philanthropic contributions from individuals and institutions. For more information, visit www.ucpress.edu.

Unless otherwise noted, all photographs are by the author.

Parts of chapter 6 originally appeared in different form as "Scoring Men: Vasectomies and the Totemic Illusion of Male Sexuality in Oaxaca," *Culture, Medicine, and Psychiatry* 29(1): 79–101 (2005), and are reprinted here with kind permission of Springer Science and Business Media.

University of California Press
Berkeley and Los Angeles, California

University of California Press, Ltd.
London, England

Library of Congress Cataloging-in-Publication Data
Gutmann, Matthew.
 Fixing men : sex, birth control, and AIDS in Mexico / Matthew Gutmann.
   p. cm.
 Includes bibliographical references and index.
 ISBN 978-0-520-25262-2 (cloth : alk. paper)
 ISBN 978-0-520-25330-8 (pbk. : alk. paper)
  1. Men—Sexual behavior—Mexico. 2. Men—Mexico—Attitudes.
 3. Sex—Mexico—Public opinion. 4. Mexico—Public opinion. I. Title.
 HQ28.G88 2007
 306.7081'0972—dc22   2006039800

Manufactured in the United States of America
16 15 14 13 12 11 10 09 08 07
10 9 8 7 6 5 4 3 2 1
This book is printed on New Leaf EcoBook 50, a 100% recycled fiber of which 50% is de-inked post-consumer waste, processed chlorine-free. EcoBook 50 is acid-free and meets the minimum requirements of ANSI/ASTM D5634-01 *(Permanence of Paper).* ⊛

To Liliana and Maya,
and to Cathy

Contents

Illustrations

FIGURES

Acknowledgments

My thanks to all the men of Oaxaca who told me about their experiences with sterilization, AIDS, and sexuality, their feelings and fears and fantasies. My gratitude as well to the women in their lives, who made evident time and again how central they are to so many men in the major decisions of their sexual lives. This book would have been impossible were it not for the generosity as well of medical personnel in clinics and hospitals in Oaxaca, who allowed me to sit in their waiting rooms, corridors, and theaters of operations and who shared with me their thoughts and described practices in patient detail.

Several friends and colleagues in Oaxaca provided help in logistics, orientation, and comfort. I would like to single out especially Alejandro de Ávila, who for most of my years in Oaxaca was the director of the Ethnobotanical Garden there; were it not for Alex I would never have become a *zorra jardinólogo*. As with other *hombres marginados* in Oaxaca, I could always count on my compadre Michael Higgins for his wise counsel. Gudrun Dohrmann, my oldest friend in Oaxaca, was caring and helpful in all respects. Paola Sesia, Margarita Dalton, and Nacho Bernal in particular have been confidantes and critics extraordinaires over the years.

In Mexico, thanks also to Raúl Alavez, Julia Barco, Blanca Castañón, Doña Hermila García, Paco González, *mi tocaya de alma* Estela Guzmán *y mi hermano de alma* Pedro Lewin, Alberto Martínez, Sergio Navarrete, Tere Pardo, Leonardo Pino, Nemecio Rodríguez, Esteban Schmidt, Tere Sosa, my dear friend Lynn Stephen, Lucero Topete, Toni Vizcaino and other colleagues at CEMyF, and Lulu from Docuprint. Thanks to our wonderful *vecinos* in Fraccionamiento Casa del Sol for *tequios* and neighborliness, Melania Aquino and Murad Musalem for our summer rituals with Etiqueta Negra, Beto Sánchez and Araceli Jiménez for good *mezcal* and so much more, and Eduardo "7 Pisos" Torres for a monster machete. Thanks as well to Modesta, Nacho, Manuel and Ester, and Miguel. Elsewhere in Mexico, Ana Amuchástegui, Roger Bartra, Mario Bronfman, Federico Besserer, Teresita de Barbieri, Benno de Keijzer, Orlandina de Oliveira, Juan Guillermo Figueroa, Mary Goldsmith, Soledad González, Susana Lerner, Ana Luisa Liguori, Alfonso López Juárez, Nelson Minello, Mirka Negroni, and Ivonne Szasz were most helpful with suggestions and good discussions.

I was fortunate enough to count on institutional affiliation during my year in Oaxaca, 2001–02, with Centro de Investigaciones y Estudios Superiores en Antropología Social—Pacífico Sur, the Instituto Nacional de Antropología e Historia—Oaxaca, and the Welte Institute. I am delighted I have been able to renew my affiliation with CIESAS since that date as well.

My gratitude to the incomparable Elia Aguilar—without her careful transcriptions and thoughtful commentary (including periodic injunctions not to interrupt quite so often in my interviews), this study and my previous ethnographies could never have been written.

Thanks to Michelle McKenzie, with whom I shared life for sixteen years, including in Oaxaca during our year there, and with whom I still share the immense pleasure of parenting. So many facets of my understanding of masculinity, sexuality, and vasectomy I owe to her; I also learned much about AIDS through her own brave work in Providence. My gratitude always.

I have learned over the years from fertile dialogues and/or received bibliographic suggestions about masculinity, sexuality, and reproduction from those living outside Mexico, including Katherine Bliss, Philippe Bourgois, Stanley Brandes, Carole Browner, Manny Campbell, Fernando Enrique Cardoso, Héctor Carrillo, Sylvia Chant, Raewyn Connell, Norma Fuller, Gloria González López, Cori Hayden, Judith Helzner, Gil Herdt, Michael Higgins, Michael Kimmel, Roger Lancaster, Ondina Fachel Leal, José Olavarría, Richard Parker, Teresa Valdés, Mara Viveros, and Vanessa Woog. Thanks to all. Robin Tittle kindly tracked down some material for this and other projects. Family and friends were crucial in giving life focus and meaning.

At Brown, this study has benefited from discussions on specific and related topics especially with Cathy Lutz, Dan Smith, David Kertzer, Nick Townsend, Pat Symonds, Kay Warren, Jim Green, Sal Zierler, Rich Snyder, and Jody Rich. Thanks as well to Kathy Grimaldi and Matilde Andrade at Brown.

A University Professor Fellowship from the National Endowment for the Humanities, a sabbatical leave from Brown University, and summer research grants from the Population Studies and Training Center and the Center for Latin American Studies at Brown made fieldwork financially possible.

Never have I felt as blessed by the generosity of colleagues as I was in the comments on the manuscript of this book. Richard Parker and Carole Browner were the formal reviewers for the University of California Press, and they are indeed each responsible for many improvements in the argument and presentation of the book. At the Press, thanks once again to Naomi Schneider for her insight and enthusiasm, as well as to Laura Harger. Several other colleagues read through earlier drafts: Marcia Inhorn, Raewyn Connell, Stanley Brandes, and Michael Higgins. I am beholden to all these friends and colleagues for their indispensable and incisive comments; as recipient of their gift of critique, in the finest anthropological sense I know my debt is enormous.

This book is dedicated to my children, Liliana and Maya, who throughout our first year in Oaxaca and then on our summer sojourns back to "our other home" have shown me the meaning of delight. Then, in the last two years, you have inspired me in more ways than I imagined possible, with your radiance and wit and most of all with the kindness of spirit you have each in different ways embodied as we embarked on new journeys together.

This book is also dedicated to Catherine Lutz, for life itself, as in her infinite goodness she has rejuvenated and redefined life and love for me. The research for this book began before we knew each other, and it was completed as we began life together. Cathy, your own ethnographies and your impatience provided the motivation to finish this chapter of my professional life, knowing that the next book will bear both our names.

Providence, May 2007

ONE Taming Men's Natural Desires in Oaxaca

At the bedrock of our [Western] culture's thinking about
sexuality is the assumption that a given pattern of sexuality is
native to the human constitution.

R. W. Connell and G. W. Dowsett (1992:50)

"Well, you know, they did it to *me* a few years ago. . . ." That is how I
began my interviews with men who wanted vasectomies in Oaxaca, conducted during their operations. It seemed to break the ice and get the
men talking. They told me why they decided to get sterilized, about discussions they had had with their wives before the procedure, and, invariably, about anxieties as to what would happen with their postoperative sexual desire and performance. Sometimes a man would get jumpy
and I would excuse myself. The last thing the poor guy needed was to be
interviewed, I assumed. But the doctors and the men themselves would
insist, "No, stick around!" I became the anthropologist-as-emotional-
anesthesiologist.

Vasectomies were not common in the mountainous provincial capital
of Oaxaca, in southern Mexico. But I was not looking for common men—

whatever that term might mean. I wanted to know why men who got sterilized decided to do so. The answer turned out to be deceptively straightforward. For many, if not all, of the men I spoke with in Oaxaca, the most common explanation for getting vasectomies was that their wives had already suffered enough—taking birth control for years, getting pregnant, giving birth—and now it was their turn. When I asked these same men why they had long relied on their wives to use contraceptives in the past, and why they had not used a male form of birth control, the men responded with a simple incredulous question: "Like what? The condom?" In Oaxaca, as elsewhere in the world, most artificial, modern forms of contraception—and all the most reliable ones—are for women. The men asked me if I thought they had much of a choice about what form of birth control to use. I responded honestly that the choices available to the men of Oaxaca were part of a larger picture that involved, among others, the international pharmaceutical industry that develops and manufactures birth control devices and medications. Unless a modern contraceptive is made and marketed by these companies, it will not be available in Oaxaca or anywhere else in the contemporary world.

International pharmaceuticals were also involved in the lives of other men I spent time with in Oaxaca, those who traveled to the United States as migrant workers, became infected with HIV while living there in new labyrinths of solitude, and returned home, whereupon they infected wives and girlfriends. When I lived in Oaxaca on and off in the period 2001–05, fewer than two hundred men and women received the life-saving antiretrovirals manufactured by the multinational drug companies and sold to the state-run clinic in Oaxaca. Unlike some countries in the world, in Mexico the government health sector paid the pharmaceutical companies top prices for AIDS medications. As a result, thousands of men and women in Oaxaca who were HIV+ or had AIDS were inevitably going to face premature deaths, many without ever knowing what disease was killing them. I spent time with these dying patients, and I attended the Wednesday-morning meetings with the medical personnel where decisions were made about exactly which men and women would be given the drugs and who was doomed to an early demise.

In Oaxaca, doctors said the migrant men had become infected with

HIV after having sex with other men in the United States. When I asked one doctor how he knew this and why he was so sure, he told me, "That's what Mexican men do: they have sex with other men." When I asked him if he had sex with men, he looked startled. When I asked if his father or brother or son or uncle or neighbor had sex with other men, he began to get annoyed. It turned out that a lot of what passed for knowledge in this realm was based on common sense and cultural folk wisdom. The notion of "men's natural sexual desires" was blamed for a host of health problems like AIDS in Oaxaca. And if these generalizations were not necessarily accurate for all men—"That's just the way men are!"—then at least they were true for men who grew up in Mexico. Mexican culture and Mexican male culture were considered the culprits in many a Mexican medical schema.

Surprisingly to me, the medical people who seemed least taken with dichotomous views of men's sexuality and women's sexuality as entirely and naturally distinct were the men and women who called themselves traditional indigenous midwives and healers. From these *médicos tradicionales* I also heard of techniques that women can employ to keep their men from straying, and I learned why men go on sexual diets after their wives give birth. In distant rural communities along the coast and in the mountains of the state I often discovered a far more expansive and self-conscious understanding of what culture means for the diagnosis and healing of illness than I heard in the various biomedical clinics in Oaxaca City where I spent time.

My arrival in Oaxaca coincided with efforts launched from Mexico City—and the implementation of an earlier 1993 report by the World Bank—ordering that health care throughout the country be further privatized and decentralized. These stringent measures further exacerbated an already inadequate situation in providing care to those most in need, which in Oaxaca nearly always means the nearly two million indigenous people, most of whom live in poverty and some in extreme poverty. The conditions of poverty and miserable health care are the same as those that propel so many people to try their luck as migrant workers in the United States. Seen in this context of scarcity and suffering, issues of impotence, infertility, and infidelity among men might seem inconsequential. I can only affirm that none of the men and women with whom I spent time in Oaxaca from 2001 to 2005 belittled my questions about sex, birth control, and AIDS.

MEN AND WOMEN TAKING POLITICS PERSONALLY

Many studies on reproduction to date have focused on women. This book provides the stories of certain "missing" players in most accounts of the reproductive process. Nonetheless, rather than compound the error of viewing the essential (though certainly not universal) human activity of procreation as a matter of *either* women *or* men, this study examines negotiations between women and men with respect to men's reproductive health and sexuality, as part of a larger effort to address questions of gender differences and inequalities in line with expanding notions of gender and sexuality.

Important steps have been made since the early 1970s in understanding women and gender inequality in a diverse range of cultural situations. There are still few parallel studies of men. For example, we do not yet have a clear understanding of how men in different cultural contexts utilize formal and informal health services, including with respect to contraception, AIDS care, and other matters of reproductive health. My purpose here is not to replace studies of women with those of men or even to suggest that studies of men should be seen principally as a complement to studies of women. Instead, in *Fixing Men,* I argue that studies of men's reproductive health and sexuality must be developed as central to understanding gender relations overall. This is because men, too, are engendered and engendering beings.

When I use the term *gender*, I refer not just to women but also to men, and to the ways in which differences and similarities related to all human physical sexuality are understood, contested, organized, and practiced by societies. With Susan Bordo, in studying men as engendered and engendering, I am especially interested in "the 'direct grip' (as opposed to representational influence) that culture has on our bodies, through the practices and bodily habits of everyday life" (1993:16), including here in relation to birth control and sexually transmitted infections (STIs). How is culture inscribed on male bodies through beliefs and practices associated with their sexuality? And more pointedly for the present study, how do women as themselves gendered and engendered beings affect men's sexualities?[1]

Unless we understand the subtle cajoling, the vehement rage, and the abject frustrations of daily interactions—to say nothing of love—between women and men in households throughout history and in different cultural milieus today, we will continue to analyze intimate gender relations simplistically. Until we view such everyday interactions as productive and not simply reductive sources of culture change, we will persist in underestimating intersubjectivity as a basis of socially significant collision and collusion. The shifting moods and sentiments of men and women are indicators and also, potentially, critical catalysts imparting novel ways of understanding gender identities and relations, and, sometimes, new manners of living together as women and men in households and society.

Fixing Men develops these arguments through ethnographic portraits of three topics related to men's reproductive health and sexuality in Oaxaca—AIDS, vasectomy, and traditional medicine for men. In chapters on these subjects, and others that focus on the theoretical issues of men's sexuality and the history of family planning in Mexico and Oaxaca, my aim is to address five interrelated issues.

Although women have been conceptually "denaturalized" and biology and destiny disengaged in feminist and other writings in the last several decades, attributing ubiquitous and uniform qualities to men's sexualities is still curiously in fashion. In this book I ask why such commonplace notions of male sexuality persist, in Oaxaca and elsewhere, and examine why men's sexual desires and activities are treated as if these were "natural" and uniform among all men in the state, despite the fact that even many medical practitioners seem to accept same-sex desire among men as sufficient proof that men's biologies do not dictate their sexual destinies.

A second area of attention relates to the negotiations between men and women as couples, especially with respect to birth control and safe sex practices to protect each other from HIV. In academic gender studies, women's participation in the construction of masculinities and practices associated with these identities has been extensively discussed in the literature of mother-son bonding, Oedipal conflict, and mother-son estrangement.[2] Yet I think we need to challenge the tacit assumption in the social sciences that women have a negligible influence on males beyond infancy and childhood, and that male identities and practices are necessarily and uniformly grounded in homosociality alone, that is, in the identities and relations of men among themselves. On the intimate level of families and households, for example, we know too little about how women and men discuss, debate, and decide on sexual behavior and make reproductive decisions. And in general scholars still lack detailed information on how changing affective relations between men and women in turn alter cultural values concerning reproductive health and sexuality.

The research for the present book evolves from previous studies of mine focused on changing masculine identities and cultures in Mexico City and extends an earlier examination of the ways that couples cope practically with sexuality, childbearing, and child rearing.[3] In Oaxaca, one of my aims was to learn about women's relationship to men's reproductive and sexual lives and decision making around contraception, and in this way gain new insights into the ways through which men and women enact and transform gender relations rooted in power disparities.

Because I wanted to carry out most of the research in clinics, where different people come and go every day, there were certain inherent limitations in my ability to develop long-term relationships with patients, though of course I spent much time with the same doctors, nurses, social workers, psychologists, and other medical personnel. Thus, when I wanted to document and chart negotiations in couples about birth control and sexuality, I was obliged to rely more than I wanted on what people remembered and were willing to share with me about their histories of using contraception, deciding when to get pregnant, and associated events. And, truth be told, I started my research with the somewhat unrealistic expectation that I could "isolate" the process of decision making in couples by learning of the specific events and discussions and personal histories in their lives. Nonetheless, decisions about what forms of birth control to use, how many children to have, the spacing of children, and

A variety of contraceptive methods promoted on wall in San Agustín Tlacotepec in rural Oaxaca, 2002.

where to give birth cannot be understood as decisions made in isolation from the larger issues of political economy, cultural prejudice, and social networks. I knew this in a general sense, of course, but I had to bang my head against a few walls in Oaxaca for the implications of the broader political and economic influences and constraints to become more clear for me. In this book I trace how I came to understand these decision-making processes that appear so personal and yet clearly are so intimately linked to broader social pressures and restrictions.

The third theme I address in this book concerns a process known as medicalization, and here I am especially interested in the medicalization of men's sexuality. Among health care specialists and the population at large several beliefs concerning male sexual practices and urges that have little basis in biologically established fact nevertheless become enshrined as scientific truth. In this process of medicalization, men's sexualities are pathologized; it is taken for granted by many medical practitioners that men's sexualities are more or less similar, that men are in some sense "controlled" by their sexualities, and that their sexualities are innately problematic. Further, in considering health problems associated with male sexualities, like impotence and infertility, a medicalized model considers as secondary broader social and political relationships—for example, between women and men and between men themselves—and instead accentuates what are considered individual bodily malfunctions and abnormalities, for example, a lack of sexual desire on the part of men. This study considers the ways such ethnomedical beliefs among biomedical personnel about male sexualities are grounded in folk wisdom yet presented as innocent scientific truth, and the relationship of medicalized thinking about male sexualities to broader questions of sexual reproduction and women's sexuality.

Yet as injurious as medicalization models of diagnosis and treatment may be, an even more pervasive and pernicious problem for the world's health is, as Lock points out, globalization, characterized in part by a process in which "people everywhere adopt the concept of risk and become familiar with the disease nosologies [the classification of ill persons into groups] of biomedicine" (2001:483). As we will see in the chapters to follow, it is impossible to understand AIDS in Oaxaca without a broader, global analysis of international migration, multinational pharmaceutical companies, multinational religious institutions, and foreign health agencies. It makes equally little sense to talk of birth control in Oaxaca absent broader discussion of many of the same global institutions and agencies.[4] Globalization is therefore the fourth topical thread in this study. Studying reproductive health politics (around contraception, AIDS, and other issues) requires an appreciation of the international interests and involvement of governments and private organizations in the cultural construction of sexual realities and meanings. The fact that between 1920 and 1950 numerous medical doctors and anthropologists became involved in the international eugenics movement—in the process finding "Mexico's various poor populations (from rural Indians to urban workers) as comparatively deficient" (Lomnitz 2001:139)—is but one historical illustration of how global trends and pressures have influenced reproductive health in Mexico.

MEXICAN MALE CULTURE

The fifth and final theme that spirals through this book is how culture is used to explain, blame, maintain, and extend banalities about men's reproductive health and sexuality in Oaxaca. Comparisons with earlier platitudes about how women in such a Catholic country would never adopt contraceptives in large numbers are irresistible. Several decades ago, before family planning programs were launched in Mexico, "culture" was similarly invoked as an insurmountable obstacle to family planning, both because the purportedly dominant cultural ethos of machismo prescribed that couples had to go forth and multiply and because of Catholic doctrine that disallowed artificial forms of contraception that could limit the future progeny of the church.

As we will see in chapter 5, however, the actual historical role of the Catholic church, and the actions of tens of millions of Catholic lay women with regard to artificial birth control, present us with a far more complex picture. Total fertility rates plummeted in Mexico from around seven births per woman in 1955 to women having between two and three children, on average, forty years later. This rapid decline in the birth rate commenced in the 1970s, when the Mexican government abruptly shifted from a pronatal ideological stance to active family planning policies and rhetoric. When given the opportunity, people in Mexico have availed themselves of contraceptives, and birth rates have tumbled as a result, despite the fact that life expectancy rose from fifty years in 1955 to almost seventy-five years in 2005. Somehow, "Mexican culture" survived the mass expansion of modern forms of birth control.

In part, "Mexican culture" survived because it never existed in the first place. What I mean is that there has never been a single, homogenous Mexican culture. Nor is it helpful to talk of a uniform Mexican female culture or a typical Mexican male culture. Yet culture is often blamed for a variety of sins, as when *la influencia cultural* is blamed for the fact that few men in Mexico get vasectomies or when it is claimed that many if not most men in Mexico have sex with other men at some time in their lives. Lest this seem far-fetched, an e-mail message I received from an official of the U.S. National Science Foundation in 2003 invoked precisely such sweeping (and inaccurate) cultural characterizations about Mexican men, and is worth sharing here. In response to a query of mine asking about possible funding for a project comparing differential vasectomy rates in various parts of the world—why they are substantially higher in China and the United States than in Mexico, for example—the official seemed to have already cracked the mystery: "There should be some interesting cross-cultural differences, for example between machismo and non-machismo cultures (Brazil, Mexico, Spain vs. China & US?)." It would seem that in the opinion of this official, whether men in different countries get sterilized can be explained by reference to national cultural traits, as in, Brazilian-Mexican-Spanish "machismo cultures." Such a notion of national cultural traits is obsolete and this argument diminishes obvious and widely known factors of government involvement (or lack thereof) in family planning campaigns, for example, the one-child policy in China.

In a sense, notions of macho/non-macho, active/passive, traditional/modern gender dichotomies in Latin America are nothing new (see Gutmann 2003a). Confusion about macho and non-macho cultures is really just an illustration of a larger misunderstanding that says "traditional" men approach reproduction and sexuality differently than "modern" men. The polarity traditional/modern makes as much sense with respect to men as a group as does active/passive with regard to sexual behavior—that is, not very much at all. There is no such thing as a traditional man and there never has been, despite the fact that the term "traditional man" is frequently used as a shorthand to describe what are presumably a consistent set of attitudes and practices associated by the labeler as premodern—for example, if men want many children or if men do not utilize some form of modern, artificial birth control. Among the many problems with this formulation is the fact that it is rooted in stereotypes of imagined social relations and ideologies from the past, far more than it is grounded in actual knowledge of these phenomena. To speak of traditional men implies that they are people who come from a changeless and uniform cultural milieu, in comparison to those men involved in the rapidly transforming "modern world."

This traditional/modern man dichotomization is particularly harmful for the analysis of men, sexuality, and reproduction because it can easily lead to false assumptions about men's sexual relations with women (some might describe a man as sexually traditional if he shows little concern for women's sexual pleasure) or about why men may not practice birth control (it might be held that traditional men are less willing to use certain forms of contraception). Such a conceptual framework fails to incorporate diversity, change, and contestation among the very populations we late-modernists too haphazardly brand as traditional, even as we make unwarranted assumptions regarding the sexual proclivities and practices of our own families and friends. We await a well-grounded study of the modern sex habits of members of university communities.

In this book I examine these and other fallacies relating to supposed Mexican male cultural traits.

MEN AS THE MISSING (F)ACTORS IN REPRODUCTIVE HEALTH

Prior to the advent of the birth control pill that came into widespread use internationally in the 1960s, and in Mexico a decade later, two things were different for many men in Mexico. One, as with women, heterosexual sexual relations usually carried a far higher risk of pregnancy and therefore sex itself was more directly associated with anxieties and/or expectations linking the act to procreation. Two, more men were more often more responsible for contributing to preventing pregnancies, whether through slipping on a condom prior to sexual intercourse or, more often, withdrawing from the woman prior to ejaculating: coitus interruptus.

The pill and other forms of artificial contraception that tens of millions of women adopted in Mexico beginning in the 1970s transformed these two aspects of men's relationship to reproduction and sexuality. Like women, men were now enjoying sex at a time when "sexuality could become separated from a chronic round of pregnancy and childbirth" (Giddens 1992:26). Unlike women, men also now began to have less and less direct involvement in the most reliable forms of available birth control.

To take but one example, in international health and development agencies men have historically been of secondary concern in matters of reproductive health, presumably because women, not men, get pregnant—

"Family planning is a question of love." Painted wall in rural Oaxaca,
2002.

that is, for straightforward biological reasons. In recent decades, men
have been absent from efforts around reproductive health for social and
political reasons as well. This is because, one, improving the health of
women in general, including with respect to reproductive matters, was
identified as an urgent need and there was no parallel or complementary
demand for improvements in men's health, and, two, in these agencies,
as in government and nongovernmental institutions, men were in effect
excluded from participation in many health and development programs.

As Sylvia Chant and I describe elsewhere (see Chant and Gutmann
2000), in development work historically, "male blindness" was in part a
practical application of the policies that grew out of the United Nations
Decade for Women (1975–85), when the Women in Development movement emerged as a first step in the struggle against seemingly universal
male bias in development programs. Yet the tactic of focusing exclusively
on women failed to shake the patriarchal foundations of mainstream development thought and practice and it became increasingly evident that
women-only approaches to reproductive health, domestic violence, edu-

cation, and a host of other social problems were insufficient to resolve gender imbalances at the grass roots in any fundamental way.

In an analogous manner, anthropological studies of reproductive health have generally concentrated on women. Perhaps this has been true, Ginsburg and Rapp speculate, "because in our own social categories we disassociate men from domestic domains" (1995:4). Van Balen and Inhorn, in their volume on infertility, in the same way "acknowledge with dismay the relative lack of male 'voices,'" and in fact argue that "male infertility per se, as well as male experiences of partners' infertility, represents the great uncharted territory in the social science of infertility" (2002:19).[5] In addition to inserting men as the missing players in the field of reproductive health and sexuality, this book seeks to contribute to another area of study that is woefully underexamined in anthropology: contraception. Despite the fact that hundreds of millions of women and men use birth control worldwide, and despite the considerable attention paid within anthropology to new reproductive technologies, as Russell and Thompson (2000:3) point out, interest in contraception has been scant.[6]

Perhaps, in part, men have been missing from studies of reproductive health both because it was women researchers who were taking the first steps to address the problems facing women and because few men researchers were interested in exploring issues of gender and sexuality with respect to reproduction. I do not wish to imply any rigid principle dictating that women scholars will study women and men will study men. But political choices as to whether, when, and how to address problems of gendered social inequalities have undoubtedly been factors in the history of the study of reproductive health and sexuality. For all these reasons, and also in light of anthropological attempts to challenge "the mainstream demographic view of fertility as a one-time biological event (childbirth)" and to rethink reproduction as "an ongoing social and political construction" (Greenhalgh 1994:5), it should be apparent why there is a need to involve men in studies of the full range of reproductive practices in which men are so unambiguously implicated.

As I mentioned above, one intellectual puzzle I was seeking to resolve with this study revolved around decision making in couples about birth

control, how many children to have and when, and issues related to reproductive and sexual health, like impotence and infidelity. To the extent
that I began my research thinking I might discover the source of decisions
about contraception and the like among heterosexual couples in Oaxaca,
I was invariably disappointed. It was just too obvious that much of the
decision making—about what birth control methods, and about what antiretroviral treatments for people with HIV and AIDS, are available—
takes place in the boardrooms of pharmaceutical companies located in
Basel, Switzerland, and New Jersey. It is there that men, for the most part,
develop and market contraceptive products and antiretrovirals—or not.
Nevertheless, I was still able to learn a great deal about the decision making in couples that takes place in Oaxaca, albeit within a limited set of alternatives, established elsewhere, with regard to several aspects of men's
reproductive health and sexuality.

Of course, there is a broader question as to how accurately we can
study sexual practices in general. Without doubt, the principal compli-
cating factor in any research on sexuality is the uncomplicated fact that
people may not wish to tell the truth, they do not remember the truth,
they misremember, and they lie, and that it is often impossible to tell if
and when one of these conditions pertains. The central conceptual conundrum of research on sexuality is therefore the extent to which these
kinds of problems severely and irremediably limit what can ever be
known in this realm. As frustrating as it may be to admit that certain parts
of human existence in some profound way might be unknowable, no
amount of wishing it were not so, and no amount of variables run
through multiple regression analyses, will make it otherwise. Because we
cannot jump into bed with people, would not want to in most cases, and
if we did we would hopelessly skew subsequent events, we must seek indirect ways to study who does what to whom, how, and when. And we
must rely to a great extent on self-reporting. Undoubtedly, there are ways
to compare quantitative survey research, with oral histories, for instance,
in order to gain a better idea about sexuality and reproduction. But there
are limits to our ability to chart this terrain.

We can also invent ways to get a rough fix on how often people are
probably doing a range of things to each other. If we extrapolate from

condom sales, for example, we might assume we can then get an approximate count of how often men engage in ejaculatory forms of sex. Yet what can condom sales actually tell us? For example, what can we learn about men, masculinities, sexualities, and reproduction from the fact that sales are higher in Tokyo and Buenos Aires than they are in Topeka and Budapest? Without a local cultural perspective on the meanings of condom use in particular locales, and without understanding global pharmaceutical marketing practices and their local impact, such comparisons must be relegated to the realm of speculation far more than many researchers are comfortable admitting.

THREE CLINICS AND A GARDEN

This study was conducted in Oaxaca de Juárez, a metropolitan area of around 500,000 people located in a mountain region 300 miles south of the Mexican capital. Approximately half the population of the state, totaling over 3.7 million people, self-identifies as belonging to one or another indigenous group (the largest being Zapotec and Mixtec). According to nearly all indices, living standards in the state of Oaxaca are among the lowest in Mexico, especially in the countryside. In 2000, the average years of schooling in Oaxaca were 6.0 for males and 5.2 for females. The national averages that year were 7.6 and 7.1, respectively; only the state of Chiapas had lower figures.[7] Life expectancy in 2001 was 72.9 years in Oaxaca; again, only Chiapas had a lower figure, and not by much (72.8). The national figure was 75.7 years.[8] In 2001, the average hourly income in Oaxaca was 9.8 pesos, the lowest figure for any state in the country. By way of contrast, the state with the highest average hourly wage was Baja California, with 31 pesos; the national average was 19.4 pesos.[9] And, again, living standards were qualitatively more tenuous in rural areas of the state, compared to urban areas.

Oaxaca is a major tourist destination in Mexico for North Americans and Europeans, who arrive seeking a charming locale of "indigenous traditions," a place that visitors like to imagine has just emerged from an ancient, remote, and changeless purity. The cultural traditions of Oaxaca are indeed as rich as any on earth, but they are far more diverse and contentious than many tourists realize in their brief stays.

In 2006, Oaxaca the tourist mecca was severely disrupted by pitched battles in the streets, pitting a variety of civic organizations against the state government of Ulises Ruiz. It all began in May, when, as they do each year, school teachers raised demands for higher salaries. Unlike in previous years, however, the notoriously inept and reputedly corrupt governor Ruiz refused to even meet with the teachers who were occupying the downtown *zócalo*, or central square. On 14 June, police attacked the teachers' encampment, though the protestors returned and put up new barricades within hours. In response to the police violence, the Popular Assembly of the Peoples of Oaxaca (APPO) was formed, made up of teachers, clergy, and an assortment of community activists and organizers from throughout the state. Leaders of the teachers' union and APPO now demanded the resignation of the governor. On 28 October, police and local paramilitaries attacked the protestors, leaving six people dead, including a U.S. journalist.

The next day, the federal government sent troops to Oaxaca to forcibly remove APPO from the *zócalo* and a local university campus. Several more protestors were killed and more than a hundred people were arrested. In an interview conducted in late 2006, Mexican cultural critic Carlos Monsiváis offered this assessment of the events to that point in Oaxaca:

> What we see on the ground is an unarmed and bold popular insurgency that is expressing its generalized rejection of the current situation and of the neoliberal policies that have brought it to a head. In Oaxaca, neoliberalism is anything but an abstraction. It is the economic system that forces massive migration to the United States, that provokes massive dropout rates at the primary school level, and that has led to a decline in life expectancy. Savage capitalism and neoliberalism have forced far too many to live in ignorance and under conditions unfit for human beings, buttressing the abuses and crimes of machismo along the way. The poverty of Oaxaca is a terminal situation. (Monsiváis 2007:7)

Nor are the political and social struggles of contemporary Oaxaca some kind of historical fluke. Despite the absence of such history from the tourist brochures, even the street names give a taste of the cultural politics in Oaxaca City, and reflect a history that has been anything but tranquil and placid. There is one street called Mártires de Chicago (Martyrs of Chicago), in reference to the anarchists killed in the Haymarket Massacre in Chicago on 4 May 1886. México 68 Street makes reference to another politically inspired massacre, this time in Mexico City in 1968. Another street is named simply Obreros y Campesinos (Workers and Peasants). Then there are streets named after the heroes of the Mexican Revolution that began in 1910, Francisco Villa and Emiliano Zapata, in addition to Democracia, Independencia, Libertad, Joon Lokke (John Locke), and 1° de Mayo (May First) streets. All in all, the names of the streets in Oaxaca City reflect a tumultuous history that is rather at odds with the quaint, sleepy Indian villages of the tourist posters, and the political conflict and turmoil that are illustrated in the discussions of men's reproductive health and sexuality in Oaxaca that follow are thus of a piece with the overall turbulent social, economic, and political climate of contemporary life in this area of the world (see Anaya Muñoz 2004).

My ethnographic fieldwork in Oaxaca City in 2001–05 was carried out in two vasectomy clinics, in the state-run AIDS clinic, and in the Ethnobotanical Garden of Oaxaca, where I worked as a laborer clipping cactus and digging ditches for planting and irrigation.[10] To learn about AIDS in Oaxaca, I spent one or two days a week at the state-run AIDS clinic, meeting and talking with men and women who came there seeking medical services. Often these patients would have monthly appointments, and I would try to coordinate my schedule so as to coincide with their visits in order to develop an ongoing relationship with them, though in most cases our relationship remained a fairly formal one of conversations about health between patients who were HIV+ and the gringo medical anthropologist.

To learn about male sterilization, I interviewed men at the Centro de Salud Urbano #1, operated by the Ministry of Health, which is supposed to provide health care services for the rural and urban poor in the Oaxaca City metropolitan area. And I met men at another clinic, the Unidad Médica Familiar #38, that is part of the Mexican Institute for Social Security, which officially serves workers in the formal private sector of the economy. The two doctors who performed vasectomies in Centro #1 were both originally from Oaxaca and had received their medical training, including in this procedure, there. One of the doctors at the Unidad #38 was from Mexico City (where he went to medical school), and the other was from Oaxaca and was finishing her residency there. In Centro #1, one of the doctors was a man and the other a woman, and there was a female nurse generally present throughout a procedure. In Unidad #38, one of the doctors was a man, the other a woman, and nurses were rarely present.

As I describe in some detail in chapter 6, my role in these vasectomy clinics developed beyond that of passive observer and interviewer, and my tasks came to include what I call "emotional anesthesiology." Nonetheless, as in the AIDS clinic, my ongoing relationships with people were sporadic and somewhat restricted to issues of sex, birth control, and AIDS. Pleased to be learning about these issues, but frustrated by the limitations of my interactions with patients, after a few months of fieldwork in 2001, I happened to have lunch with a friend, Alejandro de Ávila, then director of the Jardín Etnobotánico de Oaxaca, the Ethnobotanical Garden of Oaxaca. When Alex asked how my work was going, I mentioned my ambivalence arising from not having more systematic and informal contact with a specific group of people and spending most of my time in the socially grim hospital clinics.[11] He then asked me, "Why not come work at the garden?" He meant I should work there as an unskilled laborer. I think I replied something to the effect of "Why? It's a magnificent garden, but what could that have to do with my study of birth control and AIDS in Oaxaca?" The garden contains hundreds of species of plants from all over the state, one of the most biodiverse spots on the earth, but what did this have to do with vasectomies and AIDS? Alex then explained his offer: "You are studying men. There are twenty to thirty men who work at the garden. Come, work alongside them, get to know them in a less barren setting than a clinic." It was the best advice I got that year.

Discussing what form of contraception a couple uses is not a topic that casually arises in my everyday conversations with other Brown University faculty and staff, or with the parents of friends of my children, or with my neighbors, or with members of my gym. But after working alongside them for months in the Ethnobotanical Garden of Oaxaca, many of my fellow laborers had a general sense of my research on sex, birth control, and AIDS, and to my surprise and delight, they were the ones who initiated our conversations about contraception and sexuality. Daniel's wife had had a tubal ligation. Before this she had used "métodos naturales."

"Like what?" I asked. "Herbs?"

"No, you know, there are days when she's most fertile."

"Oh, *ritmo* [rhythm]," I replied.

"What did you call it?" Daniel asked. "Rhythm? Oh, right."

Then there was Roberto, who told me one morning, as we were digging ditches for the irrigation system, that he had used condoms, but his wife never used anything. Roberto's father's first wife was a midwife, and she knew about herbs for not having babies. I told Roberto that I would have enjoyed talking to her. "No," he responded, "she wouldn't have talked to you. Only to women."

Another day, while we took a lunch break, Eladio mentioned "prostitutes." He probably noticed my ears prick up because he went on to mention something about a young man he knew who had visited one recently. I nonchalantly asked him to elaborate. Most young men go to prostitutes, he reported. He had, and his friends had too. In all my years living and doing research among men in Mexico City, few of my male friends confessed that they had been to a prostitute. In Oaxaca, many seemed more than willing to narrate their experiences with prostitutes.[12] Whereas men in Mexico City seemed insulted by the allegation that they ever had to pay for sex (see Gutmann 2006:133), in Oaxaca men merrily told me where they went to hire a prostitute, where they had sex with her, how much they paid, how many times they returned, and how long their sexual activity lasted. They paid the equivalent of $8 to $10 U.S. for street hookers, $20 for the ones who worked the cantinas. And after you are married, why pay? When you are still single, according to Eladio, it is sometimes difficult for a young man to find a young woman he can have sex with. Although I could have learned about such practices through a random survey of anonymous men, the nuances of the men's desires and frustrations and curiosity came into sharper relief if I simply waited for these topics to emerge in the course of the daily banter on the job at the Ethnobotanical Garden of Oaxaca.

Workers at the Ethnobotanical Garden of Oaxaca, 2003.

More than anywhere else in Oaxaca, in the Ethnobotanical Garden I could contextualize what I learned through my interviews in the vasectomy and AIDS clinics. The men from the garden who accepted the challenge of trying to teach me how to care for their plants became my mentors and friends, with whom over the years I have been able to share ideas, experiences, worries, and dreams about far more than just plants, or even sex, birth control, and AIDS. The stories of their lives and families are among the most insightful, humorous, and poignant that I offer in the pages of this book. As everyone at the garden had a nickname—at least everyone who did the shoveling, pruning, transplanting, and maintenance—before long I was given the nickname Zorra (Fox) because, I was told, foxes show up to scrounge around and then they disappear for a while to parts unknown.[13] My pattern was show up to work in the hot sun for a day, then disappear for several more.

My research on men's reproductive health and sexuality in Oaxaca was motivated not by the magnitude of the numbers—vasectomies were fairly unusual in Oaxaca, and AIDS was a growing problem there, yet by no means epidemic—but instead was sparked by a set of straightforward questions about a very human activity: sex. How did men and women in Oaxaca avoid making babies? How did they avoid sexual disease? What were their reproductive health options, and how did they make decisions about them? Over the course of several years, there was not a man at the garden who did not have something to say about these issues. And most of the men had different things to say at different times. When I heard the men contradict themselves, express ambivalent and inconsistent opinions, and challenge one another about religion, government, and family views regarding sexuality, I finally began to trust what I was learning. Instead of relying largely on what people in the clinics reported on some particular occasion after having been prompted by me as the interviewer, in the garden I was able to wait for topics to arise through casual conversation.

Oaxaca was a bit exotic for me at first. I had visited many times before 2001, when I arrived there with my family, but it was different in many ways than any place I had lived in the United States or Mexico. Although I was born and raised in the United States, I had lived for several years in Mexico City and written about changing gender relations and popular politics in a squatter settlement there (Gutmann 2002, 2006). In the Mexico City neighborhood of Santo Domingo, where I lived and worked on and off in the 1990s, most of my friends and neighbors had been born and raised in the capital, if not necessarily in that barrio. In Oaxaca, I was constantly in contact with people who had been born and raised in small villages in the countryside. In Mexico City, although a few of my friends spoke one or another indigenous language, like Yucatec Maya or Nahua as spoken in the state of Puebla, the overwhelming majority of my acquaintances considered themselves mestizos, "mixed-race" Mexicans, and did not self-identify as Indians of any kind. In Oaxaca, even my lightest-skinned friend boasted of his Zapotec grandmother's special recipe using *mole* sauce and grasshoppers.

Which is not to say that discrimination and racism are in any way absent from Oaxaca; the epithet *yope* (similar in ring to *nigger*) is spray-painted on city walls and signs. At the Ethnobotanical Garden, I quickly learned that asking someone if they are "indigenous" is akin to calling them a *yope*. *Indigenous* is a term dear to anthropologists and activists, but for most people in Oaxaca it sounds too much like *indio* (Indian), the slur used by the Spanish conquistadors. Instead, the men at the garden were delighted to inform me that they were Zapoteco or Mixe or Mixteco, and more than once I heard the older men urge the younger ones not to lose their ability to speak other languages or, as they called them, "dialectos."[14]

Following on earlier work by anthropologists in Oaxaca City, I also wanted to know what difference ethnicity made in people's health and treatment for illness.[15] Was the clear and present significance of indigenous ethnic groups and racism in rural areas of the state overpowered by issues of class and class subordination after these people arrived in the city? Doctors complained regularly to me about their stints in the countryside, which in Oaxaca is overwhelmingly populated by indigenous peoples. "Despite the best of intentions when I went out there to do my service," one callous physician snarled to me, "they pull guns on you out there. So there's no point in going to some of those areas." Nor is this a matter of a few racist public servants. In a section called "ethnographic perspective" of the official training manual for medical personnel working in reproductive health in the state of Oaxaca, practitioners are advised to discuss among themselves "who among you would like to share any experience related to popular beliefs, values, or customs that has interfered with a technical-medical indicator or intervention?" (Proyecto IMSS-PRIME 2001: sección I, p. 5). God forbid in the state of Oaxaca that indigenous beliefs, values, and customs should be found valuable. In this way, medical professionals are trained to especially denigrate the indigenous peoples they are charged to heal.

In the course of my fieldwork I came to share the view that although ethnically grounded bigotry and discrimination are clear and evident in large and small ways in Oaxaca City, in urban areas, more often than not, class trumps ethnicity as an explanation for relations of power and inequality. Ethnic identities and racism pervade urban Oaxaca, too, but I found few patterns, in terms of disease or curing, in the city that I could associate unmistakably with one or another indigenous group. Instead, I came to see class and gender as the most salient factors to explain the state of people's reproductive health and sexuality. Despite the fact that virtually every tourist to Oaxaca visits the archaeological site of Monte Albán, many of Oaxaca City's poor have never been there. Nor have they attended the Guelaguetza festival in July—the tickets are simply too expensive for most people, so they watch on television. "That neighborhood is so poor," goes the saying, "parents wait six months before they buy clothes for their babies." It is true that even in the wealthiest neighborhoods, like San Felipe, the braying of burros and the necessity of sidestepping a full team of yoked-up oxen are common occurrences, displaying a mingling of classes that is less common than in other parts of Mexico. Yet in Oaxaca, when the wealthy get very sick, although they may live alongside goat paths, they do not hesitate before booking a flight to the medical centers in Houston.

Class and ethnic divisions are rampant and blatant in Oaxaca, and I was very concerned that social stratification would impede my ability to gain the trust and friendship of people who I perceived to be from very different cultural and economic backgrounds than my own. Yet when I raised this with anthropologist friends early in my fieldwork, I was surprised that no one shared my anxieties. Yes, I was distinct from most people in Oaxaca by virtue of class, education, ethnicity, national origin, and many other visual and implicit characteristics. And, as has been true so often with research worries spawned by erroneous preconceptions, I soon learned that as much as tourists to Oaxaca find themselves fascinated by difference, so too there is never a shortage of Oaxaqueños eager to learn about the lives and cultures and experiences of long-term and short-term visitors, anthropological and other.

This situation of mutual curiosity pertains for many reasons, including the very practical one that many thousands of men and women each year journey from Oaxaca to the United States, where at a minimum another 100,000 Oaxacans live, work, marry, and die. In 2005, I carried out a little experiment: in both Oaxaca and Mexico City I asked friends the going rate for a *coyote*, a person who guides Mexicans across the Mexico–U.S. border. Despite being several hundred miles farther away from that border, many more people in Oaxaca than Mexico City could answer ($2,000 to $3,000 U.S.). Then, too, many more friends and acquaintances in Oaxaca depend on remittances from the United States than is the case for my friends and neighbors in Mexico City.[16] Men from Oaxaca go north seeking work to earn money to send back to Oaxaca. Growing numbers of these men get infected with HIV and then return to Oaxaca and infect their wives and girlfriends. The shape of AIDS in Oaxaca is therefore different than in some other cities in Mexico, where self-identified *homosexuales* continue to be the main group of people with HIV. In Oaxaca in 2005 the largest group of people with AIDS was poor Indian men who had migrated to the United States. The second largest group was poor Indian women.

HOW TO EXPAND AND ABANDON PUBLIC HEALTH

From the 1970s into the 1980s, health care coverage in Mexico increased by as much as 10 percent annually, and during this period the federal government launched initiatives, such as IMSS-Solidaridad, to incorporate unprotected groups into the health care network.[17] From 1991 to 1995, physical infrastructure was strengthened in poor rural areas; in Oaxaca, for example, hundreds of new clinics were built, including some in remote regions of the state, although, to be sure, many of these facilities were not well staffed. Thus, despite the persistence of tremendously uneven coverage and inadequate treatment and prevention programs in the 1970s and 1980s, there were discernable improvements in health care coverage—as measured by the numbers of hospital beds, the ratio of doctors and nurses to the population, per capita spending on the uninsured—and citizens had a sense that government attention to health was headed in the direction of more and better care for the poor in Oaxaca. Then, in the 1990s, the government began to dismantle the infrastructure of social security services in Mexico.

In 1996, with the Program of Health Sector Reform, many earlier efforts to expand health care were downgraded as a priority; the reform was aimed at moving to replace the previous social security strategy with a dual policy of market commodities and poor relief (see Laurell 2001). The private sector was promoted more than ever before as a key agent in health care, including for the poor, despite their lack of economic resources with which to pay for private services. Not coincidentally, the structural changes contained in the program shared much in common with the policies explored and promoted in the World Bank study *Investing in Health*, which was published in 1993. Following the announcement of the Program of Health Sector Reform and the publication of *Investing in Health*, the federal government launched the so-called Program for Extension of Coverage, to be implemented over the period from 1996 to 2000. Although the stated purpose was to offer basic health services to 10 million additional Mexicans, in practice this program was guided by the Mexican government dictum of "equal pay for equal services." This privatized approach to health care delivery stood in direct contrast to the earlier government guideline of "Pay according to income and receive according to need."

In practical terms, the withdrawal of the state from *public* health has meant that as public services became privatized, health care became increasingly decentralized. This change became marked in urban areas, as health care was shifted from public to private institutions, including from public clinic to private home. What is more, as clinic and hospital care were transferred to home care, health care practitioners necessarily shifted from medical personnel to the mothers, sisters, and wives resident in these households. As a result of neoliberal economic reforms, health care spaces, like clinics and hospitals, that had been touted as public became increasingly inaccessible to those without the personal funds to pay for health services. Although Oaxaca was not one of the fourteen Mexican states incorporated into the first phase of decentralization (1983–88), it was especially impacted in the second decentralization phase (1995–2000), as inequalities in the services provided grew and the quality of the services offered suffered. One example from the late 1990s is the decline in primary services available in the rural areas of Oaxaca, as states were expected to take over hospitals previously run by the federal government, although insufficient funds were provided to the states to accomplish these tasks.[18] Such social exclusion, prompted by structural readjustment policies, represented a reduction of citizens' rights, as the mere existence of new clinics, for example, was supposedly sufficient evidence of expanding coverage. Never mind that the actual services provided were less available to those without money to pay.

Such is the content of democracy and the democratization of health care in Mexico, all in all a fitting illustration of the roles offered to contemporary citizens to participate in Mexican society and a good illustration of the benefits they can expect based on their personal (private) ability to pay for such cultural membership. As an anthropologist from the United States, I was often asked by patients, doctors, friends, and neighbors about health care availability and services there. I found it especially difficult to explain why so many citizens of the United States consider their country as the paragon of democracy when so many of its residents have so little access to decent health care. My first research year in Oaxaca, from August 2001 to August 2002, was also a hell of a year to spend outside the United States, a unique time when people repeatedly sought explanations for the actions of the U.S. government and military following the September 11 attacks. Although everyone I and my family came into contact with following the events of 9/11 was sympathetic—"Did you have family in New York? Are they OK?"—most Oaxacans I spoke with were aghast at the war on terror launched by the Bush administration that followed. Paragon of democracy indeed.

THE LIMITS OF ETHNOGRAPHY AND FIXING MEN

The Irish poet W. B. Yeats is said to have suffered from a condition about which he once complained, "It was terrible. Like putting an oyster into a slot machine."[19] To cure his presumed impotence, Yeats sought out a treatment prescribed by some doctors in the 1930s to restore men to their "natural" state: vasectomy. The procedure was "intended to increase and contain the production of male hormone, thus arresting the ageing process and restoring sexual vitality" (Foster 2003:496).

The study of sexuality and decision making about sexual relations is inherently delicate and difficult. Men who cannot get erections are considered by many to be less manly. Men who are manly get erections easily and, I was informed on more than one occasion in Oaxaca, are *irrefrenable* (unstoppable). The subject lends itself to wonderful stories and jokes, but suffers from an intrinsic problem: people who study sexuality are always dependent on what people tell us about their sex lives. Philippe Bourgois (2002), in particular, has discussed the problem of self-reporting in public health studies, in his case with respect to drug addiction and needle use. The fact is, there are practical limits to studying sexuality and sexual relations, a point to which I return in the final chapter.[20]

But within those limits there is much that can and needs to be said. The anthropological study of human sexuality has ancient roots. But studies of sexuality and reproductive health have been propelled and guided, in recent years especially, by two new and powerful political movements within the academy, namely feminism and the struggle against AIDS. The significance of men's reproductive health and sexuality is enormous, though except for work on AIDS largely uncharted. Scholarship on these matters is scarce, and the present study aims to contribute to a broader discussion of reproductive health by focusing attention on several crucial aspects of men's reproductive health, sexuality, and sexual relations in Oaxaca in the early years of the twenty-first century, which in turn is part of the larger process of exploring those whom Rayna Rapp has called "the exotic male sex" (2000:6).

TWO

The Missing Gamete

EIGHT COMMON MISTAKES
ABOUT MEN'S SEXUALITY

The French philosopher Simone de Beauvoir wrote in *The Second Sex* that "biological facts [provide] one of the keys to the understanding of woman." Yet, she quickly added, "I deny that they establish for her a fixed and inevitable destiny."[1]

This revolutionary thesis that detached female bodies from female destinies has been a cornerstone of feminism and women's studies for several decades, sometimes captured in the aphorism Biology Is Not Destiny. Since Beauvoir wrote *The Second Sex*, our understanding of the biological facts themselves have become still more complex.[2] Some hallowed truths about bodies have nonetheless been more difficult to dislodge than others. In this book, using ethnographic research I carried out in Oaxaca, I examine the notion of men's sexual destiny, a topic that is widely taken for granted in the popular imagination, yet sadly and oddly one that is seldom studied.

Beliefs revolving around men's sexually rapacious appetites are found all over the world. In academic circles today, evolutionary psychologists claim to have uncovered the primal motives of male licentiousness—a built-in compulsion on the part of the males of the species to spread their seed. In his primer to this new science of evolutionary psychology, Robert Wright, for instance, goads, "Can anyone find a single culture in which women with unrestrained sexual appetites *aren't* viewed as more aberrant than comparably libidinous men?" (1994:45). Lest we blithely dismiss such biologistic and universalist claims (or their widespread popular counterparts), we still must reckon with the dearth of good scholarship—feminist or otherwise—on male (hetero)sexuality and reproduction. By not studying male sexuality and reproduction, we have left too unchallenged the conclusion common to evolutionary psychologists that, with respect to sexuality, "male license and (relative) female reserve are to some extent innate" (Wright 1994:46). And in case there is any confusion regarding the shortage of studies on male heterosexuality and reproduction, this situation is the product not of some reverse feminist bias against men, but of the general totemization of male sexuality (see chapter 6). In an age of evolutionary psychology and the medicalization of all manner of (alleged) bodily processes, the belief in men's hypersexuality has, in more than a few cultural contexts, become something of a totemic illusion that treats male sexuality as naturalized, something fixed, and as entirely distinct from female sexuality. Fortunately indeed, many feminist theories of gender inequality help provide the framework within which we are today able to develop the contrasting study of men, sexuality, reproduction, and masculinity as integral to a more general project of exploring the history and diversity of gender/sexuality systems in the world.[3]

Further, we might do well to remember Anthony Giddens's (1983) double hermeneutic, by which he means that, unlike the subjects of study in the natural sciences, social scientific conclusions about society and social groups have an impact on the people studied. Therefore, what health researchers say about male sexuality, for example, even if simply by implication, can and does have a chain of consequences among those we seek to represent. That so enormous and everyday a topic as male heterosexuality and reproduction has gone largely unnoticed in anthropology and the other social sciences, for example, shows both the importance and the urgency of the task at hand, because left underexamined and underanalyzed it is too easy to rely on facile biologisms that reduce men and their sexualities to man and his sexuality.

In short, if we settled (or began to unsettle) the matter of women's bodily destiny over fifty years ago, why is the myth of men's sexual destiny still so pervasive in popular culture and why does it remain largely unchallenged in scholarly venues?

A clue to the answer to this question may lie with what Carole Vance (1999 [1991]) has termed "the cultural influence model," in which cultural differences provide a patina of sexual diversity spread over primordial male and female bodies. This speaks to the central dilemma in Western sexuality research in the last hundred years: the interaction between material bodies and cultural meanings in the course of periodic licking, sucking, inserting, enveloping, topping, and bottoming one another. In Vance's formulation, the cultural influence model is utilized to describe the sexuality of both men and women, so that "sexuality is seen as the basic material—a kind of universal Play Doh—on which culture works, a naturalized category which remains closed to investigation and analysis" (1999 [1991]:44). With the cultural influence model, one may encounter a range of mutually exotic and/or repugnant sexual practices cross-culturally, but each is but a script on the basic underlying corporal essence of human beings. As a friendly amendment to Vance's critique of the view that culture is a mere epiphenomenal influence on sexuality, I would add that in much feminist research—though certainly not in the popular imagination—the male body even more than the female body is still in too many ways considered to come factory-loaded with a predictable Play Doh hard drive.[4]

The notion of sex drives, urges, and impulses, for instance, has been repeatedly challenged and explored in a sophisticated feminist literature on women's sexualities. For a similar corpus of work among men, only queer theory and studies of same-sex sex can make any claim to a wide-ranging, complex, and nuanced treatment of sexualities. It is high time to queer our dull understanding of male heterosexualities, that is, to consider the woefully unmarked category of the male heterosexual that, despite and perhaps because of its hidden dominance in models of sexuality, has nonetheless too long gone overdetermined and understudied. And, as we do this, we might also keep in mind R. W. Connell's cautionary judgment regarding social constructivists: "They face, as a group, difficulties about the bodily dimension of sexuality. Bodily processes and products—arousal, orgasm, pregnancy and birth, menarche and menopause, tumescence and detumescence, semen, milk and sweat. . . . Placing an emphasis on the historicity of sexuality, as Foucault and his followers do, often marginalizes these matters" (1997:63–64). We must not continue to ignore the confluence of biological and cultural parameters on sexuality, and how these factors feed and transform one another.[5]

The anthropological gambit of first gaining conceptual clarity in the social margins has served us well, but it is now necessary to bring lessons learned to a study within the margins. In successive conceptual waves, first closely linking sex(uality) and gender systems (Rubin 1975), then splitting them apart and not just analytically (Rubin 1999 [1984]), with more recent linking of sexuality and gender again in a feminist post-Freudian synthesis (Segal 1994), we have learned a thing or two about narrowly treating sexuality as biology and gender as culture. This is important, because if male sexuality is the biological given and the rest of what we do with it is the gendered fluff, then the wide range of manly sexual desire, dread, pleasure, worry, obsession, fantasy, experience, and practice is merely lying there to be dutifully discovered and documented and not much more.

Relatively little has been written, for example, about heterosexual men *not* enjoying sex, not enjoying it often, and not missing sex when they do not have it. Reports on such topics are exceptional indeed. Among the rare accounts, in an attempt to refute the "Freudian thought . . . that each person has a certain innate amount of sexual energy which must be expressed in some fashion," Karl Heider (1976:195) wrote that among the Grand Valley Dani in Indonesia, at least in the 1960s, when he conducted his fieldwork, there was a standard four-to-six-*year* postpartum sexual abstinence and, more noteworthy still, that no one showed any signs of unhappiness or stress as a result of such celibacy. Nanda writes that among the *hijras* in India, their "emasculation is their culturally defined 'proof' that they do not experience sexual desire or sexual release as men" (1990:29).[6] And in my own research on changing gender identities and practices in Mexico City, a male friend confessed to me, "I'll tell you honestly, sex has just never been as important to me as it seems to be for a lot of other guys" (Gutmann

2006 [1996]:144). Yet the very shortage of such accounts cross-culturally can lead us blithely to assume that (a) most men are not like this, and (b) we know what most men are like with respect to sexuality and reproduction.

Anthropologists may infrequently take perverse pleasure in recording the polymorphous philandering of males and females of all ages, shapes, and kinds.[7] They may be keen observers of sexual variety and breadth and retain a phobic allergy to ideal types and the norms of normativity. Yet they may nonetheless also harbor the suspicion that most heterosexual males feel and behave a certain way (with an innate sex drive, let's say). The usual way around this predicament in contemporary cultural anthropology is to focus on the local and avoid any presumption of pan-human experience, that is, by recourse to anthropology's localist conceit—"Beliefs and practices are sui generis in every locale at every point in history." This orientation has been particularly important and necessary in response to the medicalization of human bodies and biomedical declarations regarding corporal normality and pathology (see Scheper-Hughes 1994b). As someone who has spent a good part of the last twenty years in central and southern Mexico, I am acutely aware of the perils of generalizing for regions much less for the populations of entire nation-states, and still less for larger groupings of people when it comes to sexuality, reproduction, men and masculinity, or much else. Nonetheless, my purpose in this chapter is to raise a series of questions I hope will be relevant in more than one historical and cultural context.

As a way to explore pertinent ideas and poke fun at these misconceptions, I offer the following list of "common mistakes" about men, sexuality, and reproduction. This chapter thus takes us on a general conceptual foray before returning to the ethnography of sex, birth control, and AIDS in Oaxaca.

REPRODUCTION AND REPRODUCTIVE HEALTH
CONCERN ONLY WOMEN

Obviously, many readers know better than to think that reproduction is an affair for women alone. Nonetheless, it may be worth noting that this reality is less obvious than it should be, as evidenced by the fact that in some of the recent and important collections on reproduction and gender and health, the editors were unable to include articles that dealt substantially with men and reproduction (see, e.g., Ginsburg and Rapp 1995; Sargent and Brettell 1996).[8] To highlight the missing presence of men from discussions of reproduction, Meg Greene and Ann Biddlecom titled a 2000 review essay "Absent and Problematic Men: Demographic Accounts of Male Reproductive Roles" (see also Dudgeon and Inhorn 2003). That men have been absent in studies of reproduction is itself problematic. The trick now is to incorporate men in this field without losing sight of the politics of reproduction.

Fortunately, in discovering this missing link (gamete?) in the history of reproduction and sexuality, we are able to build on substantial literatures already in existence on topics such as women and reproduction,[9] fatherhood and men's "prior involvement,"[10] and men who have sex with other men. To be sure, the inclusion of men in any field is more than a matter of adding men and stirring the mixture, though even that can be a start.

With ingenuity and not a little flair queer theorists and second-wave feminists have embarked on the task of marking male heterosexuality as normative and nothing more. As in Rich's (1993 [1982]) classic essay on "compulsory heterosexuality," we have learned that the taken-for-granted category of male (hetero)sexuality has long been employed as a stand-in, the unmarked, for all forms of sexuality. Yet analytically outing heterosexual men from their unmarked closets, in other words, showing them to have particular and not universal kinds of sexualities, was in many ways all that was done with them. And so until recently, in feminist scholarship, they have analytically remained in the shadow of the closet, albeit rather naked in their heteronormativity.[11]

The issue is not only how best to represent the views and experiences of the population of men who are engaged in reproduction in some manner or another, and the women and men in their lives, nor simply how to discuss the diversity of male heterosexualities in relation to reproductive rights, behavior, and technologies. The challenge is to develop this field without losing the key insights from feminism and queer theory regarding inequality and privilege—in particular, the real corporal and societal constraints women and men face. In the case of men, then, we might ask what would be the obverse of the following characterization by Segal: "The com-

plexity of the social is ignored, reduced to generalizations about fixed relations of power—as though to be less powerful in society, as mothers so
often are, is to be, and to be perceived to be, simply submissive and pow-
erless" (1994:148–49). What about men perceived to be powerful: are they
automatically so in all contexts, including the most sexually intimate?

Finally, on this point, there are surprisingly few gender studies in the social sciences that focus on both men and women. Although the either/or
approach has advantages in some contexts for some topics of inquiry (for
Latin America, see Gutmann 2003a), it also has severe drawbacks when one
is examining a subject such as reproduction.[12] In the burgeoning literature
on births and midwives, for example, men are seldom given more than
passing reference, despite the central role they may play before, after, and
during childbirth itself.[13] With respect to infertility, men have long been
treated as irrelevant, or if they were incorporated into studies they were the
ones who refused to consider the possibility they had the problem. Significant work in this area is just beginning (see Inhorn 2002, 2003, 2004; Kahn
2000).[14] Following international conferences in Cairo in 1994 and Beijing in
1995, the intersection of politics and reproduction and the incorporation of
men in reproductive health matters have received state sanction in most
parts of the world. As necessary as these shifts may be, and as good as it
may be to involve men in scholarship on reproduction, as in the development field and the shift from Women in Development to Gender and Development, there are risks involved (see Chant and Gutmann 2000). Within
anthropology, only in HIV research have men, sexuality, and reproductive
health been studied and discussed extensively.[15]

REPRODUCTIVE HEALTH CONCERNS ONLY WOMEN
IN GENERAL AND MEN AND WOMEN WITH AIDS

The AIDS epidemic made men relevant to reproduction and sexuality, at
least insofar as the health of men and their sexual partners was concerned.
AIDS was initially considered a health issue only for gay men and men
who had sex with men but did not self-identify as gay: in the patronizing
language of public health, these men were flagged collectively as a sig-

nificant "risk group." Then heterosexual men and their foreskin hygiene, sexually transmitted infections (STIs), and dry-sex idiosyncrasies rather quickly came under closer and closer scrutiny, especially after epidemiological studies showed a geometric growth of the contagion in parts of southern Africa and the Indian subcontinent. As elsewhere in the world, reproductive health and concerns for sexuality in Latin America were spawned by AIDS campaigns for both medications and for safer sexual practices, and the topic has largely rested there.[16]

The relationship between male heterosexuality, bisexuality, and homosexuality is of central concern in studying men, sexuality, and reproduction for a variety of reasons, not the least of which are the theoretical deficiencies in existing models of heterosexuality. How do studies of male (homo)sexuality jibe with male (hetero)sexuality and with human sexuality in general? Nancy Chodorow has examined the psychoanalytic literature and concluded that, lo and behold, "psychoanalysis does not have a developmental account of 'normal' heterosexuality (which is, of course, a wide variety of heterosexualities) that compares in richness and specificity to accounts we have of the development of the various homosexualities and what are called perversions. . . . Most of what one can tease out about the psychoanalytic theory of 'normal' heterosexuality comes by reading between the lines in writings on perversions and homosexuality" (Chodorow 1994:34; see also Segal 1994, 1997). Commonplace assumptions and clichés about heterosexuality, however, continue to abound.

Recent public health attention in some parts of the world to problems like testicular and prostate cancer (especially affecting younger and older men, respectively), erectile dysfunction (a problem that grows with time and the appearance of pharmaceutical solutions), and premature ejaculation address certain reproductive health concerns by men, regardless of sexual orientation. Yet emphasizing male analogues to female gynecological problems will only take us so far in developing our conceptual toolkit regarding male sexualities. To give texture and vigor to the study of men, sexuality, and reproduction we must find ways to extend and develop the feminist and queer literatures on sexuality, including bisexuality, so that if male heterosexualities are no longer seen as compulsory, neither are they necessarily and generally understood as compulsive.

MALE REPRODUCTION EQUALS MALE SEXUALITY

It may be a coincidence that the penis and testicles can be the site of physical arousal and sexual pleasure and are also closely involved in male fertilization. But the fact remains that for the vast majority of time in men's lives, the penis and testicles are not to be found in a high state of excitation. The erect penis is not the default penis.[17]

Clearly one of the main problems with this equation of male reproduction and sexuality is that it leaves out all forms of same-sex sex between men, once more confirming the idea of masculinity as homophobia (see Kimmel 1994). Understanding men who have sex with other men as, yet again, an elided category involves more than the straightforward recognition that men have sex with each other without any thought of procreation. In the history of sexuality studies, the notion of activity and passivity among men who have sex with each other has also become prevalent as a proxy analytical framework for heterosexual-reproductive sexuality; these terms thus link male and female heterosexuals with tops and bottoms among men who have sex with other men. Here, too, we may learn from the recent ethnography (see, e.g., Parker 1999) of emerging homosexualities that makes clear how the active/passive dichotomy can cause more conceptual problems than it resolves. This is a valuable lesson, because until now male (hetero)sexuality has been associated too often and too cavalierly with activity (and aggression), in contrast to women's passive and aggrieved (hetero)sexuality (see also Segal 1994, 1997; Gutmann 2003a).

Still, same-sex male sex is not the only kind of nonproductive sex that takes place; not only does sex between men and women usually not result in pregnancy, but most sex between men and women is intentionally "nonreproductive." This lends further weight to not reducing all discussions of male sexuality to male reproduction, just as it is important not to reduce male reproduction to male reproductive health problems like erectile dysfunction, low motility of sperm, and impotence. Questions of pleasure and desire (and the lack thereof), of emotional comfort (and discomfort), of fantasy (and fear)—all these factors are at play in and throughout men's sexual and reproductive lives.

A recent study of men who frequent strip clubs in North Carolina provides additional evidence of why male sexuality must be separated from male reproduction and even the basic male sex act itself. In the book, Katherine Frank (2003) describes why some men may spend hundreds of dollars each week *not* to have sex with women, and in the process she uncovers how, instead of direct sexual release, men pay to look at and spend time with strippers. Frank argues that the strip clubs provide a space for many men where their feelings of psychological powerlessness are given safe haven from the social world in which men have acknowledged authority.[18]

In short, as the extensive and extensively cited literatures on same-sex sex, transvestism, and transgender politics illustrate, the separation of male reproduction and sexuality as analytic categories is indispensable. The more difficult riddle is how and when to recombine these categories, and not just for analytic purposes, but, for instance, in order to explore the lives of billions of men for whom reproduction and sexuality are connected in everyday and palpable ways. It is apparent that sexual intercourse and other sexual activities as occur between men and women have been stunningly avoided and/or ignored in present-day scholarship. One might have expected anthropologists to be interested in such activities, for their habitual and ritualized qualities alone.

It is sometimes said that men's reproduction is contingent on their sexuality—and more specifically on their achieving an erection—in ways not true for women.[19] Nevertheless, to carry this argument to its logical conclusion, unless one were to argue that all erections are the same—and that all erections arise for the same reason—it is as foolish to exaggerate such features of male sexuality as to consider them wholly distinct from the ways in which women's reproduction can be contingent on their sexuality. For both men and women it would seem that the most salient issue is not an alleged universal physiological manner of responding to sexual stimulation, but what causes what kinds of responses in what cultural contexts, and when, how, and why.

MEN DO NOT TAKE RESPONSIBILITY FOR BIRTH CONTROL

This assertion may not be a real mistake, much less a wholesale lie. Many men do not take responsibility for contraception, and never have or will.[20]

Further, who among men is demanding birth control for men? Internationally, the only coherent social movements among men that are identified with men-as-men are the multithreaded struggles for gay rights and freedoms. In particular countries, of course, there are organizations professing to advance the rights of men, like the right-wing Christian Promise Keepers in the United States. Yet in none of these movements are men seeking to gain more control over their fertility, through male hormonal implants, silicone injections in their vas deferens, or other methods of contraception.[21] Nor are men as a cohesive social force demanding more condoms and more vasectomies for the masses.

Still missing in Mexico, as in most of the world, is a history of men's participation in preventing pregnancies. To what extent have men's experiences paralleled those described by Schneider and Schneider (1996) in nineteenth- and twentieth-century Sicily, where the practice of coitus interruptus was widely practiced and regarded as an eminent sign of respectability. Given that before the introduction of chemical methods, the "reverse gear" (as it was called in Italy) was a primary contraceptive technique in Mexico as well, we would do well to learn the extent to which there, too, coitus interruptus "had less to do with an ascetic renunciation of pleasure than with empowerment," gaining purchase on life and love (Schneider and Schneider 1996:162).

Meanwhile, women in Mexico sometimes describe the contraceptive situation as "Las mujeres ya saben de eso" (Women are the ones who know about that). Women in Mexico *cuidarse*, "take care of themselves," when they employ one or more methods to not get pregnant. How much this situation exists because women, not men, become pregnant, or because men by nature will not share responsibility for family planning, or because the contraceptive options available on the global market are overwhelmingly those that women must ingest, insert, or inject is far from clear. There are, in fact, few birth control options for men. Why? To what extent are culture and physiology, for example, implicated in the lack of male contraception? Experiments with male hormonal birth control and temporary silicone plugs for the vas deferens have not led to the development and marketing of contraception for the enormous population of men who presumably avail themselves of contraceptive options for women.[22]

Widespread ignorance, misinformation, and unfounded fears are at least as significant as some unbridled and peculiarly Mexican machismo in understanding the reasons that few men in Oaxaca get vasectomies (see chapter 6). According to many men I have met and interviewed in vasectomy clinics (2001–05), lack of knowledge is one reason more men do not seek vasectomies. Some men and women learn about vasectomies from public service announcements on television, the radio, or in newspapers; some from brochures available at family planning clinics; and others from nurses and doctors who work in these clinics. Word of mouth, especially from one man to another, is often the most convincing method of publicizing the procedure. In addition, throughout Mexico, it is common to see signs painted on the outside walls of health clinics in many cities to advertise the availability of vasectomies inside, thus promoting male participation in this form of permanent contraception.

Yet in most clinical situations I encountered in Oaxaca, in state-run family planning promotion efforts, vasectomy is presented as a matter of individual choice and not in the context of overall relations between men and women in which men seldom assume primary responsibility for contraception. The official brochures, for example, do not compare vasectomy with tubal ligation for women, the latter being a far more invasive and temporarily debilitating procedure. The approach with vasectomy is that this method of birth control is available, should a man choose to avail himself of this service. Not surprisingly, perhaps, for men who do choose a vasectomy, acquiring one can be difficult.

It is a mistake to discount the active participation and empathy of men in contraception altogether. One finding from my vasectomy research in Oaxaca is that men express great relief when they no longer have cause to worry that the women they are having sex with might get pregnant. Not insignificantly, several women in the same study reported a similar release from the pregnancy worries they had shared with men throughout their sexually active lives. Nevertheless, when comparing the statistics of men's participation in what are often considered more "male forms of birth control," like condoms and vasectomy, the figures vary tremendously from country to country (and sometimes even from region to region within countries). Do these numbers represent something funda-

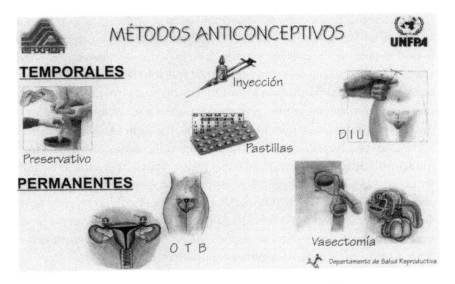

Display used in public clinics in Mexico offering different available contraceptive methods, 2004.

mental about cultural attitudes and practices with respect to male sexuality? Recalling the comments made to me by the official from the National Science Foundation, can we in a meaningful sense correlate contraceptive prevalence among men to particular national "machismo and non-machismo cultures"?[23]

Ultimately, the involvement of men in contraception is not just a matter of individual choice, of "machismo and non-machismo" cultures, nor is it a matter of men versus women, those who inseminate during spasms that last a few seconds versus those who potentially will carry a fetus for nine months. Indeed, to explain what Latin American scholars Barbosa and Viera Villela (1997) call "the introduction of a contraceptive culture," and what Colombian anthropologist Mara Viveros (2002) calls "the female contraceptive culture," in which women worldwide are overwhelmingly responsible for birth control, we must look not simply at negligent and roguish men who seek to absolve themselves of any responsibility for preventing pregnancy (see also Barbosa and Di Giacomo do Lago 1997). We must also ask about the role of government in population control, family planning, and, more recently, reproductive health and sexuality campaigns; about the role of the Catholic church in many parts of the world; and that of the United Nations Population Fund (UNFPA); the International Planned Parenthood Federation (IPPF) and its local affiliates; the Population Council; and the Ford, MacArthur, and Rockefeller Foundations in creating a female contraceptive culture. And, just as decisively, we must examine the part played by the pharmaceutical industry in demarcating the limits of what is considered by their research scientists to be biologically possible and feasible for ensuing marketing strategies (see Petryna, Lakoff, and Kleinman 2006). Clearly, some of these institutions have played a much greater role than others in finding ways to move beyond the so-called fertility regulation, in bucking the tide of the female contraceptive culture by involving men and developing a comprehensive approach to women's health.

As a final point with respect to men and contraception, it would be a shame to forget that, before the days of the pill, many men played a larger role in preventing reproduction, and that the use of condoms and withdrawal were more significant as factors in heterosexual sexual encounters than they are in most circumstances today. Clearly, this is not the situation now, when worldwide 61 percent of all "women of reproductive age" who are married or in a consensual union are themselves using contraception (United Nations 2003).[24]

MEN'S SEXUAL IMPULSE IS A (NATURAL) GIVEN

This enormous topic is so freighted with popular lore it is difficult to know where to begin unraveling the mistakes and lies. Perhaps one place to start would be to ask a question: Where did the gay gene go? One answer, of course, is that it never existed and therefore had nowhere to go. More substantially, the research that proclaimed the discovery of the gay gene was hopelessly flawed because it rested on a social construct (knowledge and consensus as to who is gay in the first place) and then attempted to trace backward to find some genetic similarity among such people. The attributive and ascriptive aspects of gayness, whatever that might be, are impossible to tease apart. Also problematic is what Roger Lancaster (2003) calls "genomania and heterosexual fetishism." As Lancaster explains: "I do not believe that homosexuality is really susceptible to even 'good' biological research. As a complex, meaningful, and motivated human activity, same-sex desire is simply not comparable to [genetically related] questions like eye color, hair color, or height" (2003:256).

The futile quest for the gay gene is relevant to the question of male sexual impulses insofar as they are similarly naturalized. Mary McIntosh (1968) helped free us from seeing homosexuals as having "a condition"; in the language of the day, she instead emphasized that homosexuals play social roles. With heterosexual men, it seems, we have not advanced much in our understanding, to the extent that they are still viewed (albeit today with the imprimatur of evolutionary psychology and hormone-level testing) as having their own kind of homogeneous sexual condition. For example, it is truly extraordinary that we have so few feminist studies on men and rape—the motives, contexts, and histories of rape—and on the relationship of power and sexuality to understanding rape.[25] Further, early second-wave feminism inadvertently contributed to the problem of biologistic reasoning. Specifically, Lynne Segal notes the "theoretical inadequacy of the scientifically respectable but nevertheless reductive model of sexuality in use in these early feminist writings, based upon the idea of drives and their repression or release" (1994:41).

In the course of exploring the pervasive influence of notions in Mexico regarding an intrinsic and totemic sexuality among men there, I have also found that the stereotype that "real men must procreate to prove themselves men" is linked historically to a state-sponsored pronatalism that developed following the Mexican Revolution at the beginning of the twentieth century and then accelerated through the early 1970s, a period in which the Mexican nation was generally conflated with men and masculinity (see Gutmann 2006 [1996]). In addition to the totemization of male sexualities that continues unabated in the twenty-first century, this national natural history has played an important role in contemporary shibboleths and truisms regarding what men in Mexico sexually want, do, seek, and need.

One implication of the totemization of male sexuality for the subject of men and reproduction is the promotion of a mechanistic understanding that "men's participation in the reproductive process is, in effect, limited to their contribution of sperm" (Marsiglio 1998:50). Marsiglio's 1998 study is among the few devoted to analyzing the relationship between men, sexuality, and reproduction, albeit largely based on U.S. data. The book is in many respects a subtle examination of "procreative man," and Marsiglio is generally careful not to overstep the limits of our knowledge about these topics. Yet though the reader may think she knows what Marsiglio really means by "limited to their contribution of sperm," I wonder if this is the most helpful way to formulate the matter. The cultural influence model at play here allows Marsiglio (1998:51) to speculate that because men do not carry the fetus for nine months, like women, this leads to an "indifference" on their part to pregnancy, and to even a general "alienation from the reproductive process" that is only now slightly mitigated by new technologies like ultrasound that allow men (in some classes and countries) to visually experience the fetal growth and impending birth of their children.

Such an approach to studying men, sexuality, and reproduction is too culturally circumscribed and ultimately supports the notion that narrowly conceived notions of biology inevitably trump all else, though undoubtedly it has a rehabilitated ring of truth today, when the role of genetic testing to establish paternity is forcing some deadbeat dads to acknowledge their paternal responsibilities. Nonetheless, even paternity, including in societies espousing normative nuclear families, has ultimately proved itself not so very reducible to consanguinity. Still less should male sexuality ever be reduced to neural firings and blood flows.

LOVE HAS NOTHING TO DO WITH MEN, SEXUALITY, AND REPRODUCTION

The claim may be patently ridiculous, but after taking stock of most scholarship on these subjects one could well be left with this impression. Part of the fault may lie with Foucault (1980), for whom love was conspicuously absent. But the lack of attention to love and the like, especially with respect to men and their sexual and reproductive life histories, is a glaring omission.[26] Obviously, terms like *love* must be thoroughly contextualized culturally and historically, yet the difficulty of such an enterprise does not in itself explain our prior reluctance to undertake this task. Instead, and following on naturalized assumptions about male sexuality, we may have unintentionally assumed that love, for men, is not so relevant to the study of sex and reproduction.[27] As absurd as this may seem, it is hard to otherwise explain our scholarly lapse.

One indication of how skewed our perspective on love and sexuality may sometimes be is illustrated by the language with which we discuss reproductive health generally, whether related to women, men, or both. In brochures and medical texts contraception is generally presented in rather negative terms, as when we talk of population and birth *control*, fertility *regulation*, family *planning*, and pregnancy *prevention*. If there is, at least for some on some occasions, a joy in sexuality that does not result in procreation and even, god forbid, reproduction, it might be worth attending to the complex meanings such pleasures might entail.

MEN WILL DO WHAT THEY DO REGARDLESS OF WOMEN

The inclusion of men in studies of reproduction reflects, in part, scholarship catching up to reality. The conceptual and empirical obstacles to this inclusion are many, and here I call attention to a particular weakness in studies of men and masculinities that has caused problems more generally than simply with respect to reproductive matters: the absence of substantial research that documents and theorizes the influence adult women have on adult men. There are many studies showing the influence of women on male children. There are studies on the influence of adult men on adult women. But there are precious few that examine what mothers, sisters, wives, and other women say and do in the lives of their men. If nothing else, this omission feeds the notion that men are not in their daily lives responding in good measure to negotiations, entreaties, threats, and seductions initiated by women.

The ad folks on Madison Avenue know better than to accept this conclusion, and following initial advertising campaigns in 1998 that were aimed more squarely at men and that announced the advent of Viagra on the global market, advertisements for newer drugs like Cialis and Levitra have made pointed use of women to promote the idea that "if you want to have sex and your male partner suffers from erectile dysfunction, get him to try this pill." In research on contraceptive decision making in Oaxaca, I discovered the influence of women on men: of the few men who had opted for vasectomy, many made reference to their wives' past experiences with contraception, pregnancy, and childbirth, and offered as a primary reason why they decided to get sterilized the justification "It's my turn to suffer" (see chapter 6). Even topics that have held long-term interest in the reproductive health studies of women might be revisited to examine the relationship of women to men—for example, with respect to postpartum sexual taboos. The meanings and experiences of such strictures for men are not often examined seriously; more likely, the are acknowledged with nothing more than a sly, sneering wink about male resentment and sexual frustration. There is more to be explored on these and related topics.

The shifting sands of feminist conceptualizing about similarities and differences in men's and women's sexualities undoubtedly is part of the picture here. To the extent that root differences are expected and given emphasis, it seems there is a tendency to assume that when left to their own sexual devices men are at most subject to female restrictions but not truly amenable to change, including at the behest of women. If the influence of adult women on adult heterosexual men is a subject of study in ethnographic research, we will find evidence of men reporting trepidation and diffidence and not just confidence and disrespect in their sexual and reproductive relations with women.

It is rather easy to ridicule erectile dysfunction, for example, as one more sob story from men unsatisfied with their sex lives; it is more difficult to develop rich and nuanced ethnographic examinations of topics like impotence and prostitution that are more often the object of jokes than serious study. Cornwall's observations of the impact that accusations of impotence can have on men in southwestern Nigeria are too brief and too rare: "Laughed at by his colleagues and accused of being impotent for not wanting to chase women, he struggled to become a man in their terms, learning to mask his shyness with alcohol and eventually to blot out his disquiet" (2003:238). The implications of the stigma of impotence are too often ignored or glossed over. Odd as it may seem, studies of men who seek female prostitutes are more unusual still, as if the only subject worthy of careful attention in such relations were women, and the only point of controversy was whether such women were more the victims or the agents of their sexual relations with men.[28]

SOMETIMES A CIGAR IS JUST A CIGAR

Sadly, this sentiment no longer applies, and not simply owing to the indiscretions of Bill Clinton and Monica Lewinsky. In her writings about women and the realities of female bodies, Simone de Beauvoir inadvertently also taught us something, by implication, about male bodies and fixed destinies. Since Beauvoir, in the subsequent decades of feminist scholarship on gender and sexuality, our assumptions about male bodies and sexuality, reproduction, and masculinity have remained surprisingly overdetermined. So perhaps we need to look back, not just to Beauvoir but to old Sigmund Freud himself, who still might have a thing or two to teach us about not following biomedicalized models of male sexualities, reproduction, and masculinities. (And, no, one must not overlook the fact that Freud, in his characteristically self-contradictory fashion, also helped to promote the stereotype of active men and passive women, and cigars that could never be smoked.) We might do well to remember that the physics and chemistry of sex do not tell us very much about desire and pleasure, or even domination and submission, the very issues that have everything to do with understanding men's sexualities and reproductive lives—or at least they should.

THREE

New Labyrinths of Solitude

LONESOME MEN AND AIDS

People died of horror and disgust at European civilization
even more than of smallpox and physical ill-treatment.

Claude Lévi-Strauss (1992 [1955]:75)

MEXICAN MIGRANT MALE LONELINESS

In contemporary Mexico, AIDS is a disease of migration and modernity. Worldwide, AIDS is a direct product of neoliberal policies that have prompted the decentralization and privatization of health care. At the same time, structural adjustments related to these changes in health care and imposed by international agencies like the World Bank foster conditions in which large numbers of people are forced to flee their homelands in search of better economic prospects in other countries.[1] This is clearly the case in Mexico, where local circumstances of impoverishment lead millions to try their luck on the other side of the border in the United States. Extrapolating from notoriously unreliable government statistics, by 2000 there were probably over 100,000 men and women from Oaxaca working as migrants in the northern parts of Mexico and in the United States—part of what Federico Besserer calls "the construction of a new diasporic Mexican nation" (2000:385). It is also estimated that by 2000, 60 percent of the 570 *municipios* in the state had experienced "significant emigration" (see Stephen 2005:97).

The political economy of AIDS in Oaxaca involves several features that are global in scope. One key factor in understanding AIDS in Oaxaca is transnational migration: the largest group of people who are HIV+ in the state are men who have worked in the United States and returned to Oaxaca infected with the virus; the second largest population are women who have had sex with these migrant men. Another key factor pertains to the international pharmaceutical industry: unlike certain other countries in the world, such as Brazil, South Africa, and India, where antiretrovirals are available for far less than the cost the drug companies would like to charge for these medications (in these countries, the drugs are either produced locally or the government has refused to pay the pharmaceutical companies full royalties on their patents for the drugs), in Mexico the government pays whatever the drug companies demand. Thus, in Mexico, instead of paying a fraction of the cost demanded by the pharmaceuticals for antiretrovirals, it is only a fraction of the people who need the drugs who are able to receive them. To the extent that people do not seek out the state clinic for AIDS in Oaxaca—because they do not know of its existence or because they do not know they are HIV+—for this reason as well only a fraction of those who need the drugs receive them.

That hundreds or even thousands of Mexican migrant men are now returning to Oaxaca infected with HIV stems largely from the fact that they seek out sexual relations with female prostitutes and fellow male migrants while in the United States. In this way, structural factors shape the vulnerability to HIV for millions of Mexican men working in the fields, factories, and construction sites of the United States. This chapter introduces a few of the men with AIDS—migrant and nonmigrant, heterosexual and bisexual—who talked with me about the virus: how they thought they had become infected; their sexual relationships with women and men in the past, present, and future; and their experiences with medications they were able to secure from the state-run AIDS clinic known as

Sign at entrance to Mixtepec, Oaxaca, in Mixteco, Spanish, and English, the last a reflection of the numerous men and women who migrate from this town to the United States, 2002.

COESIDA.[2] Most of the men and women I talked with about AIDS depended on the medical care they received from COESIDA, and I met most of them at the government AIDS clinic in Oaxaca City.

In late October 2001, barely a month after the Twin Towers were attacked in New York City, the issue of international relations came surprisingly to life in an interview with Donaciano Ramírez as we sat in a consultation room in the state-run AIDS clinic, then located on Colón Street in the center of the city. After Donaciano explained to me that he ran a little convenience store in his Mixtec-speaking village several hours away from the city, and that among other items he carried in the store were syringes, and that he was pretty sure that he must have become infected with HIV from a prick by one of those needles, he queried me: "I try to understand these things. I read magazines and everything. With all the growing problems the United States is having, and with that . . . what do you call it? The war there is now? And that other sickness that's connected to the war? Anthrax?" He then proceeded to describe to me how AIDS, too, was being brought to Mexico from the United States, and gave as an example one man who traveled back and forth and had infected his wife on one of his return visits. Throughout the Mixteca region, as in other parts of Oaxaca, it is common to find license plates that read Arizona, Utah, Ohio, North Carolina, California, New York, Florida, Texas, Illinois, and virtually every other state north of the border.

Another day, I talked with Jesús Hernández, who had worked for some years around Watsonville, near San Jose, California. There are lots of strawberries around there, he told me. He had also worked harvesting cauliflower, celery, and lettuce in the fields of the U.S. Southwest. It was scarier crossing the border now, he told me, in late 2001. "Now there's a lot of fear about biological war." He came back to Oaxaca sick one year, and they ordered blood tests for him in a clinic in his village. They told him he was seropositive and had HIV. " 'What's that?' I ask. 'Have you heard of AIDS?' 'Yes.' 'That's what this is.' I felt like dying. I thought I was dying right then. No. There was no way out for me. Not forward, not backward. They told me they were going to send me to the COESIDA clinic, where I could get help."

I asked Jesús how he became infected. He answered at length: "I was a hard worker. I worked in the fields. I killed myself in the fields! Sometimes I worked by the hour. Sometimes by contract. The bosses always looked at me like a good worker. I have a lot of experience. But I am illegal. My family was here. One day . . . because I was always responsible about what I did . . . well . . . That's why I never, well, how was I going to get through it? Because I felt so alone, right, and I wanted a little distraction . . ."

"Loneliness," I murmured sympathetically.

"I went out cruising, and went into a bar."

"In Watsonville?"

"Uh-huh, in Watsonville. I had four or five beers. Everything's cool. There was a woman dancing. 'You know what? You coming with me?' 'Yeah!' I went with her, and about five or six months later I began to get symptoms. But I never imagined that's what it was. I think that's what it was. I kept on seeing her. I would go by, and sometimes she was in the street, well, she was one of the women . . ."

"A prostitute?"

"Yeah, a prostitute. I paid about fifteen dollars."

After relating the perils of crossing the California desert, filled with rat-tlesnakes and robbers, of having walked for thirty hours over mountains after mountains, Jesús told me his wife was also now infected with HIV.

"Was she angry at you?" I asked.

"No, not at all."

"Because you didn't know you could infect her?"

"Well, I didn't know, and because she never went without money here. Every month or every two weeks, [I sent her] check after check."

"And will you go back to the United States, to earn more money to send back to your wife?" I asked.

"Well, yes. I got infected in the United States, in Watsonville. But I won't hold that against my brother country." Then he laughed. "I would like to go, to work again. But what I am scared of is my medicine. Because if I leave here they will cut off my medicine. If I get there and fight, they will do other studies, and as I am illegal there are fewer resources for me. That's why I say, 'Better here.'"

Mishra, Conner, and Magaña (1996b:8–10) provide a vivid picture of the unregistered, temporary, and makeshift encampments in California's agricultural regions where Mexican migrant laborers lived in the 1990s. The luckier men might have lived in rental housing, six or more farm workers to an apartment. Others could be found living on hillsides and in canyons, riverbeds, and the groves where they harvested fruits and vegetables for the U.S. market. Plywood covered with tar paper and cor-rugated plastic sheets or old mattresses would be pulled together to form the walls of their makeshift housing. Some men lived in what they called "spider holes" dug in the ground under thick bushes that were just large enough to sleep in and remain unseen by immigration agents. A *fayuquero* drove a van from encampment to encampment selling meals, toiletries, other goods. In the mid-1990s, few encampments had potable water, gas, electricity, or waste disposal. Leo Chavez quotes a Oaxaca migrant he in-terviewed a few years earlier, who described a similar situation: "In Oa-xaca, we live in a small village and we live the same as here. In our house there is no electricity, no water. We must haul water to the house the same as here. We use candles instead of electricity the same as here. There is no stove. We had to haul wood from the mountain just as we do here. Our house is wood like these. It is the same. The same living there as it is here" (1992:78). These conditions no doubt contributed to the chronic stomach aches and diarrhea that plagued the men, some of whom sought to relieve these symptoms by injecting themselves with vitamins and antibiotics on a regular basis, just as they had in their villages in Mexico. And needless to say, the syringes were often reused without being sterilized.

In spite of the increase in the number of Border Patrol agents, from 4,000 to 11,000 in the period 1995–2005, as many as a million Mexicans each year continue to cross the geopolitical divide to find work and to mail back as much money to their families as they can. And if their challenges were not already great enough, the modern plague of AIDS is now an additional threat to the lives of these migrants.

PATHS TO AIDS

All of these factors have for decades contributed to a transnational labyrinth of solitude for millions of Mexican migrant men living and working in the United States; what has changed in recent years is AIDS, a disease that has had severe consequences for men who are not careful enough about how and with whom they have sexual relations during their sojourns in the United States. And what has changed with AIDS is that it has become a disease of migrants and, increasingly, of women. By 2005, of the 102,575 registered cases of AIDS in Mexico, the percentage of women with AIDS had climbed from less than 5 percent in 1995 to almost 16 percent ten years later (Registro Nacional de Casos de SIDA).

One man I interviewed at the AIDS clinic in Oaxaca talked about the two years he had spent as a plumber in Los Angeles. He told me that on weekends he sometimes visited friends who worked near Bakersfield. It was common for prostitutes to visit on Saturday nights. Some men wasted so much money on these *pachanga*-parties that they had none to send home to their families in Mexico. He denied ever having sex with a prostitute—in other words, that he had ever paid for sex—but acknowledged that he would drink a lot and that he often awoke with "una mujer desconocida" (a woman he did not know). He tried to be careful and use a condom, but because of the alcohol he consumed he was not always able to do this, he said. When we talked, he was living at home in Oaxaca, suffering badly from diarrhea and body aches. He and his wife had not had sex for years and, he admitted, now she would not even cook for him any more.

Despite some excellent ethnographic fieldwork and vivid portraits of the social suffering among Mexican farm workers resident in the United States, we know surprisingly little about their sexual relationships. As Mishra, Conner, and Magaña wrote, "Little, however, is known about the impact of the HIV/AIDS epidemic on Latino farmworkers" (1996a:vii). The same authors noted, more generally, "Little is known about the health status of farmworkers" (Mishra, Conner, and Magaña 1996b:10). Around the same time, Bronfman and López concluded, "Mexico does not have enough information, based on reliable research, on the sexuality of its population and, in the case of migrants, there is no information at all" (1996:49).[3] Eight years later, Magis-Rodríguez and his colleagues were still forced to admit, "We know little about the impact of migration on the development of the HIV/AIDS epidemic in Mexico" (2004:S217). Writing about the epidemiology of HIV among Mexican migrants in California, Sanchez et al. strike the same chord, stating that "relatively few studies have examined the prevalence of HIV among Mexican migrant farm workers in California," and that "little is known about the risk behaviors and HIV prevalence among Mexican migrant sex workers" (2004:S206).[4]

Despite the paucity of reliable information, including well-grounded epidemiological studies, about the sexual activities of Mexican migrant men and about how some of them become infected with HIV in the United States, researchers believe the virus is transmitted among this population through sex with female prostitutes and through sex between the men themselves.

The primary route of transmission for the AIDS virus in Latin America is believed to be through sexual relations between men. As the PAHO/WHO/UNAIDS report on HIV/AIDS in the Americas states, "Despite increasing infection rates in women, male–male sex remains the biggest single cause of new HIV infections in several countries, including Canada, the United States and Mexico" (2001:25). Reports from epidemiological research in Oaxaca, cited in this chapter, also show that a high percentage of cases of AIDS can be traced back to men who had sex with other men. Nonetheless, although we have the broad outlines about male–male sexual transmission, we still lack details on sexual relations among migrant men. Absent better ways of verifying other possible vectors for the transmission of the AIDS virus, like sex with female prostitutes, those who study Mexican male sexuality are still too often left only with speculation, rumor, and accusations.

The focus on male–male sexual relations has been fueled in part by a desire of researchers to counter widespread homophobia, both in the United States and Mexico, and to acknowledge the many Mexican migrant men who have sex with other men. Yet in the age of AIDS the mere assertion of pervasive patterns of male–male sexual relations among Mexicans and Mexican migrants to the United States can inadvertently overlook, or at least underestimate, other possible ways that these migrant men may have become infected. Although my focus in this chapter is not mainly on male–male transmission among men from Oaxaca, this should not be interpreted to mean that men having sex with other men is no longer the primary vector of infection of this "epidemic with many faces." Rather, along with Magis-Rodríguez et al. (2004:S215), I am especially concerned with "an emerging pattern of increased [hetero]sexual transmission." The official figures for category of transmission of new AIDS cases in Mexico for the period 1983–2005 were 28.4 percent homosexual sexual transmission, 20.2 percent bisexual, and 46.0 percent heterosexual. But for just the year 2005, these figures were 21.8, 17.4, and 58.6, respectively, indicating a dramatic rise in the potential importance of heterosexual sexual transmission of the virus in Mexico (see Secretaría de Salud 2005: table 5).

Sanchez et al. (2004:S206) write that Mexican men are undoubtedly having sex with female prostitutes who originally became infected as a result of intravenous (IV) drug use or male sex partners. Not only are the rates of IV drug use higher on the U.S. side of the international border, but in Mexico, where prostitution is essentially legal if prostitutes go for monthly medical examinations, it has been reported that if registered sex workers suspect they are infected they move into the underground, unorganized, unregistered sector of sex work, where prostitutes undergo serologic assessments only when they are apprehended for selling sex without legal credentials (see Mishra, Conner, and Magaña 1996b:16–17). This same study reported higher seroprevalence rates among African American farm workers, as well as higher rates of IV drug use among this population, and speculated that Mexican migrant farm workers might have become infected with HIV through casual sex with the African Americans with whom they worked; it is possible, too, that racist stigma influenced the Mexicans not to report such sexual experiences.

In an early paper on AIDS and farm workers, J. Raul Magaña (1991) talked of men who called themselves "hermanos de leche" (milk brothers), referring to the fact that they had had serial sex with one woman "in rapid succession" and thus had contact with each other's semen. Magaña raised the possibility that, in a single sexual act, HIV could be transmitted from man to woman, from woman to man, *and* from man to man, the last without the men having had sexual or other bodily contact directly with one another except through their seminal fluids. In a later paper on Latina sex workers in cantinas, Ayala, Carrier, and Magaña (1996) show that men were having sex one after another with the same prostitute but without condoms, thereby undoubtedly "sharing" semen with one another.

Another possible vector of transmission of the AIDS virus is through the sharing of infected needles. According to all available studies, intravenous (illegal) drug use is not a serious problem among Mexicans, certainly nothing on the scale that is found in other populations in the United States. Nonetheless, there is ample evidence that Mexican men and women do use *legal* drugs like antibiotics, as well as injectable vitamins, at far higher rates than is true for other people in the United States. Facing a gamut of legal and logistical obstacles to regular, reliable, and inexpensive health care, and given their deplorable living conditions which can lead to gastrointestinal disease and much more, Mexican migrants routinely seek ways to self-medicate, including through IV injection using non-sterilized hypodermic needles.

Regardless of whether HIV is transmitted through sex or with dirty needles, for Mexican men who never make it to the United States but only migrate to other parts of Mexico, loneliness is also an important aspect of life. In January 2002 I interviewed a very chatty widow who was only twenty-eight years old. Her husband had died of AIDS the year before. She had been worried about social (and physical) ostracism and had been pleasantly surprised by the warmth and support of her family and friends. She told me she would never remarry, not because she didn't enjoy sex, but because she just did not see it happening.[5] Her husband had left to go work in a jeans factory in Mexico City. He told her he probably got infected after getting tattoos there. Eventually, he also admitted to sleeping with another woman—he just could not *aguantar* (endure) not having sex with someone. After he died, the widow told me, some other woman showed up in Oaxaca, claiming to have lived with her husband during his time in the capital city.

Loneliness is associated with the issue of male sexuality because health care practitioners, in Oaxaca and elsewhere in the Mexican republic, tend to assume that men everywhere will normally seek sexual pleasures, and that lonely men will seek these any way they can. In other words, even self-identified heterosexual men who would "normally" seek out women will succumb to sex with other men if they have no other options.[6] Unfortunately, we still lack detailed studies of what is happening in the migrant camps and apartment complexes where migrant workers live and have sex and, for the unluckiest, become infected with HIV. We know more about sexual regulation and stigma than we do about the sexual scripts written on migrant bodies in furtive and transgressive and, for the luckiest, loving ways. We need this kind of study of Mexican migrants in the United States to be able to do more than offer stories about dying and sexual malaise. In Oaxaca, a recurring theme in my interviews with infected men and women was that the former no longer had *ganas* (desires) and that this resulted in the cessation of sexual relations, with or without condoms, altogether for the couple. Not everyone with HIV stopped having sex, by any means, but many reportedly did because there was no longer pleasure in this kind of activity. Assuming the epidemiologists are correct and well over 90 percent of people in Mexico with HIV or AIDS contracted the illness through sexual transmission, we would do well to learn more about men's and women's lives when they still did want to have sex.

Given the fact that many Mexican migrant men now return to Oaxaca infected with HIV, the question remains, Where did they pick it up? Because even if they have wives back in Mexico, they are "single" in the United States, and because, according to doctors in Oaxaca, woman-to-man transmission of HIV is next to impossible, the assumption in the AIDS clinic in Oaxaca is that there must be a lot of Mexican men having sex with one another in the orchards and construction sites of the United States (see chapter 4). To further bolster their argument, the AIDS doctors in Oaxaca point to low seroprevalence rates among female prostitutes in Oaxaca, the presumption being that rates for female prostitutes in the United States are similar, despite all evidence to the contrary (see Bellis 2003; Sanchez et al. 2004; Magis-Rodríguez et al. 2004).

There is evidence that prostitutes who are infected stop going to get checked and simply work in a more clandestine fashion. One report (see McKinley 2005) noted that although 5,000 prostitutes with registration booklets received checkups every month in Tijuana, more than 8,000 women and men had once been registered there but no longer returned for medical examinations. In addition, the booklets are not given to prostitutes who are under eighteen; who are from another country (for example, those from Central America); or who do not have proof of identity (e.g., a birth certificate or driver's license), which is a less common possession for people from rural areas. Low seroprevalence among registered female prostitutes in Mexico is not necessarily a good indication that heterosexual transmission of HIV from women to men is of negligible significance, as I was routinely assured in Oaxaca by medical personnel there.

David Bellis writes in a recent study comparing Mexican and U.S. street prostitutes, "The differences between the Mexican and American FSW [female sex workers] were startling. The Mexicans were *choir girls* compared to their beaten up, sick, toothless, heroin-addicted Southern California sisters" (2003:x). In particular, Bellis finds that drug addiction is a major component in the spread of HIV from U.S. street prostitutes to clients, including Mexican migrants, and represents a factor in transmission that is largely missing among Mexican prostitutes and their clients (72–74).

Numerous men I interviewed in Oaxaca who had spent time working in the United States talked of meeting *gabachas* (white women), "going out" with them, and giving them money and other things; whether these women actually called themselves prostitutes was irrelevant to most of the men with whom I discussed these matters.

I asked Francisco López, who worked as a construction laborer in California in the 1990s, who were these women he talked of "going out" with. Were they prostitutes?

"Well, who knows? You never know."

"Did you have to pay?"

"No, sometimes not. The deal is that some of them were drug addicts. And the fact is that it makes things easier, and you just go, 'Here's some fun' [Ay viene el placer]. And when you put it all together, it's too late."

We also talked of the camps in the countryside where he had lived while working the fields around southern California. He talked of the prostitutes who showed up on Saturday nights looking for business in the rooms of the migrant laborers. "That's really common. It's normal." Francisco came back to Oaxaca in 1999; by that point, he was infected with HIV, and he then infected his wife.

Francisco's story was similar in some respects to that of Zósimo, who told me he believed he became HIV+ after having sex with female prostitutes and not using protection. He was living in Oaxaca with a young woman, who was also in the room when I interviewed Zósimo in the COESIDA clinic. I asked her how she became infected.

"Well, I hooked up with him and . . . he infected me. Still, his mother says I infected him. She shouts at me, she goes around telling me, and . . ." She began to cry, then added, "She blames me when he gets sick. She's really a fool." I asked Zósimo what he does when this happens, and the young woman responded, "What's he going to say? His mother is his mother. He doesn't say squat when she talks to me like that." When Zósimo began wasting away and could no longer work, they had to move in with his parents; they could no longer afford a place of their own, even though she worked selling used clothing. One of Zósimo's brothers moved out after the couple moved in, because he did not want to have any contact with people who were HIV+.

Several people I spoke with at the COESIDA clinic related the stigma that comes with being labeled sidoso or sidosa by neighbors and family who learn of their HIV status. "Society doesn't accept us," María Núñez, the widowed mother of three children, told me one rainy afternoon in the clinic. "They call us promiscuous," she complained, explaining that pamphlets she read from her daughter's school showed prostitutes with the sickness and explained that having multiple sexual partners was the frequent cause of AIDS. For Araceli and her husband, Santiago, who had traveled hours to reach the clinic from their home in Huajapan, the stigma of AIDS made them afraid that people in their small town would learn about them being HIV+. "They would probably run us out of town, because people are ignorant and they think they can get sick if you touch them. That's why no one in our town knows—except us and our family."

My study explored the aftermath of infection, but, as mentioned above, we know too little about "hermanos de leche," men who "share" semen by having sex one after the other with the same woman; too little about intravenous antibiotic and vitamin practices and other possible ways HIV might be spread among Mexican migrants living in labor camps, construction sites, and overcrowded apartments. Most of all, we know too little about the sexual lives of Mexican migrant men—and women—and are thereby forced to rely too much on popular lore about men's escapades with prostitutes and their furtive sexual release with one another, in short, their presumed natural sexual desires and habits.[7]

In the most candid sense, providing care for Mexican migrant men who have AIDS requires they be viewed as vital citizens whose lives are both worth saving and able to be saved. As the space of health care in Mexico is shifted from public to private, and from clinic to home, the underlying false choice of "either prevention or treatment" comes into clearer focus. Whereas primary prevention is more cost effective, the space of healing is both more costly and requires that there be people and resources to actually heal the afflicted. The view that only the developed countries can afford adequate AIDS care is shortsighted. With direct reference to the growing importance of migration, studies conducted by the University of California's Universitywide AIDS Research Program in 2004 went so far as to warn that "HIV infection is potentially on the threshold of rapid increase in this [Mexican migrant] population," and that Mexico could "rapidly become the next India or China" (see Rense 2004).

PRIMITIVO'S DESPERATION

International and national migration is deeply implicated in the spread of the AIDS virus in Oaxaca, but as mentioned, men and women who have not traveled in search of work or adventure have become infected under a variety of other circumstances that also illustrate the modern roots of the disease. And regardless of the etiology of the disease, the vast majority of people in Oaxaca do not have sufficient funds to pay private doctors for diagnosis and treatment, especially for antiretroviral medicines. Thus, if they learn about the nature of their illness and the existence of the COESIDA clinic, they may arrive in search of urgent care to save their lives and those of others they may have infected. One man with whom I spoke on several occasions at the clinic was Primitivo Sánchez, and his stories and speculations as to the origins of his affliction provided a searing indictment of the desperate measures he and countless others have employed throughout their lives to provide for their families.

A slight man of forty-eight years when we first met, Primitivo told me he had been infected for six years. He recounted moments in his life when he had begged for money to live and to pay for blood tests and other treatment at various state-run social service agencies. Working as a cook's assistant in a local restaurant, he supported a woman and his three children from a previous relationship.

"How did you get infected?" I asked.

"Well, look, I think, I don't remember, I'm not sure it was the blood bank. Back then—I am talking about more than seven years ago—there were a lot of clandestine blood banks in Mexico. And I think it could have been that. They took blood. I gave several times. One time they took plasma. They paid 300 pesos for 500 grams of blood. In a month I did it like three times."

"Did a lot of people go [to the blood banks]?"

"A lot of people! Tons of people! There were as many as thirty or forty people in lines. There were rooms with as many as fifty beds."

So that was one possible way Primitivo became infected.

Later in our conversation I asked if he had ever had sex with other men.

"Well, yes. Yes."

"With men?"

"Yes, with older men. Not young ones. I am the 'active,' not the 'passive,' one."

It was suddenly clear that he had been a prostitute with other men, so I asked, "Where do you meet them?"

"Wherever. In the Zócalo [main plaza], for example."

"I've heard about this," I commented, "but I've never noticed it."

"Because it's done discreetly."

"The ones who pay, they're Mexicans? Foreigners?"

"Foreigners and Mexicans."

"Where do you go to have sexual relations?"

"The public bathrooms or to people's apartments if they have them. In the bathrooms, they leave the stall door a little open, and someone walks by and says, 'Aha, I like that!' And then, . . . then, we're off."

"So you've earned money from prostitution."

"Well, prostitution . . . well, not all the time, because that's not all I do. But sometimes, now and then."

"Why now and then?"

"Money."

"Have you been doing this for a long time?" I asked, thinking again of the fact that he was forty-eight years old.

"Since I was fifteen or twenty."

When he has needed money, he has resorted to seeking out older men who will pay him to stick his penis in their anuses, or to let them suck his penis. Primitivo talked about sex with female prostitutes—he has had to pay on these occasions—and about other intimate aspects of his sexual history. I asked him if he always was the penetrator, never the penetrated. He said he had been screwed before, but he did not like it. Maybe it stemmed from his first experiences of being penetrated.

"Look, when I was a kid, from the time I was eight, my brother, my half-brother, the one who died recently, he raped me. He was eighteen. He did it a lot. And I was scared, so I never said anything. I was ten when my parents died. So for all intents and purposes, I was a 'child of the street' [niño de la calle]."

He never wanted to be passive after this. I asked Primitivo if he used a condom when he had sex. With the woman he lived with, for example.

"Yes," he replied.

"Always?" I pressed.

"Yes," he repeated.

"Sometimes?" I cajoled him.

"Hmm . . . well. Like two times."

"Is she infected?"

"She is also. Only thing is that there's a problem with her: she doesn't want to take care of herself."

"Why?" I asked.

"Because . . . since she was eight years old . . . she was eight when . . . crossing a river [the Río Atoyac], the one across from the Central de Abastos [the giant market]—they lived on the other side—she crossed barefoot and stepped on some glass and got infected. Her father had to take her to the Centro Médico [Nacional] la Raza in Mexico. They cut off her foot there. Her leg only goes to here. This gave her a tumor. And really they were so outrageous with her there, the doctors and her father, who was an alcoholic and abandoned her. The doctors stole some of her spinal column. What did that have to do with her foot? Nothing."

"Can she walk today?"

"Yes, she walks. With difficulty. She doesn't have a prosthesis. She doesn't use a cane or anything. She used to use crutches, but then she didn't want to anymore. She chucked them and began to walk like this."

Primitivo may have become infected from sex with female prostitutes, or from sex when he prostituted himself to other men, or from selling blood in an illegal clinic, or from a host of other reasons, all of which speak eloquently to the misery of poor men and women in Oaxaca, who must place their own bodies in jeopardy if they wish to subsist and provide for their families.

FILEMON'S CREDIBLE TALES

I thought Primitivo's stories were astonishing and revelatory until I met Filemon and his wife, Amaya. Filemon already had AIDS; Amaya was just HIV+. His tales about his stint in the Mexican Army, though never confirmed, in their very fabulousness revealed to me the wretched possibilities of human existence as have few other experiences in my life. Even if his fables were entirely the products of an AIDS-deranged imagination, what remarkable images he was able to conjure, and how consequential were the social implications of the three ways he speculated he might have become infected with the AIDS virus.

After learning a little about Filemon and Amaya—that they lived in the coastal resort town of Huatulco, that he suffered from diarrhea, vomiting, headaches, fever, cramps, and a lot of other stomach problems—I asked, as I always did, how they thought they had become infected. "I was in the Army, and that's where unfortunately I got infected," Filemon told me. "I infected my wife." I asked what being in the Army had to do with AIDS. "In the Army . . . the truth, well, it's like this . . . I had sexual relations with several partners [*varias parejas*], and, well, one of them [*una de ellas*] . . . I guess one of them infected me. And I didn't realize it, and unfortunately then I infected my wife." In a voice full of tender and grateful tones, Filemon told me that his wife had never reproached him for what he had done; nonetheless, sometimes he felt guilty, felt bad, because he was responsible for infecting her.

"When did you join the Army?" I asked Filemon.

"At the beginning of 1996," he replied, adding that he had remained in until the end of 1998 or so.

"Where were you stationed?"

"I was in Chiapas more than anywhere. I was in Tabasco. [The state of] Mexico. Mexico City. I was in the desert of Sonora. In the mountains of Chihuahua. I was in Sinaloa, too. I was in Chiapas for six months. It was incredibly tough there. Still is. It looks peaceful but there are always . . . problems. You try to defend yourself because they come . . . they, the masked people [*los encapuchados*] and they want to attack you and of course you don't want to let them."

"Were you in a city or in the jungle?"

"In the forest, in the Lacandon jungle. That's where I was. There were tough [military] engagements."

I asked Filemon, who was almost twenty-four years old when I met him, to tell me more about how he thought he had become infected with HIV. Filemon had three incredible stories to tell, each one involving events that could have led to his contracting the virus. As he began his stories, I sat in amazement and not a little disbelief: Were these accounts credible, or were they figments of a mind already ravaged by delusions related to the virus?

"I don't know if it's good or bad if I speak about the Army as good or bad," he continued. "What happened is that sometimes we asked the commanders to bring us some women to the detachment. And they brought us four or five Guatemalan women or from El Salvador."

"Mexicans?"

"No Mexicans. We never found out why. Well, because we were on the border of Mexico and Guatemala. So a lot of women became prostitutes, so the Army would let them get through Mexico. They came on weekends, sometimes every two weeks, every month. There were twenty-eight of us, twenty-nine with the officer. And five or six women would have [sexual] relations with all of us. And I used protection. . . ."

"What do you mean protection?"

"When I went with them I carried condoms. So that's how I covered myself. But sometimes I didn't have any, so, well, I just didn't."

"So you soldiers asked the commanders to bring you women?"

"Yeah, there would be another detachment, and they'd call on the radio and say, 'Well, send us the women.' And they would go over to that detachment."

"Guatemalans and Salvadorans."

"And Hondurans."

"So who knows how those women became infected, and then they infected soldiers, and a whole . . ."

"It became a chain."

Filemon paused. He looked at me. Then he looked at his wife. Then he began a second story about how he might have become infected with HIV. I still have no idea why he told me.

"Well, look, I don't know, I don't know if it's true or not true. But I am going to tell you something that I did. Look, I . . . and you know that here in Mexico there are people who ask questions. No? They talk to you about your past, who is harming you. Well, I went to someone like that. After those months in Chiapas, I went to someone like that.

"In Chiapas, the first few months I was in contact with civilians. Then

I wasn't. And where I was, they stopped sending us food [for resupply]. They didn't send water. They had been sending them in by helicopter. Well, we were really hungry. And one of the solders began to be really bad. He had a fever, sores, aches, diarrhea. And the commander, well, saw that we were all delirious, we were seeing things, we saw so many things, and we killed the soldier."

I thought I had just heard Filemon say that he and his fellow soldiers killed one of their own. No, I told myself, that was ridiculous. In a matter-of-fact way, I just asked him, "What?"

"We killed him so he wouldn't suffer anymore. Because we didn't have any food. So we killed him. . . . Because of hunger, you could say."

"You what?! How?"

"Because of hunger."

"With bullets? Like that?"

"Yes, like that. We just shot him."

"But another soldier . . ."

"Yes, one of the soldiers. The commander ordered us to kill him and eat him, because there was no food. So . . ."

"Sorry, it's just that . . . I want to be sure that you are talking about your own experience, in your unit, there, during your six months in Chiapas. The commander told you that you had to kill someone who was suffering. . . ."

"Yeah, he couldn't. . . . Exactly, we did it calmly. What fell from the heavens one night, we picked up and we took it. We killed the soldier who was . . . he had a fever, headaches, stomachaches, all that. And we ate him. So we ate him as if he were an animal, well, like eating an animal."

"But one day he was your friend and the next day he was your food?"

"He was our food. It's just that we didn't have any. They didn't come anymore [to resupply us]. We were incommunicado and lost in the forest."

"What year was this?"

"In 1997, the middle of 1997."

"What was the name of the soldier?"

"The soldier's name was Agustín . . . Agustín García Mendoza."

"Where was he from?"

"He was from the state of Toluca.[8] He was a Toluqueño. That's why I told you, I don't know if it's good or bad what I am telling you, because . . . What I am telling you is very delicate. If the government finds out that I am talking to you, who is not a Mexican, what I am talking to you about, they could throw me in jail. I've told her [pointing to his wife, Amaya] about it. And the truth is that we ate monkey meat, because there are a lot of monkeys, lots of monkeys. And that meat fed us a lot of the time. But then it didn't, not anymore."

"And what did they tell the parents of the soldier? That he died in combat?"

"That he died in combat. Yes. In the end, some said . . . all of us said that there had been an engagement and that he had died and that we had not been able . . . that there was no communication. Six months in the forest without communication."

"How many men participated in the murder, well, the . . . ?"

"You could call it a sacrifice. Twenty-nine, the whole unit."

"But there wasn't a lot of meat."

"No, well, after roasting the meat, less. Sometimes I remember this. And I feel bad."

After Filemon got out of the Army he went to see a seer and healer, someone he called a *curandera*, in Huatulco, on the coast of Oaxaca. The woman told him, " 'Look, I don't know, but you know where you've been. And you got infected from eating human flesh.' She . . . I had never told her this. I never told her." But somehow she knew, Filemon reported, and he thought this was the most likely reason he was stricken with AIDS.

And yet we were not done, because there was a third story Filemon told me that day about where he might have picked up HIV. I had asked Filemon about sex between the soldiers when he was in the army. He replied with another amazing tale:

"Well, yeah, there's that, or there was . . . one time (my wife knows about this, too), one time in Chihuahua [in the north of Mexico] we came on a drug trafficker [*narcotraficante*], and he was carrying . . . he knew where the drugs were. To get him to tell us the truth, the commander ordered me to 'work on him' [*trabájalo*]. He says, 'Do what you want but get the truth out of him.' "

"So more or less you raped him to get the information."

"Practically. But the man . . . certainly I . . . . I realized that . . . that he was a homosexual. Because he didn't refuse, he didn't say anything. A man who is, you could say, normal, well, he wouldn't like to be raped like that. And since two of us couldn't get the truth out of him, another three tried, and we ended up beating him and all that . . . but he never talked. And that was the only time I had relations with a man."

Sex in Chiapas with Central American prostitutes without using a condom might be the reason Filemon became infected with HIV. Or it might have been the fellow soldier he helped kill and eat in the Lacandon forest. Or it might have happened when he raped a drug trafficker in the northern state of Chihuahua. Or all these stories might have been sheer fantasy and Filemon might have contracted the virus some other time. We talked again, and I tried to put him into contact with a journalist who had reported from Chiapas for *La Jornada* newspaper. But Filemon died a few months after I met him. Even if every one of these stories was pure fabrication, they still reveal social horrors that undoubtedly are part of the lives of many in this part of the world: international migration and forced sex work, armed conflict that pits the poor against the poor, and the global trade in drugs that has brought such violence to so many parts of Latin America.[9]

NUMBERS AND VECTORS

Thousands of people in Oaxaca are sick and dying with HIV and AIDS. How these people are identified (and ignored) and treated (and ignored) is grounded in cultural beliefs about men's sexuality and a culturalist resignation that men who engage in dangerous sexual practices may die as a result of AIDS. Although it is true that, in a narrow biological sense, the AIDS virus knows no class or ethnic boundaries, and that many mestizos of means have succumbed to the disease, even casual acquaintance with the COESIDA clinic in Oaxaca City makes it evident that the patients there are disproportionately poor and indigenous. Having money and social standing are not in themselves sufficient barriers to prevent infection, but men and women from the upper strata are far more likely than those from the ranks of the dispossessed to know about AIDS, know how to avoid contracting the virus, or know what to do if they become infected.

Table 1   Diagnosed Cases of AIDS in Oaxaca, Selected Years,
1986–2006

Year	New Diagnoses
1986–96	710
1997	202
2000	182
2001	201
2002	230
2006	269
TOTAL for all years, 1986–2006	3,356

SOURCE: www.salud.gob.mx/conasida/ (accessed 22 January 2007).

According to official figures, in Oaxaca the total number of people, living and dead, who had been diagnosed with AIDS as of 2006 was around
3,400 (see table 1). Off the record, state officials put the number at anywhere from 7,000 to 20,000 people. Of great significance, despite being the
tenth largest state in population, by 2005 Oaxaca had more new cases of
AIDS than all but three other jurisdictions: Mexico City, Mexico State, and
Veracruz (Secretaría de Salud 2005: table 8).

Early research suggested that AIDS in Oaxaca was a stable and fairly
minimal problem restricted to urban middle-class men who had sex with
other men. In other words, it was regarded as a gay disease. This outlook
persisted through the 1980s and into the 1990s. Then gradually in Oaxaca,
as elsewhere in Mexico, in the 1990s it became clear that those testing positive for HIV were increasingly to be found among three new, interrelated
groups: men who had migrated to the United States, women who were
having sex with these men when they returned to Oaxaca, and people living in the rugged countryside in the state. In addition, according to statistics from the Pan American Health Organization (1998:76), in the 1990s
the average age for people with AIDS dropped in Latin America as a
whole, indicating that HIV infection was occurring in younger populations, probably during adolescence.

Table 2   Diagnosed Cases of AIDS in Mexico, 1983–2006

Year	Diagnoses (cumulative)
1983	64
1987	2,892
1992	19,578
1997	44,043
2002	72,382
2006	107,625

SOURCE: www.salud.gob.mx/conasida/ (accessed 22 January 2007).

Table 3   Diagnosed Cases of AIDS in Mexico, Selected States, 2006

Selected States and Mexico City	Number of AIDS Cases to 2006	Rate per 100,000 in Total Population
Mexico City	20,398	231
Jalisco (including Guadalajara)	9,257	135
Baja California (including Tijuana)	4,962	164
Chiapas	3,575	80
Oaxaca	3,356	90
TOTAL	107,625	100

SOURCE: www.salud.gob.mx/conasida/estadis/2006/tasa15nov.pdf (accessed 22 January 2007).

The first case of AIDS in Mexico was reported in 1983. In 1986, the Mexican federal government issued a statement confirming 63 suspected cases of AIDS in the country, 17 of which had been confirmed. By 1992, there were 19,578 confirmed cases of AIDS in the country, and by 1997 the government reported there were 44,043 diagnosed AIDS cases in Mexico. By 2006, the number of persons on the official list of those with AIDS was 107,625 (see table 2).

From the perspective of witnessing human tragedy, it matters little how the people who shared their life experiences with me contracted the deadly virus. From a public health standpoint, however, I became increasingly concerned in the course of researching AIDS in Oaxaca that health practitioners were (re)living in the past. The history of AIDS in Mexico is following a pattern common to other lands and peoples: the main vector of transmission early on was through men who had sex with other men.[10] Intravenous drug use transmission—through "dirty needles" and the like—was a problem for HIV transmission along the U.S.–Mexican border, but far less frequently in the interior of Mexico. Although health workers acknowledged that by the late 1990s self-identified heterosexuals in Oaxaca were key "vectors" for the transmission of HIV, in Oaxaca heterosexual transmission of the AIDS virus was said to always follow an "original" male–male sexual transmission. This is a basic belief that underlies the history of AIDS care in the state (see table 3).

In Mexico, in recent years, migrants who are HIV+ and the sexual partners whom they infect are labeled in a process similar to what Charles Briggs and Clara Mantini-Briggs (2003), in their study of cholera in Venezuela, call "medical profiling." In the case of Oaxaca, since the late 1990s, AIDS has come to be ever more associated in the state with migrant men and their female sexual partners. This is more than a simple epidemiological and demographic issue, as the public discourse within the medical community treating AIDS patients shows an acute awareness of the fact that the individuals who migrate are from very specific socioeconomic backgrounds: when one talks of migrant men and their spouses, in Oaxaca this means *indigenous* and *poor* men and women. The professional middle class is never implicated in the label "migrants." Thus, the population is divided, again borrowing from Briggs and Mantini-Briggs (2003), into "unsanitary subjects" and "sanitary citizens," that is, into those who are, potentially at least, carriers and transmitters of disease and those about whom the health authorities have little cause for worry. The stigmatizing implications of such typologizing, even when it is just implicit, are severe for AIDS care in Oaxaca, which is the subject of the next chapter.

FOUR

Frisky and Risky Men

AIDS CARE IN OAXACA

Janie had robbed him of his illusion of irresistible maleness
that all men cherish. which was terrible.

Zora Neale Hurston (1990 [1937]:75)

WEDNESDAY-MORNING PRAYER MEETINGS

In 2001, when I did my fieldwork, doctors and epidemiologists at the
state-run AIDS clinic in Oaxaca admitted they were not sure how many
people were HIV+, how many had AIDS, or even how many had died of
AIDS. Officially, around two thousand people had been diagnosed with
AIDS by 2001, although authorities were convinced that as many as fifteen thousand men and women were HIV+. And as of 2005, there were
only enough funds to provide antiretroviral, life-prolonging treatments to
fewer than two hundred people in the entire state. In other words, unless
something dramatically changed, the vast majority of people in Oaxaca
who became sick with HIV would die from complications resulting from
AIDS. The fortunate few who could afford to purchase the AIDS anti-

retroviral (ARV) cocktails themselves were able to extend their lives. But because costs ran between $800 and $1,000 U.S. per month, an amount well beyond the reach of all but a few people in Oaxaca, those without such resources had to try their luck with the state agency in charge of AIDS, COESIDA. Thus, although AIDS had become a chronic but manageable disease instead of a fatal one for those who received ARVs, it continued to be a sure killer for the majority of infected men and women in Oaxaca, for whom treatment with the AIDS drugs would always be no more than an unrealized dream.

The decision as to who among the thousands of poor men and women from Oaxaca would receive the precious few ARVs allocated for the state—who would thus be allowed to survive—was made in special meetings held on Wednesday mornings at the offices of COESIDA. At these meetings a team of doctors, psychologists, and social workers literally decided who among the poor with AIDS in Oaxaca would live and who would die. I was allowed to attend these Wednesday meetings.

As will be explored in more detail later in this chapter, with the development of triple-therapy regimes, in the mid-1990s, that allowed HIV+ people to considerably extend their lives, Mexican men and women who lived and worked in the United States without legal permission were able to receive medical treatment in some parts of the United States. Yet within a short time, in many U.S. states with high numbers of Mexican migrants, guidelines for programs were rewritten to make health care delivery to "illegal aliens" itself illegal except in cases of emergency. By 2006, even if undocumented Mexicans were able to determine which states in the United States would still provide AIDS drugs to them at no or low cost, few had the ability to move to those locations to live and work. Thus, Mexican migrants resident in the United States, in effect, faced the same constrictive forces of a neoliberal and racist health care policy that increasingly limited their ability to get proper diagnoses and treatment for HIV and AIDS. That the period from 1995 to 2000 was also when the privatization of health care in Mexico took place made it all the more difficult for the same men and women to receive such services in their homeland.

After earlier blaming male homosexuals for AIDS, by the late 1990s male migrants had come to represent the new risk group in Oaxaca. In both cases, men having sex with other men was the biological route held to be responsible for the actual transmission of the virus from one human being to another. Poisoned semen and abused anuses were the more specific sites of infection. Although they were not in the same category as the primary "AIDS vectors," those individuals who were offered medications and then proved themselves incapable of "compliance" were in turn faulted, both for wasting precious state funds and for their own deteriorating health and ultimate demise. Thus, "individuals and populations with little access to power and resources" (Briggs and Mantini-Briggs 2003:xvii) were medically profiled and categorized as unsanitary subjects.

The consistent theme in the medical profiling that has driven epidemiological and medical thinking regarding AIDS in Oaxaca is the labeling of men of one kind or another as the most contaminated, or unsanitary, subjects and the casus belli of the pandemic in general. Thus, the common cultural and medical assumptions about "unclean women" being responsible for infecting (innocent) men with sexually transmitted infections, of degenerate harlots leading men to (sexual) ruin, have become reversed. Men are the sinful inseminators of this modern disease, and women, if they know what is good for them, will treat men as infected suspects until proven faithful and sanitary lovers. Men believed to seek sex in culturally inappropriate ways, and especially with unsuitable people, are stigmatized. Male sexual infidelity is treated as promiscuity, which in turn is held up to ridicule and scorn. Nor is this phenomenon unique to Mexico. Raewyn Connell writes, in a survey on men, masculinities, and gender equality in the global arena, "In discussions of gender and HIV/AIDS, men are commonly construed as being 'the problem,' the agents of infection" (2005:1806).

It was within this context of pervasive medical profiling that the procedure I observed at the Wednesday-morning meetings must be understood. It seemed fairly straightforward: everyone in attendance was informed as to how many "slots" had opened up on the list of those who might be eligible for antiretroviral treatment since the last meeting of these medical personnel. Perhaps someone had died, perhaps someone else had disappeared, or other people had been dropped from the list for one reason or another. A list-of-the-living, consisting of people in dire need of antiretrovirals, was then presented. The physicians and others reviewed each person on this list-of-the-living to determine which ones were the best candidates to be moved over to the to-be-saved list, those who could then begin to receive the life-saving medications. With limited slots available, patients were reviewed according to strict criteria—no one wanted to waste the drugs on a patient who was deemed unreliable or, in the words of the clinicians, "noncompliant."

Was an individual punctual and responsible about showing up for appointments? Too many no-shows would automatically keep someone from the to-be-saved list. Men seemed most suspect from the beginning and had to prove themselves negatively: to be not alcoholic, not living alone, not noncompliant. Did a particular man live with other people who could be relied upon to make him take the required medications, in the proper dosages, at the proper times, and help ensure that he showed up for appointments? A man who lived alone was usually regarded as a riskier "investment" for ARV therapy. Was a man a known alcoholic or drug user? Such behavior was automatic grounds for exclusion from the to-be-saved list. In general, had the person seemed sincere and responsible about all aspects of the treatment required? "¿Tienen el apego o no?" (Are they committed [to treatment] or not?) was a question frequently asked about the men and women who were being considered for the to-be-saved list, those who would receive antiretrovirals from the state. In sum, as one doctor put it to me, a patient would not receive AIDS cocktail therapy "when we observed that they did not make their appointments, did not take their medications satisfactorily, or exhibited conditions like alcoholism, or in some other way showed that they were not committed to the treatment." There was no sense in squandering good money on bad patients, he said.

Alcoholism, weak family ties, and not showing up for appointments were all signs of a noncompliant attitude on the part of the patient, and generally even one of these factors was enough to eliminate an individual from the pool of those who could be potentially saved. For example, one man, forty-eight years old, was rejected for the AIDS cocktails after it was revealed that despite active support from family members, including his children and siblings, and their commitment to helping him take the medicines on schedule every day, he was an alcoholic. The source and nature of his alcoholism was not discussed, nor would it have mattered, given the exigencies of the triage system. "Does he know he is going to die?" asked a doctor, incredulous that the same man was balking at beginning antiretroviral therapy, despite the "guarantee" of relatives that they would monitor his adherence to the drugs.[1] In this way, the medical personnel performed a detailed vetting of the long list of potential recipients in order to determine the select few upon whom trust and costly medicines would be bestowed. The process was a classic case of medical triage, in which doctors with limited resources choose who has highest priority based on their assessment as to who is most likely to benefit from care or treatment.

On several occasions over the course of the three years from 2001 to 2004, the head of the state-run AIDS clinic in Oaxaca City told me remorsefully but firmly that he hoped to hell that the vast majority of people who were HIV+ never, ever learned of the existence of his clinic, COESIDA, or even the name of their illness. His reasoning was deceptively simple: What was the point? He hoped most of those with AIDS would just stay away. There were deplorably insufficient funds to help those in need, so it would be better for all concerned if the people just died, as they were going to anyway, without the benefit of knowledge of the exact nature and terms of their illness. It was far less painful for all concerned if the vast majority of those suffering from AIDS just died without having to go through the futile exercise of trying to cure themselves.[2]

Between 1983 and 2006, according to the most conservative official figures, 107,000 Mexicans had been afflicted with AIDS, of whom at least 50,000 had died. At least 150,000 men and women were diagnosed as infected with HIV in this same period (see www.salud.gob.mx/conasida). While attending a meeting in St. Petersburg, Russia, of the Group of Five (Mexico, China, India, Brazil, and South Africa) in July 2006, President Vicente Fox lied to the world when he claimed that all Mexicans with HIV/AIDS were receiving full and free treatment from the government-run health agencies. In fact, according to the government's own AIDS agency, less than one in six people infected with the virus in Mexico received ARVs at that time (see Monsiváis 2006); nor does this figure include the officially acknowledged under-registration in Mexico of people who are HIV+. Despite claims by the federal authorities that those need-ing them were receiving ARVs in the country overall, the situation in Oaxaca as of summer 2005 had not changed: local health officials had se-verely limited supplies of the life-extending drugs and could not hope to treat most of those in need of them in the state. Hence, the reluctant, in-advertent incentive to conceal a key public space of healing in Oaxaca.

Compared to some areas of the world, particularly parts of sub-Saharan Africa, where as many as 25 to 30 percent of entire populations are infected with HIV, the numbers in Oaxaca are small. In 2006, the sero-prevalence rate in Oaxaca was, at most, 0.5 percent of the population, though for the population that has migrated to the United States it was greater than 1.0 percent. Nonetheless, treatment in Oaxaca was available for only a tiny fraction of the people who were HIV+ or already in the stage of AIDS. State officials who dedicated their lives to serving the thou-sands affected by AIDS in Oaxaca made reference to the discourse on poverty prevalent in development agencies worldwide when they talked about budgetary restrictions on their ability to treat these women and men, pointing out that they had limited funds locally and federally and so must make do with whatever was provided. And they prayed that most of the sick with HIV and AIDS never came looking for treatment.

Such were the exigencies of local AIDS care in Oaxaca. Despite the fact that the problem of AIDS arose in good measure as a result of the inter-national migration of men from the region to the United States, where they had contracted the virus, the palliative options for these men and the women they infected after their return to Oaxaca were remarkably local. The local health care providers did what they could with limited means, and this included dispensing their meager supply of ARVs to the chosen few who were deemed reliable enough to be good investments, while in effect concealing from broader public view not only the medications but even their existence. Without enough medicine to go around, they saw little purpose in having thousands of needy but doomed patients seeking out the life-giving care that they could not provide.

CULTURAL CONDOMS

Regardless of their scientific, objectivist pretensions, health care practitioners involved in AIDS care in Oaxaca utilized a variety of culturalist explanations to guide their work. Sexual beliefs and practices associated by these personnel with culture were used to describe and explicate who had AIDS, how they had gotten it, and why they had gotten it. In this sense, then, culture was used as a sheath to enclose and contain the contagion in Oaxaca. In particular, medical employees in Oaxaca were convinced that virtually all men who got infected with HIV did so after having had sex with other men. On the clinic's intake forms, known as Encuestas Centinelas, many men reported they had had sex with homosexuals. Others, with bisexuals. And a plurality stated they had had sex only with women. Without exception, every doctor, psychologist, and social worker at the state-run COESIDA clinic believed that virtually every man claiming to be exclusively heterosexual had actually had sexual relations with another man and had become infected in this way. When asked about their reasons for holding this belief, they pointed not to epidemiological studies but instead to their cultural knowledge of Mexican men, their own extensive conversations with men who claimed to be heterosexual, and, finally, to their understanding of male and female anatomy and physiology.

When men reported different sexual proclivities to different medical personnel, the default listing usually became "bisexual" and any earlier notation on the intake form that the client was "heterosexual" and "only had sex with women" was whited out.[3]

According to official statistics provided to me in 2001 by the Subdirección de Salud Pública, Departamento de Epidemiología y Medicina Preventiva, in the period 1986–2000, 255 men with AIDS had reported they were homosexual, 247 bisexual, and 393 that they were heterosexual. Of the self-identified heterosexuals, more claimed to have had sex with farm animals than with other men. Nonetheless, the medical personnel were convinced that these men were lying. The most common explanation I was offered for this conclusion ran something like this: "Mateo, you are not from here, so you don't understand. Mexican men have sex with other

FORMATO DE NOTIFICACION Y ESTUDIO EPIDEMIOLOGICO DE VIH / SIDA

IMSS · **ISSSTE** · **DIF** · ⬤ · ⚕ · ▲ · **INI** · ⬛

? TIPO DE PACIENTE   SEROPOSITIVO (SI)   CASO (SI)

I — UNIDAD NOTIFICACION

Nombre (Hospital, Clínica, Centro de Salud, Otros) _____ Clave Unidad _____

FECHA DE NOTIFICACION [ ] [ ] [ ]
Día   Mes   Año

Institución _____ Localidad _____ Estado _____ Municipio _____ Jurisdicción Sanitaria _____

Nombre del Médico Notificante _____ MATRICULA _____ Firma _____

II — DATOS SOCIODEMOGRAFICOS

No. AFILIACION [ ]   R.F.C. [ ] ,   UNIDAD DE ADSCRIPCION [ ]

NOMBRE:
Apellido Paterno _____ Apellido Materno _____ Nombre (s) _____

FECHA DE NACIMIENTO [ ] [ ] [ ]
Día   Mes   Año

SEXO (M) (F)   EDAD [ ] [ ]
Años   Meses

OCUPACION: _____ (Actual u Ultima)   Especifique la labor que desempeña _____

ESCOLARIDAD _____ Ultimo año aprobado

ESTADO CIVIL   SOLTERO ( )   UNION LIBRE ( )
CASADO ( )   DIVORCIADO ( )

¿HA TENIDO HIJOS EN LOS ULTIMOS 2 AÑOS? (SI) (NO)   ¿CUANTOS? [ ]

RESIDENCIA HABITUAL:

CALLE _____ NUMERO _____ LOCALIDAD _____ COL. O MUNICIPIO _____ ESTADO _____

LUGAR DE RESIDENCIA POR MAS DE SEIS MESES A PARTIR DE 1980
(Si son diferentes al habitual y si han durado más de 6 meses)

MOTIVO DEL CAMBIO DE RESIDENCIA
ESTUDIO   TRABAJO   OTROS

Ciudad _____ País _____ Meses [ ]   (1)   (2)   (3)

Ciudad _____ País _____ Meses [ ]   (1)   (2)   (3)

III — ANTECEDENTES EPIDEMIOLOGICOS

1 SEXUALIDAD

A. Ha tenido relaciones sexuales (SI) (NO) (?)
Con hombres (SI) (NO) (?)   Cuantas Parejas: [ ]   Con Mujeres (SI) (NO) (?)   Cuantas Parejas: [ ]

B. A partir de 1980 ha tenido relaciones sexuales con:

Homosexuales (SI) (NO) (?)	Prostitutas (SI) (NO) (?)	Hemofílicos (SI) (NO) (?)
Bisexuales (SI) (NO) (?)	Prostitutos (SI) (NO) (?)	Donadores (SI) (NO) (?)
Heterosexuales (SI) (NO) (?)	Usuarios Drogas I.V (SI) (NO) (?)	Infectado de VIH/SIDA (SI) (NO) (?)

C. El paciente ha practicado la prostitución   (SI) (NO) (?)

2 HA SIDO TRANSFUNDIDO.   (SI) (NO) (?)

No UNIDADES TRANSFUNDIDAS DESPUES DE 1980 [ ]

UNIDAD 1   Año Mes Día   INSTITUCION

UNIDAD 2   Año Mes Día   INSTITUCION

SI   NO   NO SABE
(1)   (2)   (?)

3 HEMOFILICO   (1) (2) (?)
4 USUARIO DE DROGAS INTRAVENOSAS   (1) (2) (?)
5 DONADOR REMUNERADO   (1) (2) (?)
6 HA RECIBIDO TRASPLANTE DE ORGANOS O TEJIDOS   (1) (2) (?)

Tipo de Trasplante _____ Año Mes Día   INSTITUCION

7 SOSPECHA DE TRANSMISION PERINATAL (pase a la sección IV)   (1) (2) (?)
8 EXPOSICION OCUPACIONAL A SANGRE O SECRECIONES CON VIH   (1) (2) (?)

EXPOSICION A: SANGRE (SI) (NO)   OTRAS SECRECIONES _____   FECHA DE EXPOSICION [ ] [ ] [ ]

PRUEBA BASAL: (?) (-) (+)   FECHA DE SEROCONVERSION [ ] [ ] [ ]
Año Mes Día

9 ENFERMEDADES DE TRANSMISION SEXUAL.

Año Mes Día

1 _____ FECHA [ ] [ ] [ ]
2 _____ FECHA [ ] [ ] [ ]
3 _____ FECHA [ ] [ ] [ ]

Standard intake form used for patients in Oaxaca who are *seropositivos*, 2003.

men. They just don't like to admit it." When I pressed several of the staff, I was given a figure of "50 percent" of Mexican men who have had sex with other men. The basis of this claim? Cultural knowledge. "Have you had sex with a man?" I asked each man who offered such a cultural explanation. Each man denied that he had. "Your father? Your brothers? Your sons?" Without exception, men who were convinced that same-sex sex among Mexican men was widespread denied that they themselves had ever partaken.

Several of the psychologists and social workers also related stories of men who had denied on the Centinela intake forms that they had ever had sexual relations with other men, but who later, in the course of treatment, after trust and confidence had been established between the patient and the practitioners, admitted that they had had same-sex experiences.

When I became a bit pushy regarding the scientific basis for claims about self-identified heterosexual men's mendacity, the fallback position of the doctors at COESIDA was a mini-lesson in physiology and anatomy. The vagina is "made" for sex, the anus is not. Vaginal mucous is better at killing the virus than anything in an anus, they told me. Anal sex leads to tears and a greater possibility of transmission of HIV. For a woman to transmit the virus to a man, the virus must enter through the man's urethra or through a tear in the penis. Semen is deposited and remains in the anus or vagina, whereas the vaginal fluids of a woman do not remain on the penis. Female-to-male infection is nearly impossible, I was told. Allegedly because of their sexual practices, men who had sex with other men were at risk for HIV, yet what was unstated was that these same people, these unsanitary subjects, were just as much at risk because of their ignorance, because they had lived and worked in poverty in Oaxaca and the United States, because they were Indian, and because of their dirty customs. The racist analysis of AIDS was unambiguous for several doctors and a few nurses. When I asked one doctor if there were any relationship between ethnicity and AIDS, he replied that "Indians have a lot of babies. And they steal women. They are ignorant about birth control and sexuality. And they use midwives, which just puts their babies at risk." Another complained about a lack of hygienic practices: "They use dirty water because they are *indios ignorantes*. That's also why they have twelve children each." Aside from the fact that none of these claims is valid, they also show the underlying blaming of victims for their own poverty and lack of comparable access to basic necessities like water and contraception and hospitals (in case of an emergency during childbirth).

The gendered analysis of AIDS was also unmistakable: men infect, women are infected. Men infect each other and women, and women are infected by men. I began asking medical personnel why it was that heterosexual transmission—including from woman to man—was supposedly the main vector of infection in those countries in which AIDS had become a catastrophic problem very quickly in the 1990s. I was thinking of India and the countries of southern Africa, like Botswana, Mozambique, and South Africa. That was a puzzle, for sure, I was consoled. Upon returning to the COESIDA offices a week or two later, sometimes I would be confronted by a psychologist who had been "looking into" the problem I had raised in my last visit. Perhaps the level of medical expertise was not as high in southern Africa as it was in Mexico, one of them offered. Someone else speculated that if there were more heterosexual transmission in Africa, this might reflect different "types" of AIDS; this proved not to be the case, since in both Africa and Mexico, Type 1 is the rule rather than the exception. Another doctor told me that he had seen some educational programs on TV and he believed there was a lot more same-sex sex among men in Africa than I realized. Surely male–male sex was the main route of transmission there as well as Mexico, he assured me (see table 4).

COESIDA's ability to define the terms of prognosis and the prescriptions for "healing" (or letting people die) is central to its mission as the regional government AIDS center. Because the disease has never been simply a product of Oaxaca society alone, health care workers are continuously challenged by the false-choice gambit of spending money on either prevention programs or treatment programs. In particular, although primary prevention may be touted as the more cost-effective measure for the long run, maintaining (and even expanding) the physical spaces of healing depends on curing more than thwarting infection.

By the mid-1980s in Mexico, on a national level, the federal AIDS agency, CONASIDA, had been formed, though as late as 2002, when I fin-

Table 4   Accumulated Cases of AIDS in Mexico and Vector of
Transmission (Persons Fifteen Years or Older), 1983–2006

Vector of Transmission	*Percentage of Accumulated Cases, 1983–2006*
Sexual transmission	92.3%
Homosexual	46.7
Heterosexual	45.6
Blood transfusion	5.1
Perinatal	2.3
Drugs	0.3
Unknown	(36.6)*
TOTAL	100.0

* AIDS cases in the category "Unknown vector" were excluded from the sum of percentages; nonetheless, this figure is given in parentheses to indicate its magnitude. Categories are those employed by the Mexican government.

SOURCE: www.salud.gob.mx/conasida/estadis/2006/categtrans15nov.pdf (accessed 22 January 2007).

ished the first stage of the research discussed in this book, outside Mexico City there were only two state-run treatment centers for AIDS in the entire country, one in Guadalajara and the other in Oaxaca. Gay activists in Mexico City and several provincial capitals like Oaxaca City provided a key impetus to these early initiatives, and the efforts of gay rights organizations have coexisted, often acrimoniously, with official programs for AIDS prevention and treatment since that time. The enormous obstacles and stigma confronted by gay activists in these early years cannot be overemphasized; initial press coverage around AIDS throughout the country was often unashamedly homophobic.[4]

In recognition of the shifting demographic profile of persons with AIDS in Mexico, in 2001 the Mexican government launched a program focused on the migrant population in the United States and internal migrants within Mexico: "Vete Sano, Regresa Sano" (Go Healthy, Return Healthy). In the language of the epidemiologists, Mexico was experiencing a shift in which populations constituted the major "risk groups"— that is, in populations that were most at risk for contracting the virus and spreading it to others. Despite a rise in the number of women with HIV and AIDS, from the 1980s through 2006 at least, the process of identifying risk groups for AIDS in Mexico entailed distinguishing which groups of *men* were deemed most dangerous (that is, unsanitary), for their own good and for society as a whole. The possibility that, as in other parts of the world, AIDS would suddenly become just as much a disease of women was quite real in Mexico. Nonetheless, as of 2006, this had not yet occurred.

The early medical profiling and homophobia that tainted AIDS care may have contributed, inadvertently, to exaggerated attention on men who have sex with men, with the result that heterosexual transmission, and the population of self-identified heterosexuals, was believed by health practitioners and the public at large to be not a risk. In particular, the belief that it was virtually impossible for a heterosexual man to become infected from sex with a woman was widespread among health care workers in Oaxaca in the early 2000s. This was in some ways an updated version of the notion prevalent in the 1980s throughout Mexico that AIDS would not develop as a major health problem, because the risk-group populations were negligible (see Carrillo 2002:214). The updated version in Oaxaca held that even if it turned out that there were significant numbers of men who had sex with other men (and therefore constituted a risk group for AIDS), the problem was still somehow limited to these men and their sexual partners. As Schoeph has written, "A focus on risk groups implies that everyone not included within the boundaries of stigma is not at risk" (2001:338). More generally, Parker has characterized international AIDS efforts as shifting from "our early preoccupation with diverse forms of *risk behavior,* understood in largely individualistic terms, toward a new understanding of *vulnerability* as socially, politically, and economically structured, maintained, and organized" (2000:41).

Nonetheless, there are researchers and activists for whom the concept of risk group has proved more valuable. In his influential formulation linking questions of hegemonic masculinity with studies of the body, Benno de Keijzer (1998) advances the notion of "masculinity as a risk factor"; de Keijzer is referring especially to public health issues like domestic violence, reproductive health, and alcoholism, all syndromes that are directly traced by de Keijzer to hegemonic patterns of male embodiment in Mexican society. De Keijzer applies his formulation of masculinity as a risk factor across the ranks of men, regardless of their sexual proclivities and experiences. Whether this is a reasonable analysis remains to be seen; in a support group of men with AIDS, sponsored by COESIDA, the arguments between self-identified homosexual and heterosexual men over who was most prone to "risky behavior" more than once led to the meetings having to be abandoned.

The issue of risk groups and unsanitary subjects is in turn related to questions of priorities in health care funding. In a discussion in the fall of 2002 with the head of a government clinic in the town of Tlacolula, outside Oaxaca City, I heard the complaint "Look, we lost two people to AIDS last year in our district. In the same period, we lost thirty-seven children to diarrhea, malnutrition, and other childhood diseases of poverty." The doctor added, "If everyone were infected [with HIV] and infecting others at the rates some people claim, half the world would be HIV-positive by now." The problem of AIDS remained of far less significance for health care in his district than more widespread causes of mortality, he informed me.

In these ways, identification of the so-called cultures of particular populations in Oaxaca was used to explain AIDS there. Cultural analysis was utilized by medical personnel like a cultural condom, to contain the disease and help prevent its spread to other populations with presumably less susceptible cultures. If culture was to blame, and if culture could not be changed through institutional remedies, then the best that medical personnel at COESIDA could hope to accomplish for most AIDS patients was to give comfort.

COESIDA

I arrived at the offices of COESIDA (Consejo Estatal para la Prevención y Control del SIDA) in the summer of 2001 and was quickly introduced to Dr. Miguel Vargas, then director of the SEAI (Servicio Especializado de Atención Integral), the clinical facility of COESIDA. "Dr. Miguel" proved to be an enthusiastic and generous host for the dozens of interviews I would conduct with women and men there over the next few years. He and a psychologist, Mónica Cervantes, suggested I stop by on Mondays in the late morning because that was the busiest time of the week, when sometimes a dozen or more people lined up to see the social workers, psychologists, nurses, and doctors, to get blood tests, and to receive medications and counseling at the center. At the time, COESIDA was seeing approximately four hundred patients each month. Although no one had firm numbers to prove it, it was the general consensus among the health care workers that the overwhelming number of people who came in already had AIDS. People around the state often "waited," I was told, until they were truly dying before coming to the clinic.

When I would arrive, on Monday mornings, there were usually several people asleep on the blue benches in the front lobby. Many had taken all-night bus rides, which had been preceded by long walks along mountain paths before arriving at the buses, to arrive at dawn in Oaxaca so as to show up early for their monthly appointments at the COESIDA clinic. Old people with AIDS often were brought in by children and grandchildren. Some of the older men and women, who spoke only an Indian language, also needed translation help in order to communicate with the medical personnel, who spoke only Spanish. To make their COESIDA clinic appointment, Azabel and Fabiola, for example, had left their village, in "the last piece of Oaxaca," near the border to the north with Veracruz, at 11 P.M. They had traveled through the night, arriving in Oaxaca City at 6:30 A.M. When I asked why they didn't go to the closer Veracruz clinics, they told me that as residents of Oaxaca the only way they could receive any free medication was to travel to Oaxaca City. At the government clinic in Veracruz, "It would cost you between eight and twelve thousand pesos every month," Azabel told me. "Who's got that kind of money?" I murmured. "Really," they concurred. "They told us that this illness is for rich people," Fabiola recalled.

In 2002, the COESIDA clinic was each month conducting approximately 250 ELISA blood tests to check for seroprevalence and 10 Western Blots for those who had received two positive ELISAs. Until they moved to a new building, in 2002, blood had been drawn in the reconverted kitchen of the house where the clinic had been housed for several years. The ELISA tests could be read locally, whereas the far more expensive Western Blots (which that year cost 2,500 to 4,000 pesos each, between $250 and $400 U.S.) were sent off to Mexico City, where more precise CD4 counts and viral load testing could be done; results from the Western Blots could take as long as six months because of the backlog in the capital.

My activities at COESIDA during the year 2001–02 mainly involved interviewing people who arrived for appointments with various members of the staff. We would find a spare room and sit and chat for anywhere from a few minutes to an hour or more. With some people, I was able see them again on return visits a month or a few weeks later. With others, the information I gleaned from our initial talk was all I would ever know about them. After hearing the stories of dozens of women and men, I asked the director of the clinic, Dr. Miguel, if I could review the intake forms, the Centinelas, to see if the information I had been given in the interviews I had taped was the same as what people had told the social workers and psychologists. My request was denied, for reasons of patient confidentiality, but Dr. Miguel did come up with a way around this problem. He allowed me to sit on the other side of a desk from Mónica, the clinic psychologist, and have her review the files while I asked questions and took notes. I was not allowed to know the identities of those whose files we reviewed, but as I explained to them, I had no interest in knowing that information. In particular, I was curious how many men had reported both that they were heterosexual (they had to choose from the three categories of "have had sex with" homosexuals, or heterosexuals, or bisexuals) and that they had never had sex with another man. Some men who reported sexual relations with other men also said that because they had penetrated these men, this meant they were still heterosexual.[5]

In May 2002, I also decided to get tested for HIV. My decision was motivated by anthropological curiosity, and I am pleased to say that it paid off in at least two respects. One, although I never had reason to fear I might be infected, once I took the test I began to get anxious about the results. Two, I shared the embarrassment of other patients, perhaps, when Mónica, whose job it was to ask the standard questions, inquired, "When was the last time you had sex?" I was not comfortable answering the question and I hesitated. She prompted me, "Five days ago?" "Yes," I lied. We then headed for the lab, where she joked with the technician that he should see if there was a clean needle to use to take my blood.

It is by now evident that in this chapter I quote a number of medical personnel who are in the forefront of the fight against the modern plague of AIDS in Oaxaca. Some of their comments will seem, I hope, caring and dedicated. Others may seem misinformed. Because most have the best intentions (and nearly all could make more money and have more prestige doing other health work), I have changed certain details so that statements are not always attributable to individuals. This is more than a matter of protecting people's feelings. I have done this because the ideas expressed by them to me are not theirs alone, but more profoundly arise out of relations of inequality locally, nationally, and globally. To take the most obvious illustration, the unavailability of antiretrovirals and the decisions of local practitioners to give the scarce medicine to one patient and not another is not evidence of local lack of concern; it is because that choice is anything but a local, individual one.

MEN'S NATURAL DESIRES

Given the lack of knowledge among researchers who have studied the sexual practices and the spread of AIDS among Mexican migrant men, the insistence of medical practitioners in Oaxaca that all the migrant men who have returned HIV+ or already with AIDS must have become infected through sex with other men may seem all the more remarkable. I am not saying I am privy to any better information, or that medical personnel are necessarily wrong; I am simply arguing that there is too little reliable epidemiological evidence regarding routes of transmission of the AIDS virus among Mexican migrant men in the United States, and thus we should concede that we all rely largely on common cultural knowledge and hearsay. Cultural assumptions about sexuality and AIDS guide AIDS care in Oaxaca, including the assertion that AIDS is a disease of "non-heterosexual men," that is, risk-taking homosexual and bisexual men. Such thinking is a way of attributing disease to those who are deemed by some to be outside the cultural bounds of normativity. It is also a way of associating sexuality, especially male sexuality, with AIDS and disease (see Vance 1999 [1991]:47).

A generalized fear of return migrants is also a byproduct of slipshod medical profiling. As one indigenous midwife insisted, when we spoke in summer 2004 about men's reproductive health in her Zapotec-speaking village in the mountains north of Oaxaca City, "Look, people who come from the United States, you'd better not trust them. Better not trust them. Because from one minute to the next, in an instant, they infect us, and then what happens? You die!"

The employment of cultural models in AIDS intervention worldwide cannot, as Sobo (1999) insists, be underestimated. "But blaming cultural differences for situations clearly linked with class and the unequal distribution of power, money, and authority can represent a disingenuous attempt to ignore or to mystify the facts and to support the status quo" (Sobo 1999:7). With respect to the case at hand, to attribute the contagion of AIDS so overwhelmingly to men who have sex with men is to blame assumed cultural practices for the spread of a disease that is rooted in international relations of inequality. A similar trajectory took place in Africa earlier in the 1990s, when culture was designated as the culprit in the spread of HIV and when sweeping statements were made about a special "African sexuality" and, especially, "African promiscuity" (Schoeph 2001:340).[6]

In this sense, what is at issue is both the assertion that Mexican men as a group share so-called natural desires for sex and the implicit corollary argument that some Mexican men's sexual desires have led them to have sex with other men. The idea that Mexican men have difficulty controlling their sexual desires is thought to lead them to have sex with other men, according to medical personnel, and thereby constitutes the root problem of the AIDS pandemic in Oaxaca. The fact that Mexican migrant men in the United States may have less "access" to women is understandable but unfortunate, they say, because this leads to men having sex with other men, a practice considered by the medical specialists to be riskier than heterosexual sex.

Of course, there are contradictory beliefs regarding what is natural about men's sexuality. A slogan promoted by government AIDS workers in the summer of 2005 contributed to fostering a biologized concept of homosexuality: "La homosexualidad no es un resultado social. La homofobia, sí. No discrimines" (Homosexuality is not a product of society. Homophobia is. Don't discriminate). The underlying conceptual framework for understanding Mexican men's sexualities that is evident in this slogan and that directs AIDS care in Oaxaca extends common truisms and, by mere virtue of their association with health practitioners, transforms them into medical conviction.

As has been true in Africa, blanket statements about a special kind of Oaxacan male sexuality, or sometimes a Mexican male sexuality, are frequently offered without qualification. One of the clearest instances of the lack of reserve evident in concepts about male sexuality accepted at COESIDA is the fact that same-sex sex is tied indexically and sentimentally to the Isthmus of Tehuantepec in the southern reaches of the state. I was repeatedly surprised by how widespread and uniform was the belief within the medical community regarding the ubiquity of sexual relations between men in that area and, by extension, in the rest of the state. With respect to homosexuality in the Isthmus, I was often told, "Allí está más abierto" (It's more open there) and even that it is "bien visto" (well regarded).

One social worker at COESIDA reported to me her impression that most men who arrived at the clinic and initially called themselves heterosexual later stated that they had had sex with men, too. When we reviewed the actual medical files, however, the opposite seemed true, and she expressed surprise, because she was so convinced these men were lying.

"Why do you think most men lie when they say they have never had sex with other men?" I asked.

"Because they are all liars" (Porque todos son mentirosos), she replied, in a sweeping commentary on men in general. She was sure that half the men in Oaxaca had had sex with other men.

"How do you know?"

"Because people say so." (Porque la gente lo dice.) "As in communities

Wall in Oaxaca City warning people to "Protect yourself!!!" because the
AIDS virus is deadly, 2003.

in the Isthmus [of Tehuantepec]; most men there have first sexual relations with other men," she asserted.

"How do you know?" I asked again.

"We know," she replied.

"How?"

"More men are infected. And it's harder physiologically for women to
infect men. The virus has to enter [a man's] urethra. We see men not infected even after they've lived for years with women who are. Even after
three or four years, men don't get infected. We also know all this from the
transvestites who come in here." In other words, the transvestites who are
HIV+ or who have AIDS tell people at the clinic there are a lot of straight
men who are having sex with them.

"Why do you believe them?"

At this point, another social worker came into the room and answered,
"Well, it's the only base [of information] we have." In other words, because there is no conflicting information available, and because this information coincides with popular belief, it has become the guiding conceptual framework for understanding men's sexual behavior in Oaxaca.[7]

Talk of urethras, like talk of vaginas and anuses, is a central component
in the physiological explanations that are used indiscriminately to prove
what often is no more than a complex of cultural certainties.

THE CULTURAL SEXUALITY OF THE ISTHMUS
OF TEHUANTEPEC

> The women were the most beautiful in all Mexico.
> and they bathed naked in the river every
> morning. . . . Whenever we mentioned Tehuantepec
> to the Mexicans. we found that they agreed.
> although none of them had visited the place.
> Paul Bowles (1937 [1995]:69–70)

Undoubtedly, many of the youth in Oaxaca experience sexual initiation neither with female prostitutes nor with girlfriends, but with male prostitutes or other men. Many researchers have noted that in various parts of Mexico young men try out their sexual urges and abilities for the first time with other young men. Still, even if adolescent sex between male youth is not a phenomenon unique to Oaxaca, we do find particularities there, especially a set of famous cultural traditions in the Isthmus of Tehuantepec revolving around people known as *muxe'*. The quick-and-dirty translation of *muxe'* is "transvestite gay man." The full scope of how this category is employed is far more complex and interesting.

The mythology of the *muxe'* in Oaxaca, and especially in the Istmeño cultural capital of Juchitán, has its origins in primordial sensationalism, imaginative sentimentality, and some culturally creative forms of social organization not found in many other parts of the world. The influence of the mythological image of the *muxe'* extends to other parts of Oaxaca, including the capital city. As Macario Matus wrote, "In Juchitán homosexuality is regarded as a grace and a virtue that comes from nature" (cited in Miano 2002:149). For youth in the Isthmus the image of the *muxe'* inevitably mixes with the fame of the Istmeñas. Also, among these youth there is resentment about what *fuereños*, "outsiders," might think of the men and women of the Isthmus. According to my friend nicknamed Cubano, who is originally from that part of the state, "Here [in Oaxaca City], there's more work for men than in the Isthmus. There, on the other hand, there are no jobs. Women have the work, the ones who work in the market, who sell their products in the streets, that kind of work, like selling tortillas, making tortillas, which men can't do. That's why *fuereños* who don't understand what's going on there think that women are the ones who work more and run the show."

The relation between the famous Istmeñas—renowned for their sovereign and boisterous demeanor—and the *muxe'* was clear for my friend: "Another thing is that there's another important point in the Isthmus area, and that's . . . a lot of . . . as I was telling you that time, a lot of . . . they call them . . . they have a nickname, well, they call them *'putos'* [faggots] and *'mampus'* [sissies], and in their own language, Zapoteco, they call them *muxe'*. In Zapoteco it's *puto; muxe'* is *puto.*"[8]

My friend Cubano (whose real name is Fidel) taught me about what he saw as general and significant Juchiteco and Istmeño customs. According to him, for example, "80 percent" of the young men in the Isthmus have their first sexual relations with a *muxe'*. The *muxe'* pay teenagers to screw them ("They give you food, or clothing, or money—*te atienden muy bien, pues*" [They take real good care of you]). When I asked if sometimes the *muxe'* penetrate the youths, he answered that sometimes they will rape youth. "At least with the devious ones, well, if they're devious they grab you by force and they rape you. Because the *muxe'* are grown up, and it's fun for him, and sometimes he does it by force." Fidel's scorn for the *muxe'* was both anxious and perplexing; he usually voiced generous opinions about people who were unlike himself.

The *muxe'*–adolescent youth relationship was important in the Isthmus for mythological and ordinary reasons that had a recognized cultural antiquity. The image was also exploited for more mundane purposes. When the medical personnel at the AIDS clinic in Oaxaca City made reference to the Isthmus in an attempt to explain more general sexual practices among men in the state, they based their comments on two implicit assumptions: one, that the Isthmus was somehow representative and/or culturally determinative for sexual practices among men more generally in the state; and two, that widespread beliefs about the sexual practices in the Isthmus involving young men and *muxe'* were based on unimpeachable facts and did not simply represent pervasive folk wisdom.

In this fashion, the seduction by *muxe'* in the Isthmus of young men there became a way to divert attention from the heterosexual transmission of HIV and to connect the virus rather exclusively with young men who have sex with other men. Doctors and the public in general then projected risk away from female-to-male infection. When I asked Cubano and his cousin Gordo about their own experiences with *muxe'* in the Isthmus, and if they had bedded down with any, Gordo told me, "No, really, no. One time, yes, I was about to, but . . . it didn't happen. What happened is that . . . there are *muxe'* who are really older and they say that . . . if you go with him, the two of you get locked in together and some say that he will turn you [into a *muxe'*]."

The conviction among medical practitioners in Oaxaca that homosexual sex was the nearly exclusive vector of transmission of the AIDS virus infecting men was grounded in cultural models—Mexican men like to have sex with other men, and this is even more true for some Mexican men, such as those from the Isthmus of Tehuantepec in southern Oaxaca—and when these cultural explanations seemed too flimsy, the argument for same-sex sex among men relied on earnest physiological "evidence"—anuses, vaginas, mucous, and other bodily fluids. Regardless of the rationale, the upshot was a fixation on certain bisexual and homosexual groups of men, to the near obsessive avoidance of recognition of the possibility that heterosexual men, too, could become infected and could infect others without ever revealing themselves to be homosexual or bisexual.[9]

THE BIRTH AND CONCEALMENT
OF THE NEOLIBERAL CLINIC

Undocumented "illegal alien" men living and working in the United States became infected there with HIV in rising numbers. Many sought treatment in the North; the unlucky ones often went back to Oaxaca to die of AIDS. Before they died, some of the men learned about COESIDA and began making monthly pilgrimages to the clinic to receive whatever medication they could. Some got ARVs. For most, this was not possible and they received painkillers and anti-diarrheal medications.[10]

The emergence in the 1990s of AIDS as a growing public health problem in Oaxaca coincided with major institutional changes in the health care delivery system throughout Mexico at that time, when the infrastructure of social security services began to be dismantled (Laurell 2001). Decentralized public spaces meant an increasing privatization in urban health care, resulting in a shift from services being provided in clinics and hospitals to a greater expectation that this care would occur in homes and be managed by women in the household.

In practical terms, in Oaxaca at the time of my research (2001–05), there were rarely more than four or five *promotores de salud* (health care outreach workers) with AIDS as a primary responsibility. In a state with over 3.5 million people, of whom as many as 20,000 may have been infected with HIV, even the appearance of AIDS care was sorely lacking, especially in remote rural areas. This was true despite new "specialized services clinics" *(módulos de extensión de servicio especializado)* that had been established on the Pacific coast and in the Isthmus of Tehuantepec around 2003, and other efforts, like the AIDS informational booths set up at the international airport, especially from October through December, when many migrants return from the United States for the holidays.

The United States clearly falls outside the geopolitical borders of what is commonly considered the public space in urban Mexico. Nevertheless, the relevance of describing at length the place where Mexican men get infected is relevant, because lurking behind any discussion of AIDS and the public space in Oaxaca is a shadow state. In this case, I mean not the Mexican state but rather the United States.[11] Given the growing population of migrants who returned to Oaxaca infected and then infected their sexual partners, we may fairly ask how the United States could be factored into any equation regarding AIDS care in Oaxaca.

With respect to AIDS in Oaxaca, the United States performs as a shadow state in at least three ways: one, it is the site of infection, albeit one that is sometimes curiously regarded as incidental to the spread of the contagion, as if millions of Mexicans just happened to be resident in the United States, and as if the living conditions of these men and women were insignificant as to how and why they became infected. The United States is a shadow state because were it not for the political economic factors that compel these men and sometimes women to migrate from their homeland, the issue of AIDS would not exist for them on this kind of scale or in this way. AIDS is, we will recall, a disease of modernity and of global population movements.

Another way we may view the United States as a shadow state intimately implicated in AIDS among Mexicans is that, despite their illegal status, Mexicans might still have received more adequate treatment for their suffering in some states, and thus many stayed in the North as long as they could, often only returning to Oaxaca and other parts of Mexico in the final stages of the disease to die in their natal land. But by 2005 this was quickly changing, as state legislatures across the United States sought to cut noncitizens' access to health care and other public services. In 2005, in fact, around eighty bills were introduced in twenty states to curtail such services or to require benefit agencies to inform migration authorities about applicants for health benefits who appeared to have immigration violations (see Bernstein 2006).

The third sense in which the United States is a shadow state in the matter of AIDS in Oaxaca concerns the policies of the Mexican government and payment for antiretrovirals. Unlike several other countries in the world, as of 2006 Mexico was still paying whatever the U.S., British, and Swiss pharmaceutical companies demanded as the "full price" for the dozen medications on the international market that could potentially enable those with HIV to live relatively long lives. Ostensibly a decision made by the Mexican government alone, few doubted the pressure exerted by the North to pay top dollar for these ARVs. In simple economic terms, the higher the cost, the fewer the patients who could receive medication.

The situation in Mexico stood in stark contrast to that of Brazil, for example, where in the early 1990s the government decided that the lives of its citizens trumped the proprietary rights of transnational corporations and that it would manufacture the drugs locally and not pay for the right to do so (Biehl 2004). Whereas in the United States a full year's course of AIDS cocktails could cost $15,000 or more, in Brazil the same medications were dispensed at a cost to the state of less than $1,000 U.S. per year. In Mexico, the drugs came from companies that manufactured them abroad and payments were made based on what the companies charged. The cost in 2002 was approximately 6,000 to 12,000 Mexican pesos a month, or roughly $7,000 to $14,000 U.S. per year.[12]

Thus, the notion at COESIDA in Oaxaca that nothing could be done for those who would never be included on the to-be-saved list—those two hundred chosen people for whom antiretrovirals were available—was ultimately based on the globalized triage model that in effect accepted that this was the only way social life could be lived *in Oaxaca* at that time. This was in part a reflection of the underlying conundrum by which the U.S. economy continued to depend on Mexican migrants at the same time that it took steps to heighten security measures against "illegal aliens" following September 11. In a sense, debates about health care—who was responsible for providing services to Mexican migrants, where could they receive the best care—were similar to recent arguments regarding the remittances sent by these same men and women to their home communities in Mexico: Does such transfer of funds ultimately alleviate or reinforce the impoverishment of Mexico's countryside?[13] Regardless of the ethical issues involved in assigning blame and responsibility for healing the sick, the fact remained that it was the underlying subordination of Mexican migrant labor power to transnational flows of capital that provided the historical context in which thousands of Mexican migrant men became infected with HIV in the first place.

In a passage relevant to my argument here, Fernando Coronil writes, in a review of James Scott's (1998) *Seeing Like a State* (the review is titled "Smelling Like a Market"):

> The opposition between state and market that structures the book is itself a thin simplification that obscures the mutual historical constitution of "state" and "market," their close interaction, and their ongoing transformation. The modes of objectification, homogenization, and abstraction that Scott attributes to the state are inseparable from conceptual, technological, and social transformations linked not just to the constitution of modern state bureaucracies but to the development of global capitalism and the generalized commodification of social life. (Coronil 2001: 124)

Similarly, the funding of health care in Oaxaca—in this case for AIDS treatment and, more specifically, for access to medications that would allow people to live relatively healthy and long lives—may best be understood as part of a globalized and commodified practice of states and market (including but not limited to a discourse about these entities) that was rooted in cost-benefit analysis of human lives. Such was the state of public space and everyday life in urban Oaxaca in the early twenty-first century.

In documenting the growing problem in Oaxaca of treatment of AIDS among return migrant men who in turn infected their sexual partners, the impact of extremely limited funds for ARVs in the state was of obvious significance. Public space in this sense may be construed broadly as a matter of the public good (health care) as well as a physical location. With respect to the public good, in the period of neoliberal reforms of the 1990s, expanding coverage to a greater number of people had been a key element in the proclamations issuing from the Ministry of Health and other institutions charged with providing health care to the public in Oaxaca and Mexico as a whole. For those in the know, the COESIDA clinic in Oaxaca City, where patients from all over the state of Oaxaca had to come for diagnosis and treatment, sometimes traveling great distances on a monthly basis, existed as a site for health care pilgrimage.

Yet the health care providers at COESIDA rued the day the pilgrims became too numerous. Said one, "What would happen if all those still living arrived one day? Well, there isn't enough money. No one could sustain an economy like that, because it's an economy of waste [desgaste]." That is to say, it was a waste to spend money on people who would die anyway in a few years at most. New manuals in use at COESIDA in the summer of 2004 emphasized the need to pay closer attention to "costo-beneficio" and to adherence to medications in AIDS care in Oaxaca.

For obvious reasons, differential diagnosis and treatment fuels or diminishes the transmission of the disease and delays diagnosis and treatment, including for institutional reasons, and capitation rates inevitably cost more in the long run than ARVs. Several people I spoke with at the AIDS clinic told me that the first family member to be diagnosed was one of their children. Araceli and Santiago said that after their baby died of AIDS-related illnesses, they learned they too were HIV+. Prior to this, if the parents had showed symptoms of sickness they were tested for one medical problem after another, often wasting the precious little extra money they were able to gather, all to no avail. Some men said they had been diagnosed with HIV in the United States and had tried to remain there as long as they could; treatment was not always easy to obtain in El

Norte, but they thought they had a better chance of receiving medication there than in Oaxaca. Two men said they had been confused by the diagnosis of being "seropositivo." They had heard this term as the invented homonym "zeropositivo," that is, not HIV+, and had not followed up with any of the treatment offered because they thought they had tested negative for the virus.

The "lucky" patients are the ones who see a doctor in their pueblo who sends them to the Hospital Civil in Oaxaca City for tests, whereupon they are sent to the AIDS clinic. If they are even "luckier," they live close to the city, within a few hours by bus, and can arrive punctually and without fail for their monthly appointments.

Neoliberalism was associated by health practitioners generally in Mexico with less money to heal. This was linked to the expressed wish by COESIDA personnel in Oaxaca City that only a limited number of men and women afflicted with HIV/AIDS might discover that a clinic like COESIDA existed, because there was no money to provide them with the medicines necessary to sustain their lives. Although it was certainly not the goal of any health care practitioners to deny services to those in need, *the concealment of public space* where people might turn for treatment in effect had become public health policy in a time of limited financial health resources.

Yet as a critical epidemiology in Latin America has demonstrated, the critique of the state in promoting a narrow vision of what constitutes public health and the use of state statistics to "lie with precision" has too often tended to obscure the bifurcated nature of health in the Americas (see Morgan 1998). Was AIDS in Oaxaca best viewed as a problem for the Oaxacan state to prevent and treat? What part could be reasonably expected for the Mexican state to play? Should the United States, in a practical and moral sense, have been held responsible for AIDS care for Oaxaca migrants who became infected in El Norte?[14] Locating the public space of healing in Oaxaca was often difficult. The assumption that developing countries simply could not afford to provide care and treatment for more people living with HIV and AIDS was based on the approval of an arrangement whereby the international pharmaceutical companies received full market value for their AIDS medications.

The dozens of men and women who arrived at the COESIDA clinic barely able to walk because of aches and pains and weariness from all-night bus rides, the ones who were vomiting and running to the toilet with diarrhea—those were the lucky ones. They were the ones who had discovered the clinic that might provide relief of some kind. For thousands of others afflicted with HIV and AIDS in Oaxaca, the clinic remained essentially concealed under a disappearing screen of neoliberal health care reforms and abject poverty. The shadow state to the north remained a key player in the moral regulation of life in Oaxaca, though it too remained concealed behind the paternalistic disguise of "transparent health care reform," and the broader reasons for global migration were left out of health care.

LETTING DANGEROUS MEN DIE

In 2005 it made little sense, if it ever had, to talk about local solutions to AIDS care in Oaxaca, absent a coordinated and consistent national and international program of prevention and treatment. At a time when romantic talk of democracy in Mexico flowed freely from the lips of pundits and the populace at large (see Gutmann 2002), we could well ask if the example of AIDS care in Oaxaca was an example of democracy gone amiss. It was not. On the contrary, it was a typical, if tragic, example of democracy in action. Decision making with respect to paying ARV prices to the pharmaceutical industry, for example, was conducted in the most democratic of traditions: elected officials appointed health care administrators who took into account not simply their own personal needs but those of a variety of public and private sectors in Mexico. Based on their assessments, they decided to not challenge the United States or the other countries that manufacture the more than a dozen antiretrovirals that were on the market.

At the same time, given widespread obsession on the part of health care practitioners in Oaxaca with male–male sexual transmission and a fixation on men who have sex with other men as the defining risk group, these most unsanitary of subjects were held responsible for the spread of AIDS. The fact that AIDS care in the state was based on cultural beliefs about male–male sex more than on epidemiological evidence—and the fact that this conviction was validated with a specious biomedical analysis that female-to-male transmission was all but physiologically impossible—could lead these same devoted providers to miss potentially significant routes of infection between heterosexuals, including from women to men.

This chapter has discussed two central conundrums in understanding AIDS care in Oaxaca and how certain cultural ideas about proper and improper male sexual behavior are linked to broader political economies of health care in the world. Given the willingness of the Mexican government to obey pharmaceutical market dictates, only some of those in need got antiretrovirals. In summer 2004, I was again informed by clinic staff in Oaxaca that fewer than two hundred people in the state were receiving ARVs from them, and that—despite official statistics that were used to pretend that most Oaxacans who needed the medications received them—there were at least one thousand individuals in the state who should have had access to antiretrovirals.

This is what democratic public space looks and feels like in twenty-first-century Mexico. Democracy is not in itself a panacea that will resolve human plagues and poverty in Mexico. Nor have global information flows about the mere existence of medications that can keep people with AIDS alive led to greater practical accessibility of these drugs to treat those who are suffering from the syndrome there. These are the fruits of neoliberal transformations in the public space of health care. The regulation of healing is ever more clearly guided by the dogma that it is easier to replace wage labor with new bodies than to save the ones that have become diseased.

FIVE Planning Men Out of Family Planning

The spread of contraception has ruptured the previously
existing physiological fatalism.

Lourdes Arizpe (1990:xv)

HISTORIES OF MEN — SUCH AS THEY ARE

Histories of family planning and reproductive health usually focus on
women, and men are rarely addressed except with respect to AIDS and
sexually transmitted infections (STIs). Occasionally, men are mentioned
in passing, almost as an afterthought, as if men might have something to
do with reproduction, but the implicit assumption is that men probably
have little to do with birth control because they are generally reluctant to
share responsibility for preventing pregnancy from occurring during
their few seconds of ejaculation. The absence of men from the history of
family planning is customary in academic disciplines that have pioneered
research in reproductive health, such as medical anthropology, public
health, and demography,[1] and men are so remarkably missing from re-

ports and teaching materials produced by governments, international health agencies, family planning associations, and other educators that we might almost consider this to be a conspiracy of silence with respect to men and reproductive health. The account that follows is thus unorthodox history.

International conferences in Cairo and Beijing in the mid-1990s addressed the problem of men not figuring significantly in family planning efforts internationally, but ten years out the impact at the local level was often still very limited. The present study aims in part to contribute to an emerging literature on men, contraception, and sexuality. By examining the history of family planning in Mexico in the last several decades, and especially in the state of Oaxaca, we may gain insight into how men have intentionally, or not, been excluded from most governmental and nongovernmental initiatives on reproductive health in general and birth control in particular. In this way, we will show that the expectation that men will not easily or generally participate in family planning has become a self-fulfilling prophecy.

As in other parts of Mexico, so-called modern forms of contraception became widely accessible in Oaxaca in the 1970s. Devices and methods, like the condom and the intrauterine device (IUD), were available to middle-class women and men living in urban areas before this time—in fact, the science to manufacture the birth control pill was developed in Mexico in the 1950s (see Soto Laveaga n.d.; Marks 2001)—but widespread access to and employment of these forms of contraception did not occur until a major campaign for family planning was launched by the Mexican federal government in the 1970s.[2] Although the history of family planning is similar to that of the rest of the country, in Oaxaca there is less knowledge about sexual health and contraception and less availability of medical care in general because of insidious poverty and a perennial lack of funding for health care.

Family planning campaigns in Mexico and Oaxaca in the last three decades were designed to accomplish two key goals. One, to foster a regime of "personal choice" regarding the timing and number of children a couple wanted and hence herald the advent of democratic decision making and citizenship in this realm of social life, a result in part of feminist currents internationally that began in the 1970s, when women activists asserted the need to gain control over their own bodies, reproductively and otherwise.[3] And, two, to analyze, regulate, and control populations, a reflection of efforts on the part of states and international multilateral organizations, beginning in the 1960s, to promote economic development in the southern hemisphere through the disarming of the "population bomb" by lowering birth rates around the globe.

The history of family planning in Oaxaca and in Mexico is similarly replete with this language: *control de población* (population control), *control de natalidad* (birth rate control), and *control de fertilidad* (fertility rate control). The term *salud reproductiva* (reproductive health), which is today widely employed in Mexico and throughout the world, was coined in the United States in 1980s. "Reproductive health" was meant to shift the focus from population control to efforts to improve women's health, contraception, maternal and child health, midwifery, sex education, and access to abortion, and to help prevent problems like sexual violence, infant mortality, and sexually transmitted infections. As used in public health, development, and academic studies, the expressions "reproductive health" and "reproductive rights" generally refer to women's reproductive health and rights. Men's reproductive health, if it is raised at all, usually refers to problems of the male organs, like the prostate, and to STIs. Indeed, the term "men's reproductive health and rights" seems to many an oxymoron.[4] Raewyn Connell discusses the contradictory history of "men's relational interests in gender equality" policy (2005:1813), finding that early assumptions that men and women had the same interests in equality have yet to be confirmed in practice. She argues that simplistic approaches to equality and rights can inadvertently conceal real differences along gender lines with respect to influence and needs.

The history of family planning in Mexico thus shares much in common with the history of family planning in other parts of the world. Perhaps for this reason one remarkable feature of the history of family planning in Mexico is how quickly the country went from being a bastion of pronatal policies as late as the early 1970s, to a country in which contraceptive methods were adopted in a matter of a few years by millions of women (and few men), which then led to dramatic declines in the birth rate (from 6.7 in 1970 to 2.2 in 2003) and in the rate of population growth.[5]

Pronatalism had multiple roots and various justifications, and the impediments to widespread adoption of contraception were legion. The teachings, language, and regulations of Catholicism—for example, the sanctity of the seed—represented obvious obstacles to the use of modern forms of birth control by followers of the church's doctrinal rulings on preventing pregnancy. Others in Mexico, who were intent on guarding the country from imperialist encroachment, insisted that only foreign capitalists would benefit from fewer Mexican births, and on these grounds they decried contraception as interference in the internal affairs of the country. As Ivan Illich, the iconoclastic educator, remarked in a late 1960s polemic on family planning, "Only a strong-man could afford simultaneously to dare traditional Catholics who speak about sin, communists who want to out-breed the U.S. imperialists and nationalists who speak about colonizing vast unsettled expanses" (1969:138).

Below, I explore a few of the rationales for supporting unlimited population growth, as well as related attitudes regarding men, male sexuality, and male cultures. In particular, I wish to raise an issue from previous decades that was still evident during the time of my research: the idea that men in Mexico "naturally" and as a general rule endeavor to prove their masculinity and virility by fathering, in a procreative sense, many children.

PRONATALISM IN MEXICO AND OAXACA

Although it would change spectacularly in the early 1970s, throughout most of the twentieth century pronatalism was the official state ideology and a principle cherished by a nation that had seen millions die in their revolution, from 1910 to 1921. Population growth was not only not a problem, it was encouraged in order to repopulate the country as a whole, to expand needed workers to more remote but economically strategic areas of the country, and as part of a plan to vault Mexico into the ranks of the more important regional powers. Children represented more hands in the countryside and security during old age in the cities: the more children, the greater one's chances of survival later in life. The dominant cultural ethos held that "big families were not merely a reflection of antiquated or 'macho' values . . . but rather an adaptation to an economically extremely precarious situation in which the majority of the Mexican population found (and finds) itself" (Márquez 1984:314).

The fallow fields left in the wake of the Mexican Revolution helped set the pronatalist backdrop, as politicians and peons alike, and for their own reasons, sought to repopulate the countryside. Countercurrents were nonetheless present early on in the century, as when the First Feminist Congress, meeting in 1916, promoted contraception as one component of women's emancipation. The contradictory political demands of population growth, on the one hand, and women's right to determine the number and timing of children, on the other, were apparent in several events of 1922. First, as many as 300,000 copies of a pamphlet on "safe and scientific contraceptive methods" were distributed in Mexico. The pamphlet was written by the North American women's rights activist Margaret Sanger, who coined the term "birth control," and in the state of Yucatán, for example, it was distributed by the Partido Socialista Obrero and the government of Governor Felipe Carrillo Puerto. In April of that same year, the leading newspaper of the age, *Excelsior*, initiated a campaign to annually celebrate the Tenth of May as Mother's Day. Beginning in 1922 and continuing until 1953, the same newspaper awarded a prize each year to the woman deemed the most "prolific" mother (Acevedo 1982:60–62).[6]

The diverse political currents of the 1920s converged in the 1930s to become a monotheistic state doctrine on population growth. Beginning at this time, as McCoy writes, "pronatalism was the guiding principle of national policy" (1974:378). In 1936, a General Population Law was passed to encourage the "natural growth" of population, the repatriation of Mexicans living outside the country, and to a lesser extent the migration of foreigners to Mexico. In line with assimilationist policies of the era, *mestizaje* and mixed marriages between "Spanish" men and indigenous women were promoted, no doubt inspired in part by earlier eugenicist trends in family planning campaigns that sought ways to decrease the proportional size of Mexico's indigenous population. It should not be surprising, as Stern writes, that in addition to mandating "the fusion of all the nation's ethnic groups," the 1936 law also found that "pronatalism was a constant feature of Mexican eugenics" (2003:194–95).

Through the early 1960s, the rate of Mexico's economic growth was double that of its population growth. As long as the economy grew at a faster pace than population, government and business leaders believed that there would be no problem in sustaining the younger generations. On the contrary, a young work force was needed to fill the factories and populate the more underdeveloped cities and regions of the country. Not only was family planning unnecessary, in the view of the authorities, but as the Secretary of Public Health stated in 1962, birth control was antithetical to Mexican religious and social values. Nonetheless, despite this policy from above, the view from below was different. Popular demand for birth control in Mexico was unmistakable in a mid-1960s study of 500 women from the middle and lower sectors in Mexico City on attitudes about contraception. Specifically, the authors of the study concluded: "More than 8 of every 10 women accept the use of contraception" (see Mateos, Bueno, and Chávez 1968:148). Despite pent-up demand, contraceptive use in the early 1970s was still conspicuously low compared to other countries in Latin America with similar socioeconomic trajectories, such as Brazil and Colombia. As in other countries, Mexico's mortality rate had declined, and life expectancy had grown over the course of the twentieth century, from twenty-four years in 1895, to forty-eight in 1950, and to more than seventy-five years in 2006. A key component contributing to this rise was declining rates of infant mortality that consequently led to women and men no longer needing or seeking to have as many children to insure that some would survive into adulthood. Unlike in many other countries, however, fertility rates did not begin to decline in a commensurate fashion until the 1970s.

Worldwide, debate unfolded in the 1960s regarding the "population problem." But in Mexico, pronatalism reigned, and nay-saying academics and policy figures were largely ignored,[7] as were the voices of international organizations trying to influence Mexico's family planning politics.[8] According to the Sanitary Code in effect at that time, contraceptives were to be distributed only with a medical prescription, which was less of an obstacle for those in the major urban centers with the connections and financial means to obtain them, and more difficult for most of the rest of Mexico's citizens. At that time, there were also restrictions on the manufacture of contraceptives, and all advertising for family planning was prohibited. During his presidential campaign in 1969, Luis Echeverría went so far as to state that "to govern is to populate" *(gobernar es poblar)*. In January of the following year, he affirmed the "need to populate our country." Although as early as 1 December 1970, the date of Echeverría's inaugural address, there were hints that a change in policy at the highest levels of the government and the state party, the Partido Revolucionario Institucional (PRI), would be forthcoming, it was not until April 1972 that the government formally announced a wide-ranging family planning program for the entire country.

In other countries—for example, Brazil—modern contraceptives like diaphragms and hormonal pills became widely available and utilized by women through the aegis of private foundations and the commercial efforts of pharmaceutical companies. By contrast, in Mexico such measures were the result of a public policy aimed at shaping fertility behavior; in practice, this meant targeting women in birth control campaigns (see Merrick 1985; Potter 1999). And although in 1962 the Mexican Secretary of Public Health declared that birth control was antithetical to Mexicans' religious and social values in general, by 1976, even in rural areas where prevalence rates have lagged significantly behind urban centers, 14 percent of married women of childbearing age reported using birth control. By 1981 this figure was 27 percent, and by 1987 it was 33 percent (see Potter 1999).

Culturalist explanations that insisted Mexican women would be reluctant to adopt birth control in large numbers were thus significantly flawed and proved unable to predict the sea change in women's contraceptive practices. Yet what was learned about women and about the fallacious culturalist reasoning with respect to women's sexuality and sexual practices was unfortunately little applied to men's sexuality and sexual practices. To this day, the analysis of the monolithic and monochromatic Mexican male and his sexual attitudes, proclivities, and practices has proved far more stubborn to dislodge. To the extent that male sexuality has been taken for granted in Mexico as a cultural given, public policy, including with respect to contraception, pregnancy, and child rearing, has shown little imagination. Reproductive health policies have consequently been designed so that women and not men are held responsible for family planning. That Mexican men's supposedly uniform "negative attitudes" were seldom challenged in the early 2000s could be partially traced to the manner in which the very first family planning campaigns were fashioned, often, as we shall see, under the aegis of liberal, international, multilateral agencies and foundations.

THE 1973 ABOUT-FACE

In April 1972 a new national family planning program was announced and launched under the slogans "Paternidad responsible" (Responsible parenthood) and "La familia pequeña vive mejor" (Small families live better). Over the next two years, a series of programs and policies aimed at kick-starting "population regulation" were activated by the federal government. By December 1973, the Mexican Congress had approved a new Ley General de Población that went into effect in January 1974. The primary aim of the General Population Law was to lower the population growth rate in Mexico that President Echeverría had begun acknowledging as "one of the highest in the world" (cited in McCoy 1974:398). The General Population Law established the following general objectives for the Mexican federal government: (a) the regulation of population growth, (b) the coordination of population policies, and (c) the formation of the National Population Counsel (Consejo Nacional de Población, CONAPO). At the same time, the language of the new law emphasized population regulation and not population control; further, reducing fertility rates in Mexico was not named explicitly as a policy objective (Brambila 1998:163).

In February 1973 a new Sanitary Code abolished Article 24 of the Mexican Constitution, which had prohibited the advertising and sale of contraceptives. Even more significant, on New Year's Eve 1973, Article 4 of the Mexican Constitution was amended to read, "Men and women are equal before the law. This will protect the organization and development of the family." The amendment specified that "every person has the right to decide, in a free, responsible, and informed manner, the number and spacing of their children" (see Zavala de Cosío 1992:189–217).[9]

In a sense, it is a misnomer to call the policies that guided population policy from the 1930s through the early 1970s pronatal. There was ample pronatalism; what was lacking were truly coherent policies that could be clearly linked to state politics. More characteristic of the approach to population issues by governments in Mexico prior to the 1970s was the scant attention paid to demographic trends. Population growth was not considered a problem, and therefore was rarely addressed in a concerted and systematic manner. All this changed under the presidency of Luis Echeverría (1970–76), when state officials at all levels unfurled a full-scale effort to limit family size through birth control. The abrupt about-face in population policy led to a rapid and sharp decline in fertility rates in Mexico, a decisive refutation of the views of policy wonks who had predicted that Mexican women would not acquiesce to contraception for religious, moral, and practical reasons. The predictions of "those who thought that Mexico's high fertility was entrenched" (Alba and Potter 1986:63) were quickly dispelled. Pent-up demand for contraception and receptivity to the goal of smaller families proved the correctness of an American Enterprise Institute study from the period, which stated that "the Mexican desire for more children is not immutable" (cited in Turner 1974:11). Table 5 shows the dramatic decline in birth rates in Mexico since 1970.

What accounts for this spectacular turnaround is a key question in the history of population and family planning in Mexico and Oaxaca. Economic pressures were clearly central to the decision to staunch population growth that was made early in his presidency by Echeverría and other high officials. Although Mexico still enjoyed a healthy economy, annual rates of economic growth had slowed by the early 1970s. In addition, migration within Mexico from the impoverished countryside to the cities was getting out of control and the appearance of "overpopulation" became more worrisome to many officials. Academic demographers, in league with interested foreign foundations and agencies, at long last seemed to find a receptive audience among those in positions of power.

Table 5 Fertility Estimates in Mexico, 1970–2003

Year	Total Fertility Rate (per 1,000 women)	Crude Birth Rate (per 1,000 women)
1970	6.7	46*
1975	5.7	41
1979	4.7	36
1981	4.3	33
1992	3.2	27
2000	2.4	21
2003	2.2	19

NOTE: Fertility is defined by demographers as the number of children a woman would have during her reproductive years if in each five-year age interval from ages 15–49 she had the number of children that women of that age currently have in the population as a whole.

* In the period 1895–1900, the birth rate was 50; for 1935–1940, it was 46. Neither of these figures is significantly higher than the crude birth rate for 1970 of 46 (see Zavala de Cosío 1992:26, table 1).

SOURCES: Alba and Potter 1986:62, table 4; www.inegi.gob.mx/est/contenidos/espanol/tematicos/mediano/anu.asp?t=mpob14&c=3191; www.inegi.gob.mx/est/contenidos/espanol/tematicos/mediano/anu.asp?t=mpob16&c=3193 (both accessed 10 May 2005).

Population control became yet one more means for the ruling party, the PRI, to perpetuate its institutional regime (see McCoy 1974:399), although as Márquez (1984:315) notes, following the government massacre of hundreds of student protesters in October 1968 at the Tlatelolco plaza, Mexican politicians had all the more reason not to be seen to be promoting policies to "limit" population. The Mexican government was also at pains to not appear to be responding to demands of the United States, although here too it was difficult to conceal that the new policies were in part the result of strong international coercion, especially from the United States and affiliated funding agencies like the World Bank.

International pressure on Mexico in the 1960s and 1970s was tied inextricably to the sordid history of imperialism and colonialism, from the time of the eugenics movement in the 1920s, through the campaigns for sterilization throughout Latin America,[10] and to the subsequent dire prognoses by the CIA, among other U.S. agencies, that argued for population control as a way to reduce revolutionary movements and protect strategic U.S. interests in the southern hemisphere. In a 15 June 1972 summit between Presidents Richard Nixon and Luis Echeverría, Nixon badgered the Mexican head of state: "The biggest problem in Latin America at this time is population growth, unemployment, and the tensions provoked by international communism" (see Welti 2003:4).[11] Mexico's population growth at the time was considered by Washington a risk factor that threatened the security of the United States. In 1975, a confidential National Security Study Memorandum 200 was prepared by the CIA, the U.S. Agency for International Development (USAID), and the Departments of State, Defense, and Agriculture, and subsequently adopted as national security policy. The document suggests that the key mechanism to force governments in the southern hemisphere to cooperate with the United States was to "integrate" development assistance with population planning (see Sobo 1990; Hartmann 1995:111; Welti 2003:13).

With respect to international communism and the security of Mexico's northern neighbor, Carlos Brambila (1998:174) raises another fascinating though seldom explored factor that influenced the change in population growth policy in Mexico: the model of socialism and comprehensive family planning campaigns in countries of the Soviet bloc, China, and Cuba. The significance and success of population planning in these countries made more untenable the charge by leftists in Mexico that any form of family planning in poor regions was necessarily imperialist in aim and content. In particular, the 1977 announcement by Mexico's National Population Council of demographic targets had more in common with countries in which five-year plans were central to government planning of all kinds, including population, than it did with the policies of countries that publicly criticized "Mexico's unhindered population growth." Reductions in the rate of population growth, from 3.2 percent to 2.5 percent between 1976 and 1982, were to be followed by drops to 1.9 percent in 1988, 1.3 percent in 1994, and 1.0 percent in 2000. Federally mandated contraceptive prevalence targets were required to meet these goals and were set by Mexico's National Family Planning Program; as Cabrera writes, these targets constituted "one of the most important aspects of the plan" overall (1994:115).

How did contraceptive use become so widespread in such a relatively short time in a Catholic country? The short answer to this question is that Mexico has long had an inconsistent and flexible relation with its Catholicism. In 1859, President Benito Juárez decreed the separation of church and state in Mexico; in 1867, Mexico broke diplomatic relations with the Vatican, and only reestablished them in 1992. Throughout the Mexican Revolution at the beginning of the twentieth century, the wave of anticlericalism was given new impetus, which would hold sway in important ways for the next hundred years. In point of fact, although Catholicism in contemporary Mexico has played an enormous role in preventing the legalization of abortion, in many ways, with respect to sexuality and reproduction, it has never mattered very much.

In December 1972 a pastoral letter from the bishops of Mexico stated: "It is for the spouses to decide, in God's presence, how many children they will have in their family; not leaving it to chance or acting out of selfish reasons, but guided by objective norms" (cited in IPPF 1979:10; see also Bliss 2003a). The pastoral letter appeared four years after the papal Encyclical Humanae Vitae that provided a remarkably lenient view of the Catholic church's birth control policies. The Mexican bishops' letter continued: "The decision on the means they are to take, loyally following the dictates of their conscience, ought to leave them at peace, in as much as they have no reason for feeling cut off from God's friendship. The important thing is for man to seek, sincerely and loyally, what is the will of God for him in his particular situation" (see IPPF 1979:10). The letter further acknowledged "a very real and excruciating emergency for most Mexican families—the population explosion." Among the many harmful effects of this population explosion was a "lack of self-improvement in women." The Catholic church in Mexico thus not only did not oppose the new family planning policies of the government—many of which directly contradicted official Catholic canon—but through their pastoral letter and the conspicuous lack of any challenge, the church leaders offered their de facto *support* for the government's population efforts.[12]

Throughout most of the twentieth century, following the adoption of the 1917 Constitution in which the church was prohibited from owning property and was brought under the strict supervision of the Mexican federal government, anticlericalism has existed side by side with obeisance to Rome. And as state and church became ever more separate institutions, doctors came to substitute for priests as the ultimate authorities on family planning, according to the formulation of the former director of Mexfam, the Mexican affiliate of the IPPF (see López Juárez 2003). What is more, the lack of opposition to artificial birth control on the part of the church should also not be exaggerated. Despite pronouncements by church leaders, innumerable local priests certainly continued to counsel their parishioners against these measures. In practice, this meant targeting women once again, both because far more women than men attended church regularly in Mexico, and because in the Catholic church as well as the Mexican health system women were de facto considered most responsible for family planning and most responsive to injunctions from religious authority. The adoption of the birth control pill and other forms of contraception by millions of women in the 1970s and beyond, however, illustrates that although significant, these countervailing efforts were on the losing side of the debate. In addition, as Catholic strictures against artificial contraception became more anachronistic, undoubtedly some clergy turned a blind eye to such transgressions to ward off further dwindling church attendance and membership.

From the outset, family planning campaigns in Mexico were aimed at women far more than men. Perhaps following from its unabashedly patriarchal framework, the bishops' pastoral letter is indeed exceptional in explicitly naming "spouses" and not only women and wives in its appeal to its flock to follow their conscience when choosing whether to practice birth control and, if so, which method. The conclusion most commentators have drawn regarding the surprising change in contraceptive practices, and the subsequent decline in fertility, in Mexico is that women proved far less religiously bound and more concerned with providing their fewer children with more educational opportunities and material privilege than some analysts had suspected possible. The slogan "Smaller families live better," in short, had been well and swiftly adopted by women in Mexico as soon as the opportunities were presented to them by the government health institutions.

If they were considered by planners at all, men were seen as neutral or begrudging partners in birth control method utilization. That is, although it was (belatedly) acknowledged that women's desire to have fewer children would prevail over all sorts of other mitigating factors (like their

Catholic prejudices), it was assumed that men still had to be thwarted from their preordained natural tendencies. Representing an emerging consensus in the Mexican government, Gilberto Loyo, the former Secretario de Gobernación[13] and longtime PRI spokesman on population matters, published a paper in 1967 in which he commented, "It can be said that to some degree in the rural areas and to a greater degree in lower class urban areas women—oppressed by the number of children they have, by their poverty, and by the irresponsibility of their husbands—attempt to control birth by inducing abortion (many times with regrettable consequences) or by ineffective contraceptive means" (Loyo 1974 [1967]:187).

In this way, as Alfonso López Juárez, then director of Mexfam, the Planned Parenthood affiliate in Mexico, told me in an interview in 2002, Mexican men were officially labeled as "irresponsible" with respect to family planning. Men in the countryside and, even more, poor men in urban settings were identified as bad influences and cultural barriers to containing Mexico's belatedly recognized population explosion. Yet to the extent that irresponsibly spreading one's seed was considered natural to men in Mexico and elsewhere, culturalist assumptions about what curbing fertility rates might entail shaped the government's ensuing efforts; women were the ones targeted for change, while men were all but ignored, as long as they did not interfere with these efforts. There are good reasons why long-standing programs in family planning and, later, reproductive health have focused on women, but the exclusion of men from these projects has not only impaired men's ability to participate more fully in contraception and other practices, it has ultimately hindered the stated goals of gender equality. Though these currents are evident in Mexico throughout the period from the 1960s to the present day, Mexico is by no means atypical in this respect.

MEXICAN FAMILY PLANNING IN GLOBAL CONTEXT

In an address at the University of Notre Dame on 1 May 1969, then president of the World Bank and former U.S. secretary of defense Robert McNamara spoke about "The World Bank Perspective on Population

Growth" (see McNamara 1974). A man of vision, McNamara cut to the chase: "To put it simply: the greatest single obstacle to the economic and social advancement of the majority of the peoples in the underdeveloped world is rampant population growth." Not wishing to be misunderstood, McNamara hastened to add that stemming population growth was no substitute for "more traditional forms of development assistance," like aid for infrastructure, agriculture, industrialization, and technology. "The underdeveloped world needs investment capital for a whole gamut of productive projects," he insisted. "But nothing would be more unwise than to allow these projects to fail because they are finally overwhelmed by a tidal wave of population" (McNamara 1974:108–9).[14]

Undoubtedly concerned with insidious ideas about imperial designs and population control that were circulating in parts of the underdeveloped world at this time, and with the potential influence these ideas might have in the metropole, McNamara dismissed such fears with statements like "The notion that family-planning programs are sinister, coercive plots to force poor people into something they really do not want, is absurd" (1974:115). He also mocked the idea that anyone in the West might want to promote family planning for nefarious purposes: "Nor need anyone be deterred from appropriate action by the pernicious, if pervasive, myth that the white Western world's assistance in family-planning efforts among the non-white nations of the developing areas is a surreptitious plot to keep the whites in a racial ascendancy" (116). McNamara was responding to anxieties about not only the World Bank—an institution that in fact did not become a major player in international population politics until the 1980s—but also institutions like USAID, which began to promote contraceptive campaigns in many parts of the world in the 1960s.

Mexican officials—if they thought about it at all—applauded the untrammeled growth of Mexico's population for most of the twentieth century and then suddenly began efforts to curb growth rates through the distribution of contraceptives to women: there was acknowledgment that the demographic crisis had finally reached a boil in Mexico, too, and that the population in the country could not be allowed to grow more quickly than the economy. Mexico's participation in international conferences provided a forum for domestic wrangling over population policies and the relationship of these to the broader issues of colonialism, postcolonialism, and international relations.

The World Conference on Human Rights in 1968 in Teheran, Iran, declared that access to family planning was a human right. The United Nations World Population Conference in 1974 in Bucharest, Hungary, issued a World Population Plan of Action; writing a decade later, Alba and Potter noted that "Mexico's population policy bears a close resemblance in content and philosophy" to this 1974 document (1986:70 n. 3). In 1984 the U.N. International Conference on Population was convened in Mexico City; it is remembered in the United States as the event at which the emissary of Ronald Reagan, James Buckley, assailed abortion rights and declared that the United States would no longer provide any funds to private organizations that promoted and performed abortions as a family planning method. The impact of the Reagan administration decision was immediate: organizations active in Mexico, like the International Planned Parenthood Federation (IPPF), were denied U.S. funding that same year. The new U.S. policy, in effect, "shifted the distribution of power in the population field away from the United States" and "helped to shatter the political consensus on population by challenging orthodox views" (Eager 2004:106).

The key foreign institutions involved in population politics in Mexico in this period included USAID, the U.N. Fund for Population Activities (UNFPA), the International Planned Parenthood Federation (IPPF), the World Bank, the Population Council, and the Rockefeller, Ford, Hewlett, Mellon, and MacArthur foundations. Family planning shifted from a more strictly medical matter to a global enterprise involving billions of dollars spent annually in services, fees, and products, and population policies became central to overall economic, political, and social programs throughout the underdeveloped world (see Caldwell and Caldwell 1986; Ford Foundation 1991).[15]

In Mexico and elsewhere, women were the key to future success in family planning, though invariably, in every country and for every international agency on earth, those developing and implementing family planning policies and projects were overwhelmingly men from the ruling and professional classes. This meant that women had to be convinced not to view "modern contraceptive methods as potential threats to their health and even to life itself" (Alba and Potter 1986:64), and that it was their responsibility as women to "protect themselves" by using birth control. Remarkably enough, in Mexico, as throughout the world before the arrival of the birth control pill, men had been more "active" participants in preventing pregnancy. Indeed, they were often the key players in methods like withdrawal and condom use. All this changed with the pill and other female forms of contraception that the international agencies promoted so heavily beginning in the 1960s, spawning in turn what Mara Viveros (2002) calls a "female contraceptive culture" and the effective marginalization of men from more significant involvement in birth control.

Men as targets of policies and programs were not explicitly brought into the family planning equation until the 1994 International Conference on Population and Development, in Cairo, and a year later at the Fourth World Women's Conference, in Beijing (see Chant and Gutmann 2000), though of course men all the while had been genuinely concerned with preventing pregnancies—as well as party to making babies.[16]

DOMESTIC INSTITUTIONS IN FAMILY PLANNING

Family planning in Mexico has always been driven by public-sector institutions, meaning federal and state governments and health centers; nongovernmental organizations, the pharmaceutical industry, and the church have played a role in promoting or opposing governmental policies, but at no time have their efforts been comparable in scope or impact. By the late 1990s, medical personnel in government institutions provided most contraceptive devices in Mexico, with private pharmacists acting as the second most significant group of providers and the number one group for first-time users (see Brambila 1998:184). And in line with local application of the female contraceptive culture, from the outset of government family planning programs in 1973, women were the main targets of all public efforts. Although men were formally mentioned in certain family planning programs in the 1980s (see Brambila 1998:177), in practice men were at best an afterthought and policy makers did not judge the participation of men in contraceptive use as necessary, possible, or worthwhile, and therefore little effort has ever been made to involve men.

Historically, the Mexican Institute for Social Security (IMSS) officially served workers in the formal private sector of the economy. Together with the Social Service Institute for State Workers (ISSSTE),[17] the institution responsible for providing health care to workers in the federal civil service, these institutions covered approximately 40 percent of the population in 2005. One of the vasectomy clinics I frequented was housed in the IMSS Center #38 in Oaxaca. A larger proportion of the population, probably more than 50 percent, was eligible for services only from the Ministry of Health (Secretaría de Salud), the institution that was charged with providing health care services to the rural and urban poor. Another of the vasectomy clinics I visited was at the Centro de Salud Urbano #1, operated by the Ministry of Health. Officially, 10 percent of Mexico's population, more than 10 million people, were not covered by any institutional health system in 2005. In practice, it is estimated that only one-half the population of the state of Oaxaca actually has access to health services within Oaxaca, leaving some 1.8 million people outside the formal state health care networks altogether (*Noticias* 31VIIo3, p. 1).

In Oaxaca, the IMSS and the Secretaría de Salud both have departments with personnel who are exclusively responsible for all non-AIDS reproductive health care, including contraception and STIs. Gynecological and obstetrics services, as well as AIDS care, however, are handled elsewhere in the health care system; this provides clear evidence that the decision to target women and not men in family planning efforts reflects institutional prejudice and not simply the biological fact that women become pregnant and give birth to children and men do not. It may be obvious for biological reasons why ob-gyn services are for women, but there is no similar rationale for family planning to be geared to women to the near exclusion of men.

With respect to private institutions and nongovernmental organizations, the most important has been the Fundación Mexicana para la Planeación Familiar (the Mexican Family Planning Foundation, Mexfam), which was created in 1965 and later became the Mexican affiliate of the International Planned Parenthood Federation (IPPF).[18] By 1974, Mexfam was running some two hundred clinics, providing services and counseling not only regarding contraception but on general health issues and sex education as well. From the outset, Mexfam directed its attention to women and not men in its family planning and general health campaigns. In 1982, nearly a decade after the Mexican government began its own efforts in family planning in earnest, Mexfam decided to close many of its clinics in Mexico City and other urban areas and instead focus on the more marginalized, underserved populations unable to avail themselves of government services. Although Mexfam has shifted its target populations over the years, to include more people in the countryside and more youth, for example, men continue to be a low priority in its efforts.

As noted, the role of international nongovernmental organizations was significant in Mexico beginning in the 1960s. The IPPF, Population Council, and Ford and Rockefeller foundations developed programs to promote demographic studies and family planning. The Colegio de México, to this day the leading institution for demographic research in the country, received funds from the Ford Foundation, among others, to launch its population center (see Caldwell and Caldwell 1986:126; see also Ford Foundation 1991). Colegio scholars were later instrumental in convincing the government of Luis Echeverría to adopt the General Population Law of 1974. Sensitivity to charges of external interference in the internal affairs of Mexico prevented U.S. government agencies like USAID from direct involvement, such as financial support, involving population planning efforts. McCoy reports that in the late 1960s USAID officials rejected the idea of channeling funds to Mexican associations, for example, through the IPPF and the Population Council, "out of fear that it would be discovered and publicized in Mexico" and in this way retard population control efforts (1974:388).

The reemergence in the 1970s of the feminist movement in Mexico contributed to the focusing of attention on several issues related to family planning, such as demands for the legalization of abortion and for stronger legal penalties for rape and violence against women in general. Formally and informally, the guiding assumption in family planning, domestic violence, and other campaigns developed by feminist activists in Mexico during this time was that women could be changed but that men were largely a lost cause and not worth as much effort.[19] Mexico in the 1980s witnessed the development internationally of reproductive health as a key platform of women's overall struggles for equality. Following on this, in the 1990s within the field of reproductive health in Mexico, sexual and reproductive rights became central concerns. In 1998 one NGO published a list (González Montes 1999:21–22) delineating these rights:

- Access to complete information on sexuality and reproduction
- Access to safe and effective contraceptive methods
- Safe and legal abortion
- Freedom to express one's sexuality in safe, respectful and pleasurable conditions
- The right to not suffer violence, abuse or sexual or bodily coercion[20]

Needless to say, no comparable set of goals concerned with men's reproductive health and sexuality has ever emerged from a socially significant organization. In fact, no organization of and/or for men that focuses on men and questions of reproduction, contraception, abortion, and sexual violence has ever existed in Mexico, or any other country. The silence of men on these issues has been indeed deafening—except, of course, when men have developed and implemented programs whose aims are to make women exclusively responsible for contraception and related matters. The only groups of and for men concerned with reproductive health have concentrated on medical problems like AIDS and other STIs. As mentioned, there has never been a groundswell on the part of men for contraception for men. Nonetheless, from the international funding agencies to Mexican state-run health institutions to local NGOs working on issues of sexual health and birth control, the institutional bias to ignore or even exclude men from these arenas has had indisputable and enduring consequences. Mexico's female-only family planning projects mirror those found in other countries. Writing about the experience of family planning campaigns in Colombia, Mara Viveros notes, "The aim of family planning programs to ensure the rights of each person to decide in a free, responsible, and informed manner regarding the number and spacing of children has not been realized in practice because the guidelines of the programs have not incorporated the idea that contraception carries with it a process of interaction and negotiation between men and women" (2002:315).

CONTRACEPTIVE TARGETS AND SEX EDUCATION

In 1977, Conapo, Mexico's National Population Council, announced goals to reduce the rate of population growth in the country, so that by the year 2000 the rate was to be 1.0 percent. A crucial component in reaching these goals was the contraceptive prevalence targets *(metas)* set by the council that same year. From that date until the present, every clinic and hospital in Mexico has been assigned specific numbers of women they must try to convince to accept one or another method of birth control. The targets are method-specific, with the highest priority given to the IUD and female sterilization (see Alba and Potter 1986:65; Potter 1999:717).[21] As Potter writes: "The critical statistic for public hospitals and maternity clinics was the percentage of mothers who accepted one of these methods immediately following delivery" (1999:717). In chapter 7, I discuss the abusive postpartum practices of inserting IUDs and sterilizing women without their consent, and sometimes even without their knowledge of what has been done to them.

With the advent of the contraceptive target system, the Mexican government decided to intervene in the sex lives of its citizens—a form of *gubernatio interruptus?*—and each health center was assigned a goal for enlisting new birth control users. Sexual reproduction was further medicalized, and institutionalized medicine became the regulator of fertility and of normative reproductive practices (see Viveros 2002:318). Although called "targets," these goals were in effect quotas, as clinics suffered penalties, at least indirectly through loss of prestige and clout in the health system, if they consistently fell short of the federally established

Table 6   Goals and Achieved Results for Contraceptive Adoption, Oaxaca City,
Unidad #38, January–May 2003

	January	*February*	*March*	*April*	*May*
OVERALL GOAL	106	106	106	106	107
Actual results:					
Pill	42	27	25	33	22
Injectables	8	13	31	31	62
IUD	11	20	72	40	64
Vasectomy	1	0	10	0	0
TOTAL	62	60	138	104	148

NOTE: Carole Browner (personal communication) writes, "The clinics I worked in in the 1980s in the Sierra de Juárez invented figures for charts like these." I have no doubt that similar figure-fudging occurred in the clinics I studied in 2001–05.

SOURCE: Instituto Mexicano del Seguro Social, Subdirección General Médica, Banco de Datos Delegacional, Subsistema 31, Delegación: Oaxaca, hoja 118, 17 June 2003. Courtesy of Dr. Andrés Ruiz Vargas.

goals. Conversely, clinics could expect extra resources if their numbers were significantly over target. What is more, the target-quota system of promoting contraception among women was of a piece with other nationally mandated health care programs, such as the *oferta sistemática* (described in chapter 6) that compelled all medical personnel to encourage birth control use every time they meet with women for any other reason. Table 6 lists the contraceptive goals and "achieved results" for the period January–May 2003 in the IMSS facility #38 in Oaxaca.

As is seen in table 7, contraceptive use in the country overall consistently rose from 1976 to 1997.[22] From the mid-1970s on, contraceptive methods used were overwhelmingly female contraceptive methods (see table 8). Although there has been some variation by state in the adoption of birth control methods, as table 9 shows, there is little difference in the participation rates of men in contraception, for example, condom use and male sterilization. Similarly, although there is significant variation in the prevalence of contraception use in rural and urban areas, there are not significant and comparable differences in overall male contraceptive use

Table 7   Contraception Prevalence in Mexico (Women 15–49
           Years Old), 1976–1997

Year	Percentage
1976	30%
1987	53
1992	63
1997	68

SOURCE: www.inegi.gob.mx/est/contenidos/espanol/rutinas/ept
.asp?t=mpob32&c=3209 (accessed 2 February 2007).

(see table 10). Finally, table 11 shows some of the demographic changes that occurred in Oaxaca in the decade of the 1990s, and the relationship between contraceptive prevalence and other socioeconomic factors like education, residence, and number of children for women in the state.

In all facets of family planning campaigns and programs sponsored by federal and state officials in Mexico, a notable theme is the explicit promotion of modern methods of contraception instead of what are often labeled as "traditional" methods, such as withdrawal, rhythm, and abstinence. Yet there were problems from the beginning with these taxonomies, which are only recently being addressed. To avoid the often vapid modern/traditional dichotomy, and because too many disparate techniques are lumped together as traditional, Jennifer Hirsch proposes using the expression "technological methods" to replace "modern methods" (2003:254). For similar reasons, Russell and Thompson (2000:5) consider the term "natural contraception" also problematic. As Juan Guillermo Figueroa (1999:153) notes, the language of family planning is consistently freighted with broader connotations—for example, in Mexico contraceptive techniques known as "los locales y los naturales" (the locals and naturals) are considered "males necesarios" (necessary evils) that will inevitably be replaced by more modern methods, such as the pill, the diaphragm, the IUD, the condom, and female and male sterilization.

The decline in fertility rates is obviously not a simple result of accessi-

Table 8   Contraceptive Use in Mexico (Women 15–49 Years Old), by Method, 1976–1992

Contraceptive Method	1976	1979	1987	1992
Pill	35.9%	33.0%	18.2%	15.3%
IUD	18.7	16.1	19.4	17.7
Tubal ligation	8.9	23.5	36.2	43.3
Vasectomy	0.6	0.6	1.5	1.4
Injectables	5.6	6.7	5.3	5.1
Condoms and spermicides	7.0	5.0	4.7	5.0
"Natural" methods*	23.3	15.1	14.7	12.2
TOTAL	100.0%	100.0%	100.0%	100.0%

* The term "natural" here refers to methods like withdrawal, rhythm, and abstinence.

SOURCE: Adapted from Brambila 1998:184, table 5.3.

bility and adoption of birth control of any kind. Millions of Mexicans without doubt decided they wanted fewer children. Often the reasons people use to explain wanting fewer children are that they want to have more money for their children's education and their general well-being. At the same time, the ideology of "modern is better" pervades discussions on birth spacing, number of children, and contraception. The teleology tracing supposed progress from backward, rural, and poor (and the employment of contraceptive "métodos locales y naturales") to modern, urban, and middle class (and the employment of "métodos modernos") is unmistakable.

Particular methods of contraceptives linked to rural/urban and traditional/modern dichotomies have long been promoted in the campaigns designed to reach the federally mandated targets for each clinic and hospital in Mexico.[23] An integral aspect of these campaigns has been sex education in the schools, health facilities, and in the media. Beginning in 1974 with a nationwide Program on Public Information and Orientation (regarding "population" problems), primary school textbooks have had information on human reproduction and sexual hygiene. In 1979, a National Sex Education Program was launched to provide sex education in

Table 9 Contraceptive Use in Mexico (Women 15–49 Years Old), by Method and State, 1997

	Pill	IUD	Injectables	Condom	Tubal Ligation	Vasectomy	Natural*
Baja California	17.0%	11.3%	7.1%	6.4%	46.5%	2.9%	7.7%
Chiapas	7.4	15.3	6.6	3.7	55.7	0.9	10.3
Jalisco	14.5	13.6	2.5	10.5	38.3	1.6	18.8
Mexico City	8.3	24.4	4.3	6.8	43.8	3.6	8.2
Michoacán	9.7	20.1	4.4	6.0	42.3	1.4	16.0
Oaxaca	4.8	17.8	6.7	2.7	45.6	0.7	21.4
Puebla	4.6	24.3	5.0	5.1	41.2	1.7	18.1
Querétaro	5.8	23.2	2.7	7.2	44.5	2.2	14.0
Sonora	19.8	17.9	3.9	4.3	45.3	1.9	6.9
Yucatán	15.4	8.6	3.0	2.6	44.9	1.5	24.0

* The term "natural" here refers to methods like withdrawal, rhythm, and abstinence.

SOURCE: Consejo Nacional de Población, www.conapo.gob.mx/oocifras/oosalud/Republica/RM042.xls, accessed 31 May 2007.

schools, the health sector, and private community organizations (on this early sex education history, see Brambila 1998:175–76).

Since the initiation of formal sex education in Mexico, the influence of scientific and Catholic discourses on sexuality has been manifest (see Amuchástegui 1998:312). In the schools, for example, written materials and talks provided to youth stress the biology of sexuality and often avoid or altogether ignore the more amorphous and mercurial issues of desire, curiosity, fear, passion, and experimentation with respect to matters sexual. Sex is reduced in these instructional approaches to a question of blood flows, genital shivers, and response rates. Although it seems churlish to suggest that no sex education might be better than an exclusively biologistic sex education, it is not unfair to say that this kind of instruction may bring an awareness about certain aspects of sexuality while at the same time inadvertently promoting other forms of ignorance.

It is important here to distinguish between education in the sense of

Table 10   Contraceptive Use in Oaxaca (as Percentage of Women 15–49 Years Old), by Urban/Rural Residence, 1992 and 1997

	1992			1997		
	RESIDENCE			RESIDENCE		
Method	*Total*	*Rural*	*Urban*	*Total*	*Rural*	*Urban*
Pill	7.9%	8.6%	7.3%	4.8%	5.8%	4.0%
IUD	11.9	11.5	12.2	17.8	17.4	18.2
Injection	10.5	8.1	12.3	6.7	6.6	6.7
Condom	5.1	3.2	6.5	2.7	1.9	3.4
Tubal ligation	38.0	29.6	44.6	45.6	42.1	48.5
Natural*	26.2	39.0	16.1	21.4	25.1	18.2
Vasectomy	0.5	0.0	0.8	0.7	0.9	0.5

* The term "natural" here refers to methods like withdrawal, rhythm, and abstinence.

SOURCE: Consejo Nacional de Población, www.conapo.gob.mx/00cifras/00salud/estados/Oaxaca/OAX20.xls, accessed 31 May 2007.

teaching about of the mere existence of some aspect of sexuality and knowledge in the sense of a fuller understanding of sexuality. Unfortunately, the same word in Spanish, *conocimiento,* is often used in surveys to determine the extent to which people have heard of something—for example, do they have *conocimiento* that there are birth control devices and that one is called an IUD (see, e.g., Rodríguez, Corona, and Pick 2000:362–64)? In a similar fashion, to the extent that sex education has been geared simply toward providing the names and locations of body parts and the proper medical application of particular forms of birth control, a fuller grasp of the complexities of sexual relations remains outside the scope of most publicity surrounding sexuality in the schools and neighborhoods of Mexico.

Then, too, it may be a mistake to exaggerate the ignorance of youth or the knowledge of their parents with respect to sexuality. In a Oaxaca clinic, a man named Eliseo told me the joke about a father who tells his son that he wants to have a frank, heart-to-heart talk with the boy about sex. After the two have a seat, the son turns to his father and asks, "OK, Dad,

Table 11 Women Who Use Contraception in Oaxaca (as Percentage of Women 15–49 Years Old Who Are in Heterosexual Relationships), 1992 and 1997

	1992	1997
AGE GROUP		
15–19	20.7%	31.3%
20–24	39.9	41.1
25–29	43.8	62.9
30–34	58.3	67.6
35–39	59.4	64.0
40–44	46.6	54.5
45–49	34.6	43.0
NUMBER OF CHILDREN		
0	11.7	13.2
1	36.7	37.0
2	51.0	66.9
3	60.7	67.4
4 or more	46.7	57.5
SCHOOLING		
None	35.7	43.8
Did not finish elementary	44.4	49.4
Elementary	48.1	57.3
Junior high or more	64.5	68.7
RESIDENCE		
Rural	35.9	46.8
Urban	60.3	65.5
INDIGENOUS LANGUAGE FACILITY		
Speaks	n.d.	45.7
Does not speak	n.d.	62.2
TOTAL	46.3	55.1

SOURCE: Consejo Nacional de Población, www.conapo.gob.mx/oocifras/oosalud/estados/Oaxaca/OAX19.xls, accessed 31 May 2007.

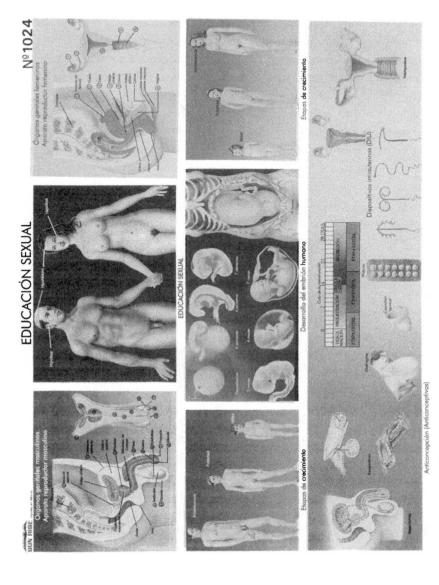

Informational flyer used in middle schools to promote sex education, 2003.

what is it you want to know?" Yet as Stern et al. (2003:S42) write in their
study on sexuality and masculinity among adolescents in Mexico City, no
matter how confused and unknowledgeable they found young women to
be about such matters, they were even more struck by the "muchachos
poco informados" (uninformed young men).

The key concern with respect to sex education is not the abstract need
to alleviate ignorance, nor even the distinction between the spread of publicity versus true information; it is the structural inequalities that exist between men and women, rich and poor, urban and rural, mestizo and indigenous. Knowledge, in the sense of awareness of some aspect of
sexuality and of particular forms of contraception, does little good in a
context in which access to regular, reliable, and affordable health care is
out of reach for large sectors of the population. Indeed, it is a remarkable
testament to women's desire to limit the number of children they have
and to have more control over the spacing of those children that so many
find the ways and means of having a certain number of children if and
when they want them.

The modern history of family planning, in Mexico and the rest of the
world, is largely the history of women and birth control. It is also an institutional history, because international and national, governmental and
nongovernmental organizations have played the pivotal role in developing family planning campaigns, contraceptive products, and promoting
the use of one or another method of birth control—among and for
women. Mexico's own particular history of benign pronatalism was followed by intensive and widespread efforts to lower population birth rates
throughout the country in a short period of time. These efforts were in
general very successful, no doubt in part owing to the common desire of
women (and men) for smaller families, as well as to contingent factors
such as the essential absence of the Catholic church in attempts to derail
the spread of contraceptives in order to prevent pregnancies. It was also
a reflection of the fact that Mexican women (and men) selectively choose
from the doctrines of the church, and, to cite Gloria González-López, that
Mexican women, in particular, "are neither submissive nor passive, but
are active individuals who mediate Catholic teachings on sexual morality based on their personal subjectivities" (2005:244).

It is in light of these peculiar institutional and historical dynamics with respect to family planning and contraception that we may best understand why some men in Oaxaca chose to get vasectomies in the early 2000s. We turn now to research on male sterilization and the totemic illusion of male sexuality in Oaxaca.

SIX

Scoring Men

All three of my daughters-in-law have had tubal ligations. I
think it was very smart of them. The boys should get them
too, that way there can be no gossip about other children.

Quoted in Michael Higgins and Tanya Coen (2000:61)

THE ANTHROPOLOGIST AS EMOTIONAL
ANESTHESIOLOGIST

I observed twenty-two vasectomies in three different clinics in Oaxaca
City, and I interviewed dozens of other men and women in clinic corridors about male sterilization. As I mentioned in chapter 1, my opening
line at the outset of a vasectomy—as I stood near the man's head, introduced myself, described the reason for my presence, and asked the man's
permission to stay during the operation—was "Well, they did this to me
six years ago. Of course, I wasn't paying much attention to what was
going on down there at that time." Most men smiled at that point and gra-
ciously gave their permission for me to continue talking with them during the remainder of the procedure. Indeed, I began to think of myself as

playing the role of emotional anesthesiologist for many of the men, my purpose to soothe the men's nerves.

Owing to the lack of surgical nurses in one clinic (Centro Urbano #38) and to the somewhat taciturn nature of the doctors operating in another (Clínica #1), before long I was integrated by the doctors themselves into the operation in various ways, and not only as an emotional anesthesiologist.[1] Frequently, I was asked to hold a bottle of the liquid anesthetic Lidocaine upside down in order for a doctor to extract more of the painkiller into a needle and thus further numb the man's scrotum.

While we chatted, I shared stories with the men as to the pain I had suffered after my own surgery. I discussed in vague terms our mutual concerns regarding postoperative sexual performance and the "garbanzo" that remained in my scrotum for a few months after the operation. And I once was asked to photograph an operation. It was a doctor who initially asked me to take the photos. I was sure the idea would be rejected by the patient, but when I raised the issue timidly with the man, a gas station attendant named Alberto, he smiled broadly and enthusiastically agreed to allow me to shoot photographs of his genitals and the vas deferens being pulled out and cut. He then asked me to drop by copies at his PEMEX workplace, on the north side of the city, so he could show his family and friends.[2] I describe below the specifics of what is entailed in a vasectomy.

This chapter discusses why some men in Oaxaca got vasectomies in the early years of the twenty-first century. Through this research, I explore broader issues relating to men's sexuality, including normative assumptions about men's natural sexual desires and practices. Clearly, numerous issues influence and determine a man's decision to get this permanent form of contraception, including cultural, historical, physiological, commercial, and individual factors. A key concern that emerged in the course of the larger study on men's reproductive health and sexuality in Oaxaca was how cultural folk beliefs about supposed male sex drives influenced men's decisions about birth control.

Among medical practitioners as well as the men who receive vasectomies, conventional wisdom treats male sexuality as a totemic illusion, such that male sexuality became naturalized as both a fixed entity and as something entirely distinct from female sexuality. In a sense, this totemic illusion presents a robust case of medicalization, as social beliefs and mores regarding male sexuality are transformed into a physiological truism. And in the case of vasectomies in Oaxaca, such a totemic illusion conferred the supposedly " 'instinctive' attitudes or beliefs" (Lévi-Strauss 1963:2) that often resulted from speculation about men's sexuality.

What occurred locally in Oaxaca was, of course, also governed by global events. In the case of men choosing to get a vasectomy, this decision took place at a time when highly effective forms of birth control for women had become widely available throughout the world, and in fact there has developed the *cultura anticonceptiva femenina*, the female contraceptive culture, that Viveros (2002), Barbosa and Viera Villela (1997), and others discuss.[3] Nowhere on earth do men participate in contraception in larger numbers than women; in most locations the percentage of men using male forms of birth control is a tiny fraction of that for women employing other methods.

Indeed, one striking feature of decision making about birth control in Oaxaca was the fact that the number of vasectomies performed there has never been great. Through 2000, according to official statistics, 3,105 men had undergone a vasectomy in Oaxaca (INEGI 2000:265), out of a population in the state of well over three million men and women. The procedure itself was unknown to most people in the region, and irrelevant to all but a few who expressed familiarity with the term. Figures on male sterilization in Mexico overall hovered slightly above 1 percent of the adult male population; by way of contrast, figures for China and the United States, for example, were 10 and 14 percent, respectively. The rate of female sterilization in Mexico (and Latin America generally) was around 28 percent.[4] Thus, the number of men who participated in birth control by getting sterilized was relatively low in Mexico, including Oaxaca, both in comparison with other countries and with the rate of sterilization for women in this area.

Understanding why some men in Oaxaca opted for this form of birth control is not dependent upon the numbers or percentages of those involved. At the outset, it is nonetheless worth mentioning two possible factors influencing men's decisions about sterilization that ultimately were less in evidence than originally anticipated. First, because the vast majority of people in Mexico are Catholic, it could be argued that men who chose to get a vasectomy must have been deliberately rejecting Church doctrine forbidding the use of artificial contraception and sterilization of any kind. Yet not only do the vast majority of women in heterosexual relationships in Mexico use some kind of birth control (see chapter 5), but, tellingly, the issue of Catholic strictures in this realm rarely arose in the course of dozens of interviews with men and women from this admittedly self-selected group. "Tres es ya un ejército" (Three is already an army), one doctor commented to me, by way of explaining common contemporary attitudes toward the ideal number of children couples seek.

Second, there is also a culturalist explanation that attempts to explain what men in Oaxaca who were thinking about the operation had to overcome. In fact, this cultural rationale was sometimes used to explain why there were fewer men getting vasectomies in Mexico compared to men in certain other countries, as well as compared to sterilization procedures performed on women in Mexico: supposedly, there were differences between "macho" and "non-macho" cultures, as if those men who do get sterilized in Oaxaca might somehow be acting in a manner unrepresentative of their macho culture. In addition to the fact that "macho" means different things to men and women of different ages (see Gutmann 2006 [1996]), such a line of reasoning skirts the larger context of decision making about birth control in Oaxaca. Building on the notion of a female contraceptive culture, it is of great significance that there were few modern forms of artificial birth control designed for men. This circumstance is not unique to men in Oaxaca. Therefore, the problem of how to understand men's participation in birth control, as in the case of choosing to get a vasectomy, is governed by the cultures of the global pharmaceutical companies and by the basic research on male hormones (see Oudshoorn 2003) as much as by specifically local gender identities and relations of inequality (e.g., "machismo").

Among the truly salient local factors influencing decision making about vasectomies in Oaxaca was a set of folk beliefs shared by health care specialists and the population at large concerning male sexual practices and urges—beliefs whose basis in fact extends no further than their wide acceptance in society. Among health care practitioners, for example, the

main source of certain foundational beliefs about male sexuality in Oaxaca and Mexico continued to be prosaic sentiment represented as scientific knowledge that served as the starting point in reproductive health
care efforts.

Finally, I should mention that I do not believe vasectomy is inherently
a good or bad form of contraception or of reproductive health policy, nor
is it necessarily a means to promote equality between men and women.
Throughout the world, vasectomy has been employed by certain individuals, institutions, and governments to encourage the expansion of
sexual rights and obligations, and by others to further eugenicist and neo-
colonialist goals. But given the scarce attention to men and contraception,
in anthropology and demography, for example, this chapter seeks to provide new information about one aspect of men's relationship to reproductive health.[5]

NUTS AND BOLTS AND SCISSORS

As I confessed to the twenty-two men whose vasectomies I witnessed,
and to scores of others elsewhere in the clinics and in subsequent conversations in their homes, although I had had a vasectomy, it was not
until I actually watched other men get them that I felt I understood what
was involved in the procedure. (Sometimes I also mentioned to the men
and women that I had observed three tubal ligations—that is, female sterilizations—and had better come to understand why this operation, at
least as it was performed in Oaxaca, entailed a dramatically more invasive and traumatic surgery.)

The most common series of events leading to men choosing vasectomy
in Oaxaca involved women receiving counseling about contraception at
one or another clinic, from either a nurse or a doctor, at which time the
idea of vasectomy was raised for the woman to consider. Often women
were shown a board on which pictures or drawings of birth control pills,
IUDs, condoms, hypodermic needles, and male and female sterilizations
were depicted. If the idea of their husbands getting sterilized appealed to
the women, they could then tell their husbands about the operation. If the

man was amenable, he and his wife then returned for a visit with a doctor who specialized in the procedure. (Unlike in the United States, in the public clinics of Oaxaca, vasectomies are not performed by urologists.) The man would have to demonstrate verbally that he understood that the surgery would be permanent and could not necessarily be reversed, should he change his mind later. As one doctor told me, "Unless I am sure the guy wants it, I turn him away. We don't want unsatisfied customers complaining later—that would be bad for business."

On the day of the operation the men were asked to shave their scrotum at home. Some men did not understand the operation well and shaved off all their pubic hair. They arrived at the clinic at the appointed hour and took a seat in the corridor with the other men who had appointments that day. At that point, it was first come, first served. When their turn came, they went into another, private room to undress. They took off their pants and underwear and put on a hospital gown. Then they were led to an examining table and they lay down face up. A desk lamp with a flexible neck was turned on and positioned so it would heat up the man's scrotum and make the skin relax and be more supple. A doctor or nurse then used surgical tape to fasten the man's penis so it faced toward the man's head, that is to say, to get it out of the way.

The operation took place behind closed doors, but noise from nearby waiting rooms, nurses periodically opening the door to ask questions about other matters, and doctors having to run out for some other urgent matter—all these events provided a rather cacophonous atmosphere, in which the men getting sterilized tried to maintain their composure and good humor.

After the scrotum was suitably pliable, a doctor would begin feeling around for one of the two vas deferens (*conductos*) under the scrotal skin, a centimeter or so below the base of the penis. When one was located, brown antiseptic lotion was applied liberally to the area. Lidocaine was injected on either side of the vas to numb the area. When the man could no longer feel pain, a clamp-like instrument was used to grip the vas through the scrotal skin. At this point, a scissors-like instrument was used to make a small hole in the skin just above the vas. (As in virtually every other country in the world, in contemporary Mexico this "no-scalpel"

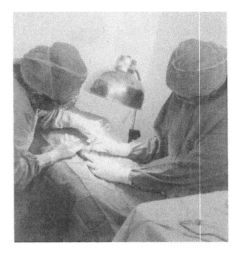

Alberto asked me to drop off photographs
of his vasectomy at the gas station where
he worked, 2003.

technique, developed in China in the 1970s, was the only one used in vasectomies. Below, I discuss certain symbolic implications of the no-scalpel
vasectomy.) Unlike a cutting or snipping motion, however, the doctor
employed this scissors-like instrument by placing the tips of the closed
blades on the skin and then gently opening them in order to, in effect,
slightly tear (rather than cut) the skin.

Once the small hole was made, the clamp was used to extract the little
white tube, mere millimeters in diameter, that is the duct through which
sperm travel from the testis in the course of ejaculation. Surgical thread
was tied around the *conducto* to close it, and then another knot was tied
approximately two centimeters apart from the first. With the same
scissors-like instrument, a section of the vas was snipped off between
what would become the two tied-off ends. In one clinic, at this point, the
ends of the vas were cauterized. The skin of the scrotum was then gently
lifted so that the ends would slip back through the little hole. This hole
was the same one that would be used for the other duct, which was then
retrieved, tied off, cut, and returned.

Because the hole in the skin was so small, only rarely were stitches required after the procedure. Generally, no more than a bandage was placed over the tear. In the twenty-two vasectomies I observed, none lasted longer than twenty-five minutes and most were finished in fifteen or twenty minutes.

After the vasectomy, men were given a sheet with postoperative suggestions. They were to place an ice pack on their scrotal area for one half hour, remove it for one half hour, and then reapply, repeating this for eight hours. The men were asked to return to the clinic in a week to check for infection. Although statistics were not kept at any of the clinics, perhaps half the men would return after a week. Finally, the men were told that if they wished to avoid making their wives pregnant, they should not have sex without contraception for the first twenty ejaculations, or three months, whichever came first. And after twenty ejaculations or three months, they were asked to bring a fresh specimen of their semen to have it tested for sperm. Only a tiny fraction of men ever returned to surrender a semen sample for analysis.

Other than how to manage any possible pain, several men wanted to know how their sexual desire and their ability to have an erection and to ejaculate might be changed. Even if they had discussed their concerns before the procedure, many men expressed renewed anxieties as they left the operating room. Occasionally, if my discussions with the men seemed to have gone well, I would tell them about my sister, who laughingly described to me how my brother-in-law was so determined to test himself that only hours after his vasectomy he insisted on having sex with her. That report seemed to cheer up some of the men as they hobbled their way into the street.

Of the slightly more than 3,000 vasectomies performed in Oaxaca as of 2000, around 1,900 of them took place at Centro #38, and slightly fewer than 500 at the Clínica #1 health facilities. In a 2001 study conducted by García Helmes et al. (n.d.) to examine the influence of social, cultural, and economic factors in the decision to get a vasectomy among patients at Centro #38, the authors concluded that the percentage of men with six or fewer years of education who opted for sterilization was only slightly smaller than those who had attended college. The widespread belief that men who decide to get a vasectomy are overwhelmingly those with higher levels of education is also not borne out in my own analysis of the

Above and right: Outside Clinic #1, where "no-scalpel" vasectomies were advertised, 2002.

records of 478 men at Clínica #1 (i.e., nearly all the men who had vasectomies at this clinic). Nor was there any discernible pattern with respect to the men's ethnic self-identification; there were numerous men who spoke only Spanish and there were many who also spoke an indigenous language or self-identified with one or another indigenous group.

Thus, both my ethnographic fieldwork with dozens of men and my archival research in the files for hundreds of others show that the men who decided to get vasectomies were not clearly distinguished by any particular demographic features related to age, income, education, or ethnicity.[6] Perhaps the only outstanding demographic characteristic of the men who were sterilized in Oaxaca is that most reported that they had sought vasectomies because they had achieved "paridad satisfecha," that is, they had already had as many children as they wanted.

PRIMORDIAL URGES

In the Ethnobotanical Garden of Oaxaca (where I sometimes worked as a laborer), workers called one young man Chaquetas (or sometimes Chaquete). *Chaquetear* in Mexico is slang for "masturbation," and the point of the nickname, of course, was that the other men in the Garden used it to tease Artemio, to use his formal name, because he was still single and therefore it was assumed he masturbated a lot. Thus, the term *chaquetas* is somewhat analogous to the North Americanism *jerk off* or the Britishism *wanker,* except that the Mexican version is heard a good deal more literally than those in the United States or Britain. It did not seem to matter that Artemio had a girlfriend and that most of the other men assumed that Artemio had sex with this girlfriend. Because he was an adolescent male, the other men were certain that he masturbated as often as he could. That's simply in the nature of being a young man. It may be worth noting that I have never heard similar casual commentary about young women who masturbate. The fact that I have not reflects more than the fact that I am a man; it is also indicative of dichotomous conceptions of male and female sexuality.[7]

Chaquetas-Artemio was a Chatino-speaker from the village of Santo Domingo Morelos Pochutla, on the Pacific coast of Oaxaca. When he arrived in Oaxaca City, in 1998, he spoke little Spanish, and coworkers still joked of the time they had sent him to the tool shed for a *pala*—shovel— and he had come back with a *barreta*—digger. They also teased him because, they said, he drank too much. Although teenage boys may drink, Artemio was considered a borderline alcoholic. Some drinking is normal, but his was too extreme and therefore had passed beyond the normal and natural. This was not so of Artemio's alleged masturbatory habits: "He has milk stored up," another worker, Felipe, smirked as he told me of this obvious male conundrum. There's only one obvious recourse to resolve such a storage predicament.

These beliefs and claims about the adolescent male penchant for sexual self-gratification—and, clearly, beliefs and claims are all that can be seriously researched on this topic—are widespread in Mexico. I found similar discussions in my own research on changing men and masculinities in Mexico City in the early and mid-1990s, for example, when grandmothers talked about nephews who still "yanked the goose's neck" and male friends related to me how they instructed their boys in the arts of onanism (see Gutmann 2006 [1996]:143). What I find remarkable is not that adolescent males in Oaxaca masturbate, but the casualness with which it is acknowledged, discussed, and joked about in a good-natured fashion.[8] As Héctor Carrillo writes in his book on sexuality in Mexico in the time of AIDS, concerning a study of Guadalajara in the 1990s: "In relation to adolescent masturbation, the main influence on peoples' opinions appeared to be the generalized perception that condoning this practice was a sign of modernity and an appropriate response to outdated moral traditions" (2002: 171). In a similar vein, Jennifer Hirsch (2003) talks of masturbation representing "a competent, modern masculinity" among Mexicans in Jalisco and Atlanta, just as Thomas Laqueur (2003) makes clear the historical relationship in Europe between modernity and masturbation.

Late modernity requires that we look at life in new ways, yet how new are these ways if they are still grounded in long-standing notions of male sexuality that is naturally out of control and must therefore be civilized by society and women (see Lamas 1996; Lancaster 1992)? The implication is that *modern* adolescent masturbation by males is a scientifically, medically, and biologically safe and sane opening toward adult sexuality, part of the virile process of adapting oneself to the sexual world of real men. How these medicalized concepts of male sexuality are applied to men in older age groups was a focus of my fieldwork in the two vasectomy clinics in Oaxaca City. How much of our naturalized and medicalized understanding of men's sexuality is based on, or at least reinforced by, biological schemata, beginning in grade school, is a question deserving attention.[9]

Vasectomies in Oaxaca took place in the early 2000s within a context of totemic male sexuality, so that certain phenomena associated with male sexuality became naturalized as symptomatic of what was allegedly unique about men in the first place. This was apparent in the medical (and medicalized) organization of reproductive health and sexuality as conceived in the Ministry of Health and other health agencies as well as in the general population. Sexuality was understood both popularly and in the medical community as a process of psychosocial compulsions and restrictions, in which ostensibly male sexual desires, needs, and satisfactions were given a naturalized and thoroughly gendered character. Further, as Parker et al. found, more generally, although there was a "demedicalization of sexuality" in social science research through social constructivist approaches in the late 1970s and early 1980s, with the HIV/AIDS pandemic, "a profound remedicalization of sexuality" has occurred (2000:3). In Oaxaca, this totemic illusion was evident in the taken-for-granted beliefs equating male sexuality with uncontrollable urges. Female contraceptive culture flourished when there was a medical endorsement of such perceptions regarding innate male sexuality.

THE OFERTA SISTEMÁTICA (FOR WOMEN ONLY)

The recent contraceptive program in Mexico called Oferta Sistemática also reveals how, based on the totemic illusion of male sexuality, state-mandated policies sought to increase the adoption and employment of birth control by women there. As Thompson (2000) shows, with the

Oferta Sistemática (roughly translated as the "Standard Offer"), every time a woman of childbearing age came into contact for any reason with a doctor, a nurse, or other health care worker, whether in a clinic or in her home, she was offered contraception. (It will be recalled that all forms of birth control are free in public health centers in Mexico.) It is significant that men were not part of the Oferta Sistemática, unless they happened to accompany their spouses, which meant that men were not as a matter of course asked about what form of birth control they might employ, unless they specifically sought information about contraception. In this way, the female contraceptive culture emerged and was reinforced institutionally, so that women were systematically confronted by health personnel about birth control in ways that few men experienced.

Although health care practitioners insisted that promotion of birth control among women was simply a reflection of the realities of the situation, in which most women expected and were expected to be solely responsible for contraception, I think such interactions in reproductive health clinics reveal a form of medical profiling (see Briggs and Mantini-Briggs 2003) in which doctors and nurses reveal their own prejudices and preferences for women to assume this obligation. In the same way, *metas* (goals) set by federal agencies for the promotion in local clinics of various forms of contraception (see chapter 5) were aimed at recruiting women as the "new users."

In an effort to examine negotiations between women and men regarding contraception—what Carole Browner (2000) terms the "conjugal dynamic"—in 2001, I also interviewed women in Clinic #1 at the family planning clinic *(módulo de planificación)*. I sat with one woman who told me that her husband had just returned "for good" from the United States and that the two of them had decided they needed reliable contraception. They might still have more children, so they were looking for temporary methods. She was in the clinic to get an IUD inserted. I asked her, "I am sure you aren't looking for your husband to get a vasectomy, because that is a permanent form of birth control, but have you thought about other methods for men instead of getting an IUD put in?" The woman looked at me as if I were confused, or maybe a little feeble-minded. "Like what?" she gently inquired.

Of course, I had little to say by way of response. Because other than condoms—and discounting withdrawal and rhythm as reliable forms of long-term temporary contraception for most men and women—there was no other method widely available on the market, in Oaxaca or in any other part of the world. There were, again, few birth control options for men.

VASECTOMIES TO SHARE SUFFERING

Whether men who opted for vasectomies expressed demonstrably more egalitarian relationships with their wives, and whether they said they were prompted to make this decision by persuasive women, is relevant to tracing patterns of decision making among men with respect to reproductive health and sexuality. Indeed, in several case histories we find what can be termed an initiating-catalytic role of women in these couples and a group of men who were willing to attend to the desires and demands of women, in other words, men who hardly fit the model of the emblematic patriarch (see Gutmann 1997). It was not uncommon for the women themselves to make the appointments for their husbands to get *la operación*.

At the same time, although the decision had the most direct bearing on the reproductive and sexual relationship between men and women, many men also recounted that it had been another man or group of men who had convinced them to seek the operation. Many men told me about their discussions with male friends, coworkers, and relatives as to what would happen during and following the procedure. And in my interviews with men during *la operación*, I occasionally mentioned that I had checked with my brother-in-law beforehand, to relieve my own concerns. Thus, one common pattern of decision making was for the woman to initiate the process by suggesting her husband consider get a vasectomy, whereupon the man might talk to male friends and relatives to get their opinions (and occasionally personal experiences). In this way, men responded to their wives' initiatives by activating their own networks and building support for the procedure from those who might potentially have negative reactions to male sterilization.

Marcos was a man whom I interviewed during his vasectomy and later in his home. After driving a taxi for thirteen years in his native Mexico

City, Marcos had recently followed his wife and moved in with her family in Oaxaca. He had also spent a year in Las Vegas, Nevada, trying to recoup his finances after the extended illness of his father. When asked about the decision making process prior to his vasectomy, after returning from Nevada, Marcos related:

> Right, more than anything, it wasn't a discussion, it was . . . in our case when she and I talked about it, she told me, "What do you think about it if I get the operation?" So I told her, "Well, whatever you want, babe, but I can get an operation, too." And she says, "You would do it?" I say, "Yeah, yeah, I would do it, because, yeah, you've already suffered in one way or another with the kids, in childbirth, so there's nothing wrong with them operating on me."

When I asked Marcos if he considered himself in any sense unusual or unique in comparison to other men who relied entirely on their wives to "take care of themselves" in terms of contraception, and why other men might be like this, Marcos replied, "It's the ideas we Mexicans have. We have ideas that are a bit macho. And if I say 'we have,' it's because sometimes I have these ideas, too. We don't appreciate that women really suffer in childbirth with our children. And all that idiosyncrasy about 'Mothers are self-sacrificing women.'"[10]

Another man, Juan, used a specific term when describing the negotiations that had preceded his vasectomy: his intention was "try to help my wife a little in family planning." She had always reacted poorly to pills and injections. As to why more men did not follow his example, Juan, like others, also thought there might be something peculiar to Mexican men: "Here in Mexico I think that because of the . . . hmmm . . . how to put it . . . the machismo, men think that having a vasectomy will put an end to everything and that you won't have . . . relations any more. Well, what do I know?" He offered a pragmatic explanation as well: as soon as his wife learned about vasectomy, she was done with trying the other methods. The next man in line for the operation nodded in agreement. That is what had happened to him, too.

Rogelio was a twenty-nine-year-old fireman with two children. Rogelio told me that his wife, having used an IUD for six years, was delighted about his decision to get a vasectomy. And, he emphasized, it had been *his* decision alone to get "la cortadita" (the little cut). But her enthusiasm was an important factor in his decision—"Just think what it's like to have kids!" When I asked Rogelio what would happen if he and his wife some-day decided they wanted another child, his answer was simple: "We'll adopt." And even more decisive, it seemed, was the role of his best friend, also a fireman, who had told him, "¡Anímate!" (Get with it!). Rogelio es-timated that ten to twelve men at work had had vasectomies in the year or two since a health care promoter named Orvil from the state-run AIDS clinic, COESIDA, had given the men a talk on safe-sex practices. Men who have had vasectomies and others who are receptive to the possibility of getting sterilized are utilized by health promoters like Orvil to induce more men to get *la operación.*

Miguel was thirty-two years old and had gone to school through the eighth grade; he has two children. At the time of our talk, he made ply-wood in a local factory. When I asked whether he and his wife had used condoms, he told me, "For about three days." Like other men, Miguel told me that neither he nor his wife liked condoms. And, like others, he gave two reasons: one, "No se siente lo mismo" (You don't feel the same), and two, "Because of machismo." When I pressed Miguel to explain the con-nection between machismo and not liking condoms, like other men, he was unable to further analyze his views. But he did insist that he wanted to "be different than most men," and that this was a key motivation be-hind his decision to get a vasectomy: "Hay que ser comprensivo con las mujeres" (You've got to be understanding with women), he counseled me. At this, Dr. Serret, the female specialist in vasectomies at Clinic #1, commented, "¡Qué bueno que ha decidido cooperar!" (It's great you've decided to support [your wife]!).

In a follow-up interview with Calixto and his wife, Patricia, a week after Calixto had a vasectomy, the conversation turned to their experience with condoms.

"Have you ever used them?" I inquired.

"No, I don't like condoms," Calixto answered. Then he laughed as he added, "I gave them back to Dr. Andrés!"

"And you?" I asked Patricia, who replied, "Me neither!"

"Her neither," Calixto agreed.

I wanted to push the point, so I asked Patricia again, "You don't like condoms?"

"Well," she now said, "sometimes you have to think about [using] them."

"She told me to use them," Calixto now confessed.

"Yeah, you know, for the illnesses," she clarified.

He stated bluntly, "But, well, no."

"It's a way to protect yourself, more than anything," Patricia murmured, and we changed the subject.

For some women and men in Oaxaca, condoms were also especially associated with migratory travels in the United States. One woman who was at Clinic #1 to arrange for a tubal ligation later that week described her experiences with the health care systems in Arizona and California, where she and her husband had lived for five years with their daughters. Before crossing into the United States, Carla had tried to use an IUD, but because of bleeding between her periods she had switched to monthly contraceptive injections. When the family had arrived in the United States, she and her husband had begun using condoms: condoms were available for free in Salinas, California, where they were working in the fields. As they had no legal papers, they tried to stay away from any authorities, including doctors and nurses who could have written prescriptions for injections and pills.[11]

A different kind of contraceptive sharing between men and women is documented in recent work on coitus interruptus among Mexican couples. As Hirsch and Nathanson (2001:413) point out, withdrawal as a form of birth control has been incorrectly classified as a "traditional" method (in contrast to "modern" methods like the IUD). As they demonstrate, many men and women who utilize this method interpret the meaning of withdrawal in ways that do not easily fall into such dichotomous taxonomies. Of the interpretations I heard regarding *coito interrumpido*, in addition to one man's admission that it was "a difficult way" to do things, women in particular bragged on their husbands, who "are able to control their ejaculation" and in this way show their love for them and demonstrate enough self-discipline to help prevent another pregnancy. In fact, the only negative comment I heard regarding withdrawal came from one of the doctors who performed vasectomies. This doctor responded to a patient's question about the method by counseling against it, on the grounds that it was not only "disagreeable," but that it often resulted in incomplete ejaculation, leaving sperm "en route" that could in turn damage a man's prostate. Needless to say, these views are not shared in any published literature on the subject, in Mexico or elsewhere. Once again, one must reflect on the extent to which medical practitioners do not merely reflect cultural biases and mores, but instead, under the guise of medical expertise, promote ideas and practices that, as in this case, could serve to undercut men's participation in family planning and contraception.

On Thursday, 4 April 2002, the IMSS (Mexican Institute for Social Security) sponsored a "vasectomy day" to help promote the procedure. Eleven men signed up for the operation, and seven showed up. One man, the forty-three-year-old father of three children and a driver on the bus line between Oaxaca and the Isthmus of Tehuantepec, several hours' drive to the south, was especially nervous about his vasectomy. But because "women suffer with IUDs," he had decided to be a "real macho" and get sterilized. He talked of machismo as characteristic of men who just want to have more children, and of real machos as those who care enough about their children to limit themselves to just a few. The experiences and thinking that brought another man, Arturo, to the vasectomy table were distinct. Arturo was thirty-two years old. Two years earlier, his baby of three months had died of hydrocephalus. Surgeons operated on the baby at six days. Then she spent a month in the hospital. Then she came home for two months to die. Arturo and his wife, a Zapotec-speaking woman from Tehuantepec, now had another baby who was one year old. Terrified they might some day experience another child's death, they decided nevertheless to be satisfied with one child, and because his wife "had already suffered" and because sterilization "is easier for the man," Arturo got a vasectomy.

From a different Zapotec region of Oaxaca, Nacho and his wife lived in a small town in the mountain zone *(sierra)*. Nacho's rationale for getting sterilized on Vasectomy Day was twofold: a tubal ligation for his wife would be more complicated than a vasectomy for him, and he was a teacher and did not have to return to work for another week—this was during Easter week—and, therefore, it was more convenient for him than for his wife. Suffering was also on the mind of a fourth man getting a vasectomy that day. Marcelo, twenty-nine years old and the father of three children, worked as a policeman on the outskirts of the city, near the famous archeological ruins of Monte Albán. He recounted to me that his wife was the one who had prompted him to get sterilized, with the admonition "Te toca un poco sufrir" (It's your turn to suffer a little).

Many men talked on Vasectomy Day, and on other occasions, about their desire to suffer instead of their wives. (One woman used the same language of suffering when she told me how she had bathed her husband, who was "suffering" from pain in his groin after the operation.) Domiciano, a resident of the rural town of Cuilapan de Guerrero, outside Oaxaca City, offered a rather more complex folk prognosis for women who receive tubal ligations, by way of explaining why he had chosen to get a vasectomy:

"What happens is that . . . when . . . they say that when a woman gets the operation . . . what I have heard is that, you know, that the woman suffers, that her temperature rises, that she can suffer depression."

"Where did you hear that? From women who've had the operation?" I inquired.

"Exactly. Well, not with men, but with my wife. Women who've had that experience, who've had a ligation, let's say. They're the ones who have commented to my wife that they suffer depression a lot. Deep depressions, or that their [blood] pressure goes up. That's why I made the decision . . . for them to do it to me," he concluded. Domiciano is not alone in believing that this is what often transpires. Men like Domiciano may believe that saving women from such health problems is one rationale for getting a vasectomy that is beyond reproach and social opprobrium.

Talking with Esteban, yet another bus driver who had a vasectomy, and his wife one afternoon under the awning of their house near the Río Atoyac, which runs through Oaxaca City, it was made clear to me that Andrea's medical condition had made sterilization a most pressing issue. "The doctor told me that it was strongly recommended I not get pregnant again," Esteban's wife said. Besides, Esteban added, they already had three children. They had thought seriously about Andrea getting her tubes tied, Esteban recounted: "It's just that she was really bad off then. I said, 'I'm going to have to take care of you, I am going to have to be waiting on you if they tie your tubes. They're going to operate on you, they're going to cut you. It would be better not,' I told her. 'It would be better if they did it to me.' "

So I asked Esteban why he had said this.

> Because I didn't want her to go through with it. I, well, the truth is that I love her a lot, no? So I don't want her to suffer. So I say to her, "So you don't have to be . . ." Because [male sterilization] is simpler, more than anything, and then the time you need to recuperate is less. First I talked with the social worker and I said to her, "What do I need to do it?" She told me to talk with Dr. Andrés Ruiz Vargas. "Talk to him and he will treat you." "Okay," I say, "good." So I go and talk with him and he asked me if I had thought about it carefully. "Yes," I say, "I'm ready." "Good," he says, "so look, all that's going to happen is this, this, and this." I say to him, "What do I need to bring or do for . . ." "No," he says, "all you have to do is think about it carefully until tomorrow, or the day after tomorrow. Or think about it as long as you want. Think about it and let me know on Tuesday." So I came home, talked to her [pointing to his wife]. We talked about our financial situation, how many days I would be laid up here, how many days I was going to be here.

WHOM TO TELL

Esteban's sister later praised his decision: "Well, I congratulate you, little brother, because you are rare among men." Domiciano's father-in-law, a man who had not had a vasectomy, similarly responded to the news that his son-in-law would no longer be siring any grandchildren for him: "Te felicito" (I congratulate you). Others were not always as inspired by the news of a friend or family member's vasectomy. When Esteban encountered another driver at the big central market, he explained that he was not working because he had had "a little surgery: they gave me a vasectomy." "¡No manches!" (Don't jerk me around!) his companion taunted him. "And now?" "Everything's fine," Esteban responded. But his friend seemed skeptical. "The hell you're really fine?" he quizzed Esteban.

"Yeah, I went into the clinic walking and I left the clinic walking. It was no big deal. It's a slight cut [*una cortadita*], maybe half a centimeter. That's all they do. *No hay problema.*"

Nonetheless, countervailing views were revealed when men and women discussed who they would tell about the man's vasectomy. Many couples were reluctant to inform family members or friends of what the man had done. Luis, a middle-aged doctor, described to me his fear of getting labeled by others as a man who was forced by his wife to get the operation, and what this would imply about his being a good man.

> As for me, well, as I always say, what do I care what others say about me? I don't care if they say good or bad things about me. As long as they don't try to stick their noses in my business it's OK by me. But I don't want them pointing, because just as I speak frankly I also have a low flash point. I have a temper, and what I really don't want to hear one day, while I am having a coffee or something, is "Look at that eunuch over there." Or something like that.

Being a good man was linked by all the men I interviewed to the inability to ever again procreate—obviously the purpose of a vasectomy. But what this meant practically was that many men sought to be good men by being two different men: the vasectomized man who did well by his wife, and the still-potent man in the eyes of friends and neighbors who did not know he had been sterilized. By no means uniform, reluctance to share the news of one's vasectomy with even close friends was nonetheless an unambiguous sign from many men that they feared not just social opprobrium but very personal intolerance. Better therefore, Domiciano told me, to leave matters "secret between my wife and me."

Teasing apart the roles of different people in the decision-making process itself commonly seemed fruitless. Although most men insisted that the decision had been theirs alone, or theirs in the final instance, the impetus had demonstrably come from wives who had learned about vasectomy as a form of birth control from health workers. As to what the women did with this information, that was another matter. A woman in the rural village of San Felipe Tejalapam, on the outskirts of Oaxaca City, told me in 2002 that, over the years, she had repeatedly urged her husband, "¡Anímate!" all to no avail. "Sometimes I talk to my friends about it," her husband confided. But the whole idea of the operation made him nervous, and no one seemed to be able to confirm the safety of the procedure.

Some cases, however, seemed clearer: Jorge related a deal he and his wife had agreed to before the birth of their third and last child. First, he said, with respect to contraception, "You don't always have to leave it to the woman." After his wife became pregnant the third time, she told him that if the baby were a boy, then Jorge would have to get a vasectomy. Their first two children were girls and Jorge badly wanted a boy, "so I can watch *fútbol* with him later. Girls get up and leave after a few minutes of watching a game on TV." And, he said, he was tired of shopping for pink clothes all the time. "If number three had been a girl, would your wife really have had a ligation?" I asked. "Yes," he replied emphatically. I was not clear if the vasectomy was seen by either of them as a form of payment for services (male progeny) rendered, or if they simply considered it a clever way to decide who would get sterilized.

Deciphering the labyrinthine circuits men traveled to arrive at the decision to get a vasectomy was made all the more complex by the challenge to distinguish between what people said and what they might mean. In recounting the comments of men and women who shared their views and experiences on vasectomy, some of the women I interviewed identified their husbands as the real decision makers. Yet, like Rapp, who studied women's decision making surrounding amniocentesis in New York City, I too "often wondered whether I was witnessing male dominance or female invocation of a classic manly privilege" (2000:99–100). Of particular interest to me were the interactions akin to what Rapp calls gender scripts that "revealed healthy doses of female manipulation." Decision making about vasectomies in Oaxaca, as with amniocentesis in New York, indicates "a complex choreography of domination, manipulation, negotiation, and, sometimes, resistance in the gender tales women tell about their decisions" (100). This tension between what people say for public consumption and the hints they give of ulterior motives and hidden rationales necessarily undergirds much of the analysis to follow.

Empathic responses to women's suffering and the couvade-like compulsion to share a spouse's pain are clearly motivations involved in the decisions of some men to get sterilized. At the same time, the influence and authority of friends who had already had the operation was often de-

VASECTOMIA SIN BISTURI
UNA NUEVA OPCION

PARA EL HOMBRE RESPONSABLE
este método es un procedimiento
rápido y sencillo, sin ningún
daño a la pareja ni a la relación
sexual .

ES GRATUITO

PARA MAYORES INFORMES ACUDA A SU MEDICO, O TRABAJADORA
SOCIAL DEL CENTRO DE SALUD MAS CERCANO.

Informational flyer about vasectomies, 2002.

scribed by the men I interviewed in Oaxaca as the deciding factor for
many of them. They checked with their friends about the pain, the turnaround time until they could return to marital liaisons, and the residual
effects of the procedure on their sexual desire and performance. There
were a few men who expressed a complete lack of concern as to potential
"side effects" from the surgery, like impotency or at least a diminished
sexual *apetito,* but they were in a distinct minority. General knowledge
about vasectomy was rarely readily accessible, and several men explained that only because they had been so determined were they able to
ultimately obtain correct information about vasectomy and secure an appointment for the surgery. All in all, if there is one thing that characterized most of the men I interviewed as to why they had opted for vasectomy, it would be their expression of sympathy for their women's
suffering in the past and their desire to have their women avoid such suffering in the future, either through another unwanted and potentially
harmful pregnancy or through a tubal ligation.[12]

Yet these were not the only reasons men chose to sterilize themselves.

AFFAIRS AND DOUBLE STERILIZATIONS

Despite such concerns on the part of most men I came to know through the vasectomy clinics in Oaxaca, and the real empathy and generosity demonstrated by men and women upon arriving at such a difficult decision as sterilization, the picture presented thus far is not complete. Indeed, there is another set of reasons men offer for getting vasectomies that also reveals much about underlying patterns of gender relations and inequalities in a variety of ways.

Some men explained their decision with the colloquialism "Cana al aire," literally meaning "[There is sugar] cane in the air," and figuratively meaning "An unusual gray hair pulled out and tossed into the air." "Cana al aire," thus, refers to an affair, something at once out of the ordinary and ultimately no more than a trifle. Having a vasectomy, according to some men, facilitates such casual *aventuras* (affairs).

Like many other men interviewed about vasectomies, Juan Miguel also talked to me about the role his wife had played in convincing him to get sterilized. Unlike most other men who opted for vasectomies, however, Juan Miguel's comments about his wife were far from flattering. In particular, he complained that she was careless about keeping track of her period and therefore that it was never possible to rely on other methods of birth control like the pill and injections. Given the additional fact that the family was poor, he felt he had to take matters into his own hands, to insure there would be no more children born to the couple. His decision had been unilateral.

Eliseo, thirty-nine years old and the father of three children, related a different set of experiences that ultimately led him to get a vasectomy. His wife had tried to take the pill and to use an IUD, but neither method was effective for her. They had tried a modified rhythm method, timing as best they could for sexual intercourse to occur five days before his wife started her period and five days following the end of her menses. Eliseo said that this rhythm method had caused more problems than it had resolved. He said he had gone to see a psychologist, who informed him that such infrequent sexual relations with his wife was causing in him a kind of "histeria." He informed the doctors and me during his surgery that "disrítmia" was the technical name for a situation in which one partner wants sexual relations far more than the other. Eliseo had tried daily masturbation, he also told us, but he found it far from adequate.

The cases of both Juan Miguel and Eliseo, then, touch on the central issue of men as "uncontrollable" and primordially driven to seek sex often and wherever possible. In his study of male sexuality in Chile, José Olavarría (2002) describes a court case in the northern part of that country in which a man was found guilty of rape and sentenced to castration.[13] The reason for this punishment was intimately related to a similar notion about male sexuality as being out of control, or as the judge in this case explained it, the rationale of the verdict was "to kill his male instinct." Thus, in this case, the male sexual drive was directly associated with something peculiar housed in men's testicles. In another case, this one closer to Oaxaca, Roberto Castro discusses how in Ocuituco, Mexico, "male desire is conceived in terms of natural forces" (2000:344), and he points out that "the equation between masculine identity and sexual desire is uncontrollable" (374).

It is in this context that an apparent anomaly that emerged in the course of my fieldwork can be explained. In my fieldwork I encountered cases of men who had received vasectomies despite the fact that their wives had earlier had tubal ligations. Here, I discuss the case of one such man.

I met Alejandro's wife and son outside the room where the vasectomies took place at Centro de Salud #1 in downtown Oaxaca City. Alejandro was outside pacing the sidewalk, while Mercedes and their child held Alejandro's place as second in line for the four vasectomies scheduled that morning. Alejandro reentered the building just before 8:30 A.M., the time he had been told to return. He was whisked quickly into the changing anteroom, then onto a padded table used for the operation. Assuming my by now standard position up at the patient's head, I began talking with Alejandro as the doctors prepped him down below.

The nurse interrupted me by asking Alejandro to provide answers for a standard epidemiological survey:

"Age?"

"Forty."

"Marital status?"

"Married."

"Children?"

"Two."

"Reason for having a vasectomy?"

"I don't want any more children."

"Previous birth control?"

Alejandro paused, finally answering, "None."

A few days later, I talked with Alejandro and Mercedes in their living room. He was still a bit sore from the operation, but he was back at work and brushing off the aftereffects of the procedure. I asked why he had decided to get a vasectomy. Mercedes responded instead.

"We'd been talking about it for eight years. Ever since our son was born."

Alejandro said he had delayed so long mainly because he was worried about "mistreating" his body with the vasectomy. But, he insisted, when he had finally determined he would go ahead with the procedure, "It was my idea. I decided to do it. I did it to satisfy her, not because I am going to 'dejar hijos regados' [sprinkle children around]. Because she's already had her tubes tied, so . . . well . . ."

"Oh, yeah?" I exclaimed in surprise when I realized that this meant that they both had been sterilized. "Then why . . . ?"

"To please me," Mercedes agreed with tenderness.

"Why was this important to you?" I pressed her.

"Better to avoid surprises" (*Más vale prevenir sorpresas*).

"So I don't go around sprinkling children everywhere, that's what she says," Alejandro added somewhat defiantly.

"Mexican men are like that, just like that," Mercedes concluded, as if little else was necessary to explain the couple's double sterilization.

When I encountered her a couple of months later at Clinic #1, where she had come for a consultation of her own, Mercedes again repeated the phrase "Más vale prevenir sorpresas," though this time she added that she did not think Alejandro was actually running around on her at the time. Even if he were, she rationalized, the fact that he did get a vasectomy was in a way a sign of love and a way to protect their marriage from "outside" pregnancies and the ensuing financial and emotional obligations.

A flip-side motivation for getting a vasectomy, expressed by two different men, was that this was a way to "controlar a su esposa" (control your wife). After a man was sterilized his wife would be even more reluctant to have an affair with another man, because they would both know that if she ever again became pregnant, it could not be as a result of sex with her husband.

In another case of a man getting a vasectomy despite the fact that his wife had already had a tubal ligation, he just shrugged when asked to explain the double-sterilization method of birth control. The female doctor operating on the man suggested it might just be a precaution, because there is always the risk of *fallas* (mistakes), even with drastic surgery like tubal ligation. The male doctor speculated aloud that it might be more related to the man's occupation as a bus driver, and he nudged the man as he noted how many girlfriends of drivers are said to be found waiting at the end of many bus lines.

Even well-intentioned doctors and others who were in the forefront of promoting vasectomy as a simple, effective, and egalitarian form of birth control, and whose message was that vasectomy should become more common than tubal ligation, made reference to "culture" as what is holding people in Mexico back in general, including in promoting egalitarian forms of reproductive health. One doctor expressed dismay that Mexican women are simply more used to suffering physically, and that Mexican men are afraid of "mutilating themselves" and therefore do not want doctors to "cut a thing" on their bodies.

And not surprisingly, perhaps, even men who described the decision-making process prior to their sterilizations as being equitable and aimed at sharing the contraceptive burden acknowledged with a wink the sexual urges that supposedly come preloaded in male bodies. Marcos, the taxi driver from Mexico City who had recently relocated to Oaxaca, insisted that he and his wife talked, and as long as his wife satisfied him sexually, there was no need for him to seek release elsewhere: "In a relationship, when one person leaves home 'well fed,' there's no point in looking for food anywhere else. No, I've got food at home. Why should I go looking for more?"

NO-SCALPEL VASECTOMIES
AND OTHER HALF-TRUTHS

In Mexico, since the mid-1990s, the "no-scalpel" method of vasectomy had been central to efforts to promote male sterilization. Introduced first in China in the 1970s, the no-scalpel procedure replaced the scalpel with the scissors-like instrument. Instead of the skin being cut with a scalpel, it is in effect torn by the scissors, whereupon a special clamp is inserted in the hole to pull out the vas deferens. When scalpels were used in the past, stitches were required; now, a small bandage is placed over the hole at the end of the procedure.

Medical practitioners insisted that the no-scalpel vasectomy represented the difference between few men and no men entering their programs. The development of the no-scalpel procedure had more to do with seeking ways to attract more men to the operation, by removing their dread of incision, than it did with any technical advantages of the scissors-like instrument over the scalpel. Sergio Navarrete (personal communication) offers the analysis that this may stem from a basic symbolic distinction that men make, so that the more metaphorically feminine scissors—more delicate than scalpels, some say—used in no-scalpel vasectomies threaten men less than the hypermasculine surgical knife. No-scalpel vasectomies were described by some health practitioners explicitly as a means by which to motivate men to get the operation. Despite the fact that many women and men referred to vasectomy as "la operación" (for men), I was frequently informed by medical personnel that some men must be reassured that a vasectomy is not really a surgical operation, which they believe must involve a scalpel and stitches.

Another example of a seemingly innocuous symbolic intervention on the part of health personnel was evident when a particular doctor began many vasectomies by asking the patients in a joshing tone, "Have you talked to your wife about this?" and when the men responded that they had, the good doctor followed up with the kicker: "And have you talked to your girlfriend, too?" Needless to say, I never heard of a woman who had chosen tubal ligation being asked a corresponding question about her husband and boyfriend.

Nor do the instruction manuals used by the health services personnel in Oaxaca talk about whether women will experience sexual pleasure after their operations. In the 1998 IMSS manual on vasectomies, however, personnel were instructed to reassure men that "the vasectomy will not take away his ability to enjoy or his sexual potency." In response to the anticipated question "Is a man less a man when he has a vasectomy?" practitioners are advised to answer: "*No.* The man continues to be the same man as before; his sexual activity and his relation with his partner do not change" (Instituto Mexicano del Seguro Social 1998:27–28). No doubt responding in good measure to genuine concerns on the part of men, these passages nevertheless reveal how concerned medical personnel were to speak to these common worries, in the process reinforcing the fears of many men. "Vasectomies . . . have nothing to do with sexual desire or masculinity," the manual insists. Needless to say, comparable concerns about femininity being dependent on intact fallopian tubes did not appear in similar teaching guides for female sterilizations.

According to many of the men I met and interviewed in the vasectomy clinics, lack of knowledge is definitely one reason more men did not seek vasectomies. Some men and women had learned about vasectomy from public service announcements on television, radio, or in newspapers. Some learned from brochures available at family planning clinics, others from nurses and doctors who worked in these clinics. Word of mouth, especially from one man to another, was often the most convincing method of publicizing the procedure. In addition, throughout Mexico, on the outside walls of health clinics in many cities, it is common to see signs painted to advertise the availability of vasectomies inside, thus promoting male participation in permanent contraception.

Yet in most clinical situations in Oaxaca, and in state-run family planning promotion, vasectomy is presented as a matter of individual choice and not in the context of the overall relations between men and women in which men rarely assume primary responsibility for contraception. Official brochures, for example, do not compare vasectomy with tubal ligation for women. The approach with vasectomy is that it is available should a man personally wish to avail himself.

Among those men who reported they had some knowledge about vasectomy on the epidemiological surveys, few men outside the vasectomy clinics had a clue as to what was actually involved in the operation. Anthropologist friends asked me what parts of the penis and/or testicles were cut in the procedure. (The answer is: none.) Men commonly told me that before their own vasectomies they had thought that the procedure was "like with animals," that it involved castration and/or the cutting off of part of the penis. Some men who had grown up in the countryside said, with varying degrees of assurance, that they knew what was involved.

Several men gave me mini-lessons in sterilizing bulls. Two men wrap a rope around the animal's girth, then pull on it hard to knock his air out, forcing him to fall and temporarily debilitating him. They then tie the ends of the rope to two trees and begin to massage the area, approximately 10 centimeters, between the body and the testicles of the bull. This will make the scrotum relax. Then they tie a string around the bull's scrotum. When the string is tightened, the vas deferens are effectively severed.

With pigs and goats, the testicles are laid on a hard surface (like a rock) and the vas are smashed with a hammer. Or, alternatively, a friend from the Ethnobotanical Garden informed me, you can twist the testicles of a goat and then smash them with a rock. You should definitely not cut off the testicles of sheep and goats, he believed, because these particular animals infect easily. Pigs, on the other hand, can be castrated without running the same risk of infection, though this involves cutting through three layers of skin in order to extract the *bolitas*.

It is a wonder more men do not jump at the chance to get sterilized themselves.

Knowledge of how farm animals are sterilized, of course, does not necessarily imply an inability to make a distinction between other methods of sterilization short of castration and the like. Some men I interviewed simply used the term *vasectomy* as a generic catch-all for any form of sterilization. Widespread beliefs regarding the methods and consequences of sterilization on other male animals nonetheless had an unsettling impact on many of the men with whom I discussed vasectomy in Oaxaca. Although castration and cutting of the penis in some way were the dominant images men who had heard of vasectomy shared, other misconceptions were frequently raised. Among these was the impression that castrated dogs no longer barked and that they gained weight. (Neither is correct.)

Years earlier, while talking with my dear friend Marcelo in the neighborhood of Santo Domingo in Mexico City, we happened to have a conversation about vasectomy. He had insisted, "You know, Mateo, if you do that, you are 'closing down the factory' forever." I asked Marcelo what was wrong with that, as long as you did not want more children. "Guys get sick and die a lot," he recounted, passing on what other friends had told him. I mentioned my own vasectomy and its negligible effects, other than sterility. After a stupid quip that this just proved that gringos were all a bunch of faggots, Marcelo began asking questions in earnest about whether my voice had risen and my hips had grown after the operation. As I had known him before and after my vasectomy, I was able to reassure him that no such transformation had occurred.

Other men in Oaxaca expressed fears that "it will take ten years off your life," "you will lose your *hombría*" (manliness), "you will lose your physical strength," and, most of all, referring to sexual relations, "they're not the same afterward."

The main fear men expressed about vasectomy was that they would never again have sexual relations with a woman. Their apprehension was twofold: many men were concerned that they would be physically unable to sexually perform after the vasectomy. As Enrique put it, "I think that more than anything it scares you, no? To think that . . . to think that afterwards it's not going to work." Some men also worried that they would not *want* to have sexual relations with women again. During my observation of numerous vasectomies, the half-joking banter devolved to a related sexual anxiety, the worry that a man might "be turned" as a result of the procedure—that is, that he might come out of it wanting to have sex only with other men.

Writing about the impact of vasectomies on some men in Colombia, Mara Viveros found men and women who recounted that vasectomy had unleashed the men sexually. One woman complained that his vasectomy had left her husband "good, too good, always demanding 'cocoa'" (2002:343).

Men's sexualized relationship with women in Oaxaca was often the thorniest aspect to analyze. "Will it work?" was not for most men simply a question of "Will I still be able to have an erection and ejaculate?" The relationship of vasectomy to manhood and *hombría*, and men's concerns about the outcome of the operation with respect to their subsequent sex lives, was described by some men as a consuming anxiety about being able to still satisfy a woman sexually in the future. For similar reasons, a man commented that his favorite word was "¡Así!" (Like that!), because when a woman in the throes of passion said this simple word to him, he felt more like a man than at any other time.

The relationship between vasectomy and manliness is thus intimately connected to that between vasectomy and sexual pleasure. And to the extent that men's sexual pleasure is associated with women's sexual desires and fulfillment, then one may well ask, again, about male sexual predilections and urges. To return to an earlier point, the meanings and consequences of men being "sexually uncontrollable" will look a good deal different if the men are understood to be "culturally uncontrolled" or as the housing for hormones out of control.[14]

It might be argued that medicalized notions of male sexuality reverse one old feminist anthropology paradigm, so that, now, men and their sexualities are far closer to nature than women and theirs. This naturalization of male sexuality occurs not only popularly but also among health practitioners; when commonsense notions and approaches to men's sexuality gain the imprimatur of scientific explanation, rationale, and rationalization as delivered by duly licensed health personnel, they become medicalized. From popular sayings and attitudes toward adolescent male masturbation to resignation to (and encouragement of) men's extramarital liaisons, the belief that men "can't help themselves" was pervasive in Oaxaca across class and ethnic lines. What constituted natural and normal male sexuality in Oaxaca was informed by both international programs regarding family planning, and local conventions and convictions that helped shape the policies that doctors and other health workers considered appropriate for the region. The language of family planning manuals was replete with references to masculinity and male sexual drives.

SHARING RESPONSIBILITY FOR CONTRACEPTION

Throughout the world today, debates are unfolding in families and public institutions regarding men's shared responsibility for sexual behavior and improving women's and men's reproductive health. Since international conferences in the mid-1990s on gender and development in Cairo and Beijing, the official policy of government agencies and NGOs around the world has been to encourage men's involvement in birth control and safe sex as part of the effort to promote the right of women and men to regulate their fertility and to have sexual relations free from fear of unwanted pregnancy or disease. Yet little headway has been made in achieving real gender equity and men's participation in this realm (see Chant and Gutmann 2000). Until we better understand the actual sexual and reproductive lives of men and women, such projects will continue to flounder.

In the more private confines of families and households, for example, we know too little about how women and men discuss, debate, and decide on sexual behavior and make reproductive decisions, and about how the changing affective relations between men and women in turn alter cultural values concerning reproductive health and sexuality. In order to better understand the couple's decision-making process regarding birth control, it is important to include men in studies of the contraceptive aspects of reproductive health. There are a host of "outside" factors—from the media to the church to public health institutions and campaigns—that influence the wrangling within couples over such decisions. Determining the impact on men and women of cultural preconceptions in the medical community—for instance, with respect to male sexuality—is crucial to chart how people are pressured to adapt to one kind of sexual behavior or another.

The relationship between globalizing and localizing factors—sexual commodification, ethnic coding, and migratory circuits of information, disease, and novel practices—in governing negotiations over men's reproductive health and sexuality is only now emerging as a significant field of study,[15] and studies of vasectomy and male contraception are still largely terra incognita. Recent scholarship on gender in Mexico and Latin America has demonstrated the relationship of engendered power identities and inequalities to culture change.[16] In line with these studies, what is most salient in the present investigation is an emphasis on viewing inequality as the *basis* of change. Some examples: the relationship that women have to men's sexuality and negotiations regarding birth control;

how to understand men's role in reproduction and why they are only just beginning to be included in studies and public health efforts concerning reproductive health; and the realities of birth control, that is to say, what roles biology, culture, and politics have in determining which forms of birth control exist, are utilized, and are developed.

Regarding the matter of choice and whether health practitioners are practicing bad faith medicine, cultural assumptions about men's reproductive health and sexuality often unintentionally sway men against opting for vasectomy. Given that Mexico in the twenty-first century is completely dependent on the products of foreign pharmaceutical companies, virtually the only other options available to men who wish to play an active role in birth control are condoms, withdrawal, or the rhythm method. There are branches of these companies in Mexico, but usually these are simply the local sales force. Occasionally, there is a clinical trial carried out in Mexico, but in those cases the trials are for products already developed elsewhere.

Marcos the taxi driver asked rhetorically in one of our discussions: "Why aren't there methods for men? And, really, a lot of folks, me included, think that the pharmaceuticals and companies like Bayer or whatever, when they see that a product is doing well for them, well, why should they worry about anything else? They must say, 'Why should I worry about you [men] if it's going really well for me with the [contraceptives for] women?'"

In 2005 there were few doctors in Oaxaca who knew how to perform vasectomies. There was widespread ignorance as to what the procedure entailed. In the absence of temporary forms of male contraceptives other than the condom, women continued to take responsibility for birth control. In the absence of widespread information, including public campaigns regarding vasectomy, it was unlikely that the number of men in Oaxaca who choose sterilization would grow. How else could one open the debate on the relationship between vasectomy, procreation, and machismo?[17]

Even if small in scale, several campaigns in Oaxaca have been aimed at simply involving men in the sphere of reproduction, and have sought results primarily in the form of participation of one kind or another in family planning programs. Yet these approaches have repeatedly failed in any but short-term bursts because they have not even attempted to re-solve the underlying causes of male reticence to use birth control. General inequalities, including in the sphere of reproductive health and sexuality, have remained concealed and therefore unchallenged. The history of va-sectomy in Oaxaca exhibits a certain aspect of the self-fulfilling prophesy: despite a lack of any hard evidence regarding men's understanding and attitudes about vasectomy, health planners nevertheless assume that men cannot be involved in any meaningful way in birth control, other than in acquiescence to the methods their wives may employ. To be sure, were men to be targeted for sterilization in the draconian ways they have been in other places, like India in the mid-1970s (see Bandarage 1997; Mistry 1997; Tarlo 2003), one might indeed expect fierce opposition on the part of men (and women) to male sterilization. But simply based on the low numbers of men in Oaxaca who have chosen to get a vasectomy, no one should presume to draw meaningful conclusions about what men there will and will not do with respect to contraception or sexual relations with women in general.

The totemization of male sexuality—from male adolescent masturba-tion to men's extramarital affairs to male participation in contraception—has similarly been a taken-for-granted attribute of the species. It is nonetheless too easy, and ultimately unproductive, to relegate sex to the biomedical sciences alone (see Amuchástegui 2001; Parker, Barbosa, and Aggleton 2000). Because there are today in Oaxaca no widely available forms of male contraception based on manipulating male hormones, we might casually assume that no method can be found, because of factors inherent in some special culture of men there, which, in turn, is believed to be grounded in male physiology. We could casually assume this. But if we did, we would miss the larger picture.

SEVEN Traditional Sexual Healing of Men

You wicked women, have done with your falsehoods!
You want your husbands, that's plain enough.
But don't you think they want you just as badly?

Aristophanes. *Lysistrata* (411 B.C. [1994:33])

MEN'S (TRADITIONAL) NATURAL DESIRES?

The tradition of anthropological fieldwork has given "cultural authority to [indigenous] people who in their own regions had been disdained or even silenced for their supposed backwardness" (Lomnitz 2001:135), including in matters of medical procedure, opinion, and therapy. More than a little romance for the "authentic" has been evident in anthropological and travel writings about indigenous healers and their magic. Yet it would be foolish to dismiss anthropological studies of indigenous medicine as merely the product of romantic illusions.

In my conversations with indigenous midwives and doctors in Oaxaca, I never felt more foolish than when I went looking for dichotomous analysis and healing of women and men, as I was repeatedly reminded by the women and men I spoke with that my starting point was itself problematic, since it was based on unfounded preconceptions about male and female "natural desires." Even approaching the subject of reproductive health and sexuality as one that divides neatly into "women's health" or "men's health" seemed at times to reflect more my own biomedicalized, feminist outlook than that of my ostensible teachers in these matters.[1]

"Is there a difference between men and women in terms of sexual relations, for instance, appetite in general?" I asked Mariana, Amparo, and Abigail, all three Mixtec midwives and healers.

"I would say it depends on the individual a bit," answered the sixty-eight-year-old Amparo.

"Is there a nature to men and is there another for women?"

"That depends as much on the woman as the man," Abigail, the youngest of the three, chimed in.

"It depends on what we already have in our blood," added Mariana. "There are a lot of people who are rebellious, too, because they drink a lot."

"And do men and women change their sexual relations over the years, with youth doing one thing and adults of fifty another?" I wanted to know.

"Depends on the person. There are women who are pretty old and—it hurts to say so, no?—and they can still . . . But we [women] are not all the same," concluded Abigail.

Amparo agreed, "We [women] are not all the same."

I persisted. "There's not a different nature, a fixed nature . . . ?"

"No. Because that depends on each person."

"A lot of people say that men are one way and women another," I persevered, "and that the man's body is one way and the woman's another."

"That depends on the person. We don't all think alike," Mariana patiently repeated what her colleagues had been telling me.

I asked Obdulia, Dalia, and Leonor, three Mazatec midwives in Soyaltepec, on the border with Veracruz, if they thought men's sexual desires were, in general, distinct from those of women. Did it even make sense to talk like that, I wanted to know.

"Well, I don't know," replied Leonor thoughtfully. "There are a lot of kinds of desire, so it depends."

"It depends on the temperament of each one," Dalia insisted.

"That's right! What they want," concluded Obdulia.

"We can't say that in general men are one way and women another?" I again asked.

"No," they all chimed in.

Rosario Gaspar, from the Zapotec mountains north of Oaxaca City, told me: "In my community we don't talk about sex very much. Because I get out of there a lot, I've learned many things. When people say, 'That's the way men are.' Well, I think instead that there are real differences from one man to the next. You know why? Because in any given community there may never have been any discussion about sex. They don't know what a caress is. There, they grab women as they can. And women don't know what an orgasm is."

"But it can happen without knowing . . . without naming it . . . ," I suggest.

"Of course! Of course! It can happen without knowing it. Maybe when she feels good, maybe she's going to look for the one she felt that good with, no? If it's not with her husband, if she doesn't feel anything with him, she might feel it with someone else."

Doña Meche had a particularly clear way of discussing the extent to which one could reasonably generalize about women and men. She told me she had on occasion been invited to training sessions for midwives at the Centro de Salud in Oaxaca, where, coincidentally, I had spent many hours interviewing men before, after, and during their vasectomies. "You know what they asked me at the Centro de Salud in Oaxaca?" Doña Meche said provocatively to me. "When I was in training sessions with them, they asked me, 'How long does it take to give birth?' I told them, 'It depends! Not everyone comes the same. Babies come at different times.' Those doctors, they don't know. They have to ask me, 'Please come help, Doña Meche,' and I go. 'Look, you help this patient because I don't know how,' is what the doctors sometimes tell me."

At the same time as Doña Meche was ridiculing the ignorance of the *médicos de bata blanca*, the doctors who wore the presumptuous white-coat uniform, she asked a niece to retrieve several notebooks from a back room. She then took pains to go over several pages in the notebooks with me that demonstrated the care with which she had documented the log of all the births she had attended and the certificates she had received from government workshops to train traditional midwives.

What stood out more than anything else from my interviews with traditional indigenous healers and midwives was that, despite all my attempts to dichotomize male and female sexual appetites, sexual problems, and sexualities in general, I was confronted with an overwhelming sense that such binary thinking along gender/sexuality lines represented far more what I was bringing to the conversations than what the midwives believed and practiced. From the first counseling they provide to young couples, as Doña Hermila related—"I tell them, 'If you want to have children, from now on both of you have to get rid of all your parasites. . . .' "—through the *cuarentena* recovery period for the new mother and child, I was impressed by the stated emphasis of the *médicos tradicionales,* or *empíricos,* I interviewed from several regions of the state: in reproductive health matters, as with all other health concerns, one first treats people as human beings, and, second, one distinguishes them as men and women or whatever else.[2]

MEDICINA TRADICIONAL

In 2001 the state of Oaxaca issued a decree in which it was announced that henceforth *medicina tradicional* would be recognized as just as legitimate as modern forms of biomedicine. As part of the new edict, the practitioners of traditional medicine, known variously as *médicos tradicionales* and *médicos empíricos,* were to be granted the same professional respect as *médicos de bata blanca* (the allopathic physicians). Each of these distinct medical systems and medical doctors was held to be equally legitimate and on a legal par with respect to healing the sick and afflicted of Oaxaca.[3]

The historic importance of this decree should not be underestimated. Indigenous rights and privileges that so clearly represent an affront to "late-modern ways" are seldom written into law. Nonetheless, the practical consequences of the new decree have been, not surprisingly, at odds with the purported intent of the law, and they reflect, as much as anything else, the continuing ability of legislators in Oaxaca, as opposed to other states, like Chiapas, to appease and co-opt demands originating in indigenous communities (see Stephen 2002).

After having spoken, over the course of a few years, with dozens of men and women I met in state-run clinics about vasectomies and other forms of "modern" contraception, in the summer of 2004 I decided to learn about how traditional indigenous healers might differ in their diagnosis and treatment of men's reproductive health problems like impotence and infertility, as well as how they approached other issues, like infidelity and birth control. As a result, in the course of five weeks, I drove over three thousand miles, crisscrossing the state to interview more than twenty Huave, Mixtec, Zapotec (from the Isthmus, Sierra, and Valley), and Mazatec traditional healers and midwives.

It required little stimulation to elicit commentary from traditional doctors about modern doctors. Ridiculing the pomposity of anyone who would call himself "Doctor So-and-So," one midwife told me, "As we all say, 'That one's a doctor. He knows, because he has a tie, he is elegant [*entacuchado*], and he lets you wait on him, but he doesn't always know what's best.'" Doña Hermila, a Zapotec healer and midwife herself, was more shrewd in her comments when she explained:

> In the first place, the white-coat doctors, as we call them, went to school, learned, and they think they know the whole human body. And then they insist to us that we are ignorant. But we are not ignorant. Maybe I don't know bones, but I know how to *acomodarlas* [reposition a fetus inside a woman], because I am a midwife, a *curandera*, a *yerbera* (I use herbs to cure). I do consultations. And I know why you have a headache, why you have something else. Maybe we don't have a title, but we have our hands. Because we didn't study, we have a sixth sense we work with, an intuition, a rain of . . . a way of healing.

Others expressed disdain for the new decree that proclaimed the legal parity between the traditional and modern medical systems, and resentment that anyone would think the traditional healers could be so easily fooled by the deception. Said Abigail, a Mixtec healer: "It's not anything like they say it is. And that's for sure. The words are pretty, on the television, on the radio, all over. That *médicos tradicionales* be treated as equals. Nevertheless, the reality is different. Why? Because the traditional doctors are still the same. They have no support. There are no rewards for them, as promised by law. Or they are not respected as they are supposed to be according to the law." The law, in other words, was a lot of fine phrasing that did not correspond in day-to-day life to any real, meaningful changes for traditional medical practitioners or in the recognition of the value and efficacy of their medicine.

Nonetheless, despite a reluctance on the part of nearly all the traditional midwives and healers I spoke with to impute great importance to the practical import of the decree, there was no doubt that it represented a larger process of rearticulation of ethnicity in Oaxaca. In an effort to conserve, defend, and extend the health care beliefs and practices associated with "our cultures" and "our communities" (these were the terms used popularly by the members of these groups to refer to what anthropologists often call indigenous ethnicities), traditional midwives and healers in Oaxaca repeatedly illustrated for me the complicated nature of contemporary "contact zones" in the state. By using the term "contact zones," Claudio Lomnitz (2001:132), for example, sought to account for the popular "traditional/modern" distinction that is at play in regions like Oaxaca. Extrapolating from this notion, we can also see how, indeed, modern medicine in Oaxaca is in part defined, albeit implicitly, by the comparison with *medicina tradicional* itself.[4] Significantly, Lomnitz's (2001:130) discussion of "contact zones" is in turn related to a broader international field of ideas and models of civilization, science, and development.

Parallel or dueling traditional and modern medical contact zones— and the 2001 decree declaring all kinds of doctors to be joined in equal status in the state of Oaxaca—existed within the larger context of the system of *usos y costumbres* that in 2005 was operational in 418 of the 570 *municipios* in the state (see Estado de Oaxaca 2005). *Usos y costumbres* refers to a collective form of political organization at the local level, through which local leaders are selected through community assemblies rather than through a system of electoral selection. In this and other ways, such as the *cargo* system, in which men and women periodically assume communal duties in their villages, indigenous populations maintain and extend political processes in parallel to the system of governance found within the electoral and party regimes that are prevalent in most of Mexico. When the decree was signed, in 2001, *usos y costumbres* continued to represent a significant form of formal, political power in Oaxaca.

Despite public recognition of their traditional healing practices, many of the midwives and healers were at first hesitant to talk with me about their knowledge and experiences. Without the assistance of my colleague Ignacio (Nacho) Bernal, I would have found it far more difficult to conduct research among traditional doctors. Dr. Ignacio Bernal Torres, a medical doctor and medical anthropologist, was director of the Traditional Health and Medicine Department of what used to be called the Instituto Nacional Indigenista (INI) and was later renamed the Comisión Nacional para el Desarrollo de los Pueblos Indígenas (CDI).[5] Over the course of more than twenty years, Nacho had developed extensive relationships among indigenous healers in his formal capacity as liaison between the government and the traditional healers. Far more importantly, he had earned respect and gratitude for consistently defending and championing the work of the indigenous doctors.

One of the traditional midwives and healers I was able to interview several times between 2001 and 2004 was Doña Hermila, who during part of this period was the president of the State Council of Traditional Indigenous Doctors of Oaxaca.[6] From the beginning of our acquaintance, Doña Hermila showed both great courtesy and sincerity in describing her organizational and personal skills within the field of traditional medicine, as well as a wariness and reserve in her interactions with me. Once, after I proposed meeting with her, she balked at setting up a specific time for the interview. Nacho intervened, explaining to her: "Doña Hermila, he's not like the guy in Chiapas. Mateo is not interested in *plantas* or *recetas* [prescriptions]." Had Nacho not vouched for me, my intentions, and the value of my research, Doña Hermila might well have refused to see me again, much less to share the stories her life with a gringo anthropologist relatively unknown to her.

This was true despite the fact that I made clear to her that I was neither an ethnobotanist—and therefore understood little or nothing about the pharmacology of plants—nor even interested in learning the names of the plants used for various purposes. Anticipating this kind of objection on another occasion, I explained to a group of Mazatec healers that I was not interested in learning specifics about the plants and was confronted by a different, but no less indignant, response: "Plants are good and it is good to know about them!" I eventually learned to state that although I was not interested in seeing the healers' notebooks and in learning the particulars of their prescriptions for how to make the remedies, I did have great interest in a general way in learning how plants and teas could cure people of a variety of ailments.

As to the "guy in Chiapas," I had my suspicions as to whom Nacho was referring to, and they were confirmed later that day. As it turned out, a particular ethnobotanist had become notorious among many indigenous healers throughout the southern region of Mexico because he allegedly had been trying to steal their knowledge for the benefit of pharmaceutical companies in the United States. All this, I was told, by Nacho and others, had earned him the Tzotzil-language nickname of "El Diablo" (the Devil). Later in the summer, another healer informed me that this ethnobotanist had also been forced to leave Ecuador twenty years earlier under similar circumstances.

On numerous occasions, "the guy in Chiapas" became a reason to initially not talk with me about traditional healing with respect to men's reproductive health and sexuality, or anything else. I have no way of determining the extent to which any of these accusations are accurate.[7] For my purposes, it is relevant, however, that the perceived exploitation of indigenous knowledge and plants on the part of the ethnobotanist and his collaborators in Chiapas, including Mexicans, became a significant obstacle in my own attempts in Oaxaca to discuss traditional healing. In addition, some of these traditional doctors were aware that the modern birth control pill was originally developed in Mexico by using the *barbasco* plant (spread on the surfaces of lakes by peasants to kill fish in such a way that they would still be edible), yet Mexico and Mexicans have been in no way the special beneficiaries of this discovery. The theft of indigenous learning and practices was felt to represent a long-term and insidious historical trend. More than a simple methodological issue of getting my foot in the door, the issue of "the guy in Chiapas" spoke to underlying issues of modern forms of neocolonialism through the global pharmaceutical and health industries.[8]

In a sense, the interviews I conducted in the summer of 2004 were part of the grand tradition of "salvage anthropology." Despite certain apparent successes in recruiting a new generation of traditional doctors, much knowledge and experience is disappearing as the older generation of healers dies. Then, too, the effort to maintain the pretense of equality between indigenous and Western medicine is itself a fitting illustration of what Roger Bartra (1999:64) calls "multicultural and segregationist paternalism." The promotion of *usos y costumbres* today in places like Oaxaca, he writes, "is the mixture of two failures in one strange cocktail: Soviet efforts to organize national autonomy and the attempt in the United States to keep ethnic and racial groups apart." Acknowledging the rich history of traditional doctors' healing, curing, and caring for millions of indigenous peoples in Mexico does not preclude our concluding, with Bartra, that with the decree of 2001, as well as the self-congratulatory boasting that accompanies reports on the widespread exercise of *usos y costumbres,* state and federal authorities are often playing the old colonial trick of manipulating decision making within indigenous communities under the guise of respecting local, autonomous governments.[9]

TRADITIONAL DOCTORS

In July 2004, I spoke with Mariana, Amparo, and Abigail in the offices of the Centro de Desarrollo de Medicina Indígena Tradicional, Chocho-Mixteco,[10] in Nochixtlán, Oaxaca. People throughout the Mixtec region of Oaxaca came to these women for help in healing one or another ailment. The women themselves held to a schedule of when they could be found in the clinic, although they normally were to be found living in the surrounding villages. One woman was from San Miguel Huautla, three hours from Nochixtlán. Another was from Tilantongo, and the third from Santa María Apazco. They were among the thirty-two *médicos tradicionales* in the Mixtec region, which has a population of nearly half a million persons. The language of Mixteco, or rather one of the dozens of local variants of Mixteco, is the mother tongue of two of the women. The third woman, Amparo, had learned Mixteco from her husband, who knew no Spanish; he spoke *puro dialecto,* as she put it, and from the time of her marriage at age fifteen she had been obligated to learn his language.[11]

We sat around a table in the "dormitory," which consisted of two consulting rooms, a makeshift kitchen, and twelve bunk beds, some with mattresses, others with straw mats lying directly on the springs, and still others with no covers at all. The women described the services they provide, like *limpias* (cleansings), *sobadas* (medicinal massages), *hueseros* (bone setting), and *baños temazcal* (steam "baths"). The cleansings happen before a woman gives birth, for example, as she begins hard labor. If the woman is suffering a lot, Mariana told me, sometimes it is because she is suffering from "airs," and a *limpia* is required so she can cope with the pain. The women talked of the seven community pharmacies, *boticarios,* in the Mixtec region, all of which have stocks of herbs and creams, and none of which, they told me, carry any allopathic pharmaceuticals. When I left, at the end of our conversation, I made a donation to their clinic, and they gave me a basket with shampoo, a cream for skin blemishes (made with *esperma de ballena,* sperm oil, they had bought at the Oaxaca City main market), two creams for rheumatism, a syrup for coughs, and another cream made with roses, for tanning. Each jar or flask was affixed with a label that read "ORGANIZACION DE MEDICOS TRADICIONALES 'XEE TATNAA'" along with the name of the preparation.[12]

Outside the building where we talked was a small garden where the healers grew the plants that were used to make the creams, ointments, lotions, and syrups which were employed to cure various ailments. The garden was remarkable for its layout, because it was in the form of a human body, outlined with small stones. Plants used especially for the head were grown at the top of the figure, and those for intestinal afflictions in the midsection of the garden, so that the more than 140 plants were spread out in appropriate locations across and along the body.[13]

List of services offered by Mixtec midwives and healers, including medicinal massages and cleansings, 2004.

Also outside the building was a *baño temazcal*, or steam bath, that had room for two or perhaps three people. Throughout much of what is today southern Mexico, and into parts of Guatemala, the *baño temazcal* has been used for centuries as an integral part of healing, including for women and their newborns who are having difficulty suckling. I took photographs in this clinic and the others I visited and sent copies back to the women and men who were kind enough to talk with me.

The women described themselves as traditional doctors who were called to their profession when they discovered they had a gift ("un don") for healing. "I do this work because I have a gift for it, not because someone has taught me," Amparo told me. "I didn't learn from my parents or anyone else. My mother doesn't know anything about healing. I remember everything I have dreamed and that's how I have been trained."

For payment, chickens and sometimes a goat or a sheep are offered them by women and men always short on money. They identify them-

Baño temazcal, steam "bath" used for medicinal purposes throughout Mesoamerica, 2004.

selves as *parteras tradicionales* (traditional midwives) and *curanderas* (healers). Some of them began as midwives from necessity, either with the midwifing of their own childbirths or those of other women who needed help through labor when no one else was available. At fifteen, Mariana said, "I gave birth to my son all by myself. Without a midwife. Alone. Thanks to God, alone. I delivered my little one, turned around and cut the umbilical cord and everything."

I asked where her husband was during all this.

"Well, he was scared. He was scared."

I also heard about husbands from another midwife, Doña Meche, whom I met through my friend Daniel, who worked at the Ethnobotanical Garden. One day at the garden I mentioned that I had visited some traditional midwives and healers in the Mixtec region and that I wanted to interview more in other parts of the state. Several people asked me questions about what I had learned in Nochixtlán and began talking about bone-setters, *curanderos*, and *brujos* they knew.[14] My friends began shouting out comments, like "Oh, yeah, there's a guy like that in my pueblo, my cousin has been to see him." Poncho, the foreman at the garden, asked me if the healers had learned their knowledge through dreams. Then he asked me if I could interpret dreams. I replied that I could seldom remember dreams, much less explain them. Chaquetas, of masturbatory fame, talked about his father dreaming of Jesús Cristo one night and that the next day his father's father (Chaquetas's grandfather) had died.

At this point, Poncho began a soliloquy that directly addressed questions of devotion, culture, and prejudice against indigenous peoples in Oaxaca's countryside. He began by saying that we should respect all people's beliefs, as long as they believed in Jesus Christ. Even the evangelists. Of course, those people who openly worship the devil are beyond the pale and should not be tolerated. (Jews and Muslims were not mentioned, but Poncho said we should also be respectful of Buddhists.) He then asked the five of us who were listening to his discourse two questions: "Who has more culture, a person from the city who's well educated, or an illiterate person from a village?"

Everyone answered that clearly the second person had more culture, which for them meant a system of "traditional" beliefs and practices. And, it was clear, this was the answer Poncho had been seeking. My attempt at anthropological intervention—"Both have culture, just different kinds"—was rejected as sincere but misinformed.

Poncho then asked, "Who will more easily get to heaven, the theologist who writes all about religion and God or the illiterate believer in the village who is full of faith and lights his candles?" It was a no-brainer, of course, as the men were both expressing pride in what they interpreted as "traditional" ways and, I assume, they were gently ribbing me and my urban-educated brethren.

In the course of our conversation that day at the Ethnobotanical Garden, Daniel invited me to San Felipe Tejalapam, a village outside the city, about fifteen minutes off the highway to Mexico City, where he lived with his wife and three children. There he introduced me to Doña Meche, who was a Zapotec-speaking midwife in her late seventies and famous in the village: her niece told me, "She's the best, the best midwife in the village. Always in demand." Moments after we had sat down in the courtyard of the place where she had been born, seventy-six years earlier, and that she shared with a dozen other family members, Doña Meche did not even wait for me to explain my purpose. As soon as we sat down on the wooden chairs hastily dusted off in the sandy courtyard of her home, she began telling me, "You know that husbands are cruel. And mine beat me. He didn't like me going to houses far away to deliver babies. And he dragged me out of the house of the nurse one day and he beat me really badly. I was pregnant, and for three months I carried the dead baby boy! I was just skin and bones. I was vomiting blood, and there was liquid coming from below."

Stories of abusive men were common in my discussions with the women who were traditional midwives and healers. So were more tender accounts of the experiences they had had working with men on matters of birth control, infidelity, and impotence.

BIRTH CONTROL, INFIDELITY, IMPOTENCE, AND INFERTILITY

"There aren't [birth control] methods for men?" I asked Mariana, Amparo, and Abigail.

"No," answered Amparo.

"Well, we are still missing a lot. Probably there are, but . . ." added Mariana.

Abigail tried to explain. "There's always more interest in women because women procreate, she's the one who has it and the one who suffers. That's why we always say that men don't suffer compared to women, and why we are partial to women. But the fact is that we have also treated men, no? Not a lot, not a lot, because I am not going to tell you . . . but maybe 20 or 30 percent we've worked with men. The fact is that in indigenous places, as they are called, it's the woman who suffers, the woman who works, the woman who raises children."

When talking with Doña Hermila about birth control, I mentioned the rhythm method as espoused by the Catholic church. "That's the method we have, too," she responded, certainly not ceding to the church the intellectual property rights of this contraceptive technique.

I talked with Obdulia, Dalia, and Leonor in the town of San Miguel Soyaltepec, located in the Mazatec-speaking region of Oaxaca, not far from the northern border with the state of Veracruz. Each woman had years, and sometimes decades, of experience as a midwife and herbal healer. When I talked with them, in the summer of 2004, they were also engaged in a struggle with local authorities to keep control of a garden they had built to grow herbs and other plants for medicinal purposes, and I was shown the scrupulously kept accounts of expenses and income for the organization of indigenous healers. Among the operating costs listed were those under a column labeled "Mordidas" (bribes)! We talked of many subjects throughout our conversation, including the contraceptive techniques practiced in their area.

"If women don't want to have children," Obdulia related to me, "they eat lemon and drink bitter tea; if they don't want children, they take Mejoral [a local variant of acetaminophen]. My father used to give them a 'salsa' for the men, the ones who couldn't 'get it up.' If women don't want babies, there is another 'salsa' for them."

Dalia added: "When men 'fail,' when a man can't be intimate with his woman or with another [woman], then there's a special plant you give the man, just to the man, so he can get things working. Do you understand?" she asked me.

"Does it take long to kick in?" I asked her.

"No, he just has to drink the tea for four or five mornings. The guy figures out pretty quickly when he goes back to his . . ."

Leonor interjected, "But he can't drink white *atole* [a porridge-like drink], he can't drink beer."

"Because they're cold?" I wanted to know.

"He can't eat fish, he has to diet, get his insides to shrink."

I asked if a lot of men sought their counsel for what had come to be known in the United States as erectile dysfunction (ED), or if few men asked for help for this affliction, because they were too embarrassed to admit the problem and ask for help.

"There are a lot of men who'd like to . . . Okay, there are bad women who ensnare them, and that's where men start to 'fail.' But there are some men who even cry because they can no longer do anything. So they say, 'Why is this happening to me?' Another way to deal with this is with colored ribbons."

"If they are ensnared."

"Yes, when they are ensnared."

"Women are very jealous of their men. So they only want them for themselves. They don't want them having relations with other women. So they say that when they are making love, they measure the penis. Later, using this measure, they put knots, knots, knots [on a strip of ribbon]. That's what's called 'being ensnared.' So when a man wants to have relations with another woman, he just can't because he's already ensnared. So a woman doesn't have to worry, because she knows that it's not going to work with anyone else, and that he has to come with her."[15]

Despite the knotted-ribbon prescription described to me, Obdulia then added, "Of course the place where they do this a lot is over around Tehuantepec; it's the Tehuanas who use this. Around here we don't do it so much."

"Do the women use a particular color?" I asked.

"Yes! It has to be seven colors. Different colors."

"Like a rainbow. He won't know what color he's been ensnared with, so we use seven so the knots have all the colors and the man can be normal. A woman knows that with her it will work with her man, and with another woman it won't work, because now she has him the way she wants him."

Dalia then described to me another technique that was used by women to "secure" men and prevent them from straying. This method gave new meaning to the term *safety pin*. "There are a lot of women who are also clever, and they put a pin on other women to keep their men from straying."

I was confused, and Obdulia tried to clarify the procedure for me.

"Let's say he goes to a hotel, no? He wants to do it [with another woman], but he can't because this woman is 'pinned up.' His woman puts a little safety pin on the other woman's skirt and the poor guy who wants to take advantage of another woman can't, because the pin thwarts him. He can't do it."

"He's impotent. He can't," Leonor stated bluntly.

"It's like an amulet. And the other woman doesn't realize she has the pin on her clothing—sometimes we don't know what we have on our clothes, right?—although she can find it and take it off. Women are always more powerful, more cunning. Women have more power. As they say, 'Women beat the devil.' They say women are always more cunning than men."

Doña Meche counseled me on what to do in case of impotence, which she described as more a problem that "no semen comes out." She recommended a remedy she called Vino de Lidia. "It's fantastic, Vino de Lidia. You have to look for it in your country. With this, with the herb they use in it, the man applies it and . . . before you know it, you've got a family!"

In Mexico City, years earlier, I had learned of a young woman who was rumored to have given her boyfriend a special tea brewed with a used sanitary napkin. She was guided by the understanding that a man can be made to fall in love and remain with a woman if he has swallowed her menstrual blood (see Gutmann 2006 [1996]:122). Aguirre Beltrán (1963:174) likewise discusses the use of "amorous material" by some indigenous groups in pre-Columbian Mesoamerica. For example, if you mix your fingernail clippings with chocolate, you can secure another's love by getting them to drink the concoction. Even better is to prepare the chocolate with one's pubic hair.

In *las comunidades*, some of the most common reproductive health afflictions affecting men are impotence, infertility, and infidelity, and there are multiple cures for each. Among many of the midwives and healers who attend to matters of impotence, for example, the pervasive remedy for such an affliction was that that men had to be "heated up" in order for them to get erections. "Calentando al hombre" was the preferred manner to achieve an "aumento del deseo sexual" (an increase in sexual desire) among men. Several healers told me that there were also "salsas" for men who cannot "stop," that is, for those who have erections too often.

If a couple is having no luck conceiving, some midwives and healers tell the man to get a clinical analysis of his sperm, and then, based on the results of the tests, they will prescribe one or another herbal remedy. Virgilio is a *curandero* from Santo Domingo Xagacía, in the Zapotec mountains several hours north of Oaxaca City. I met him thanks to my friend Claudio, who works at the Ethnobotanical Garden as a laborer and who shares a wooden shack with Virgilio and his invalid wife, Martina, also a *curandera*. The house consisted of one room with a cement floor, metal siding and roof, and a hose outside that was connected to a water spigot up the hill. A lone turkey ran around a dirt patch fenced by scrap lumber.

Experts in medicinal plants, Virgilio and Martina talked to me late one afternoon about "sterility" in men and women. "When women are sterile, they say they are blocked up where the man's milk drops," Virgilio explained to me. There are plants that women need in such circumstances to "unblock" themselves. When a man is sterile, there are various remedies, including vitamins and bee's honey. At the Ethnobotanical Garden, Claudio also professes a broad knowledge of the medicinal properties of various plants, one reason among many that his nickname there is Bruja.[16]

Doña Hermila described the problem of male infertility and its resolution in the following manner: "When the semen or sperm, when it's very acidic, and there is acidity when it enters [the woman] and gets to the egg, well, it's as if there were lime [juice]. There is acidity, and things don't jell [*no cuaja*], and if things don't jell, there is no baby. So we have to get rid of the acidity. We give him tea, and some to the woman too, to change her stomach. And there's got to be trust between the two, because even in marriages there is often not much trust between the two." I wish I had pressed Hermila on what she meant by a lack of trust in couples.

As for impotence, Doña Hermila described to me at length her counseling method. "We *curanderas* and *curanderos* insist—we're stubborn—we begin by giving him some tea. Well, I can't say I am a psychologist, but I begin working with him by asking, 'What happened? What did they do to you? What was it? Why?' I like to do it this way, to get it all out, to go through his life, close his eyes. 'What happened to you? Are you scared of something? Is it fear?' Sometimes men are very manly [*varonil*] . . . but there's something going on."

I asked if alcohol was sometimes involved.

"Alcohol, drugs, whether marijuana or [paint] thinner. But you've got to remember, it's important to get rid of the fear. Now it turns out there were problems in his house. He saw his father do different things. My grandma used to tell me (when I was grown up, not when I was little), 'There are children who see their parents [have sexual relations]. It traumatizes them! But why does it traumatize them?' He wants to know, 'How could he use [*usar*] a woman like that?!' " Doña Hermila told me she had not heard about Freud's (1989 [1918]) famous essay on the "Wolf Man," which recounts a similar historical basis for infantile neurosis.

If a man is having impotence problems, the woman often looks to intoxication as a reason. "A lot of people say that alcohol makes the sexual appetite grow, but when it comes time for relations, he can't any more," the Mixtec midwife Abigail stated. Her colleague, Amparo, concurred, "Men, because of alcohol, can't do it."

As for infidelity, of special and growing concern in the Mixtec region was the case of men who migrate to find work in the United States, become infected with HIV, and return and infect their wives and others. "There are no cures for AIDS," Mariana told me. "Look, [in healing] I have touched women who have had . . . whose husband has been on the other side [the United States] and who's been with women there. So the women who come to see me end up with *flujo* [a flow], they have *granos* [seeds] in the vagina, they have *pestilencias* [bad smells]. And I cure them all. I clean their vaginas. I give them plants to make teas with. They get better."

The United States was considered an especially noxious source of illness by other traditional healers I spoke with in 2004. Virgilio, the Zapotec *curandero*, told me, "There are a lot of illnesses in the United States, because there are a lot of microbes. You know why I say this? Because the people, the water, the pollution, there're a lot of microbes, a lot of illnesses. Here not so much, because there is more air here. There you have a lot of chemicals, weapons, gas, everything. They're not . . . they're not natural any more."

The issue of migration as an topic of concern for the traditional midwives and healers arose, as it often seems to in Oaxaca, unrelated to any discussion of medical problems or cures. One woman in Soyoltepec with whom I had gone to a photocopying store on an errand remarked that she had a son living in the United States, "in Florida or Alabama or someplace like that." Three weeks later, after I had returned to Providence, I received a call from her son, who was wondering if I could get him any work in Rhode Island.

Mariana said she knew of certain plants that were said to trap men and keep them from straying, but that they never used any of them. What they did use were other plants for the opposite situation. "For example, let's say I fall in love with her, but she doesn't love me. So I will look for a way that she will be forced to be with me. So that's what we 'cure,' we cure her so she falls in love, too."

In a study on pregnancy and childbirth in rural Mexico, Mellado, Zolla, and Castañeda state, "Let us note in passing that both at the level of field data and bibliography regarding fertility, information [on male infertility] is far more scarce than is the case for the study of female sterility" (1989:64).[17] They report that many of the men and women they interviewed for their study "take for granted that men are 'naturally fertile'" (64). Nonetheless, when a traditional healer believes a man might be suffering from infertility, remedies will be attempted. In Hueyapan, according to Mellado, Zolla, and Castañeda:

> The therapist first tried to "reduce swelling" of internal organs of the subject by massages with different herbs: *floripondio, hijas de mirtos de flor roja* and *de flor azul, cogollos de naranjo, hojas de retama* and *ramas de hijojo*. These herbs are then crushed and mixed with alcohol and clove powder. After administering the massage, the *curandera* conducts a diagnostic exam utilizing the traditional method that consists of rubbing a chicken egg over the body of the patient and then looking for signs when the egg is cracked into a glass of water. This then leads to a maneuver to "stretch the tendons to reposition the vertebrae." The man is hung from his feet with his hands behind his head and his elbows close to his face. He is raised by the elbows several times by a man positioned behind him. (64–65)

Another treatment used in Hueyapan (65) was giving the man suffering from infertility epazote tea to rid him of parasites, because it was believed that gastrointestinal problems could cause temporary male sterility.

MEN IN CHILDBIRTH AND THE *CUARENTENA*

When I inquired of Doña Meche, the president of the Oaxacan traditional healers' organization and a Zapotec midwife and healer herself, as to men's presence and participation in childbirth, she said it all depended on what the woman wanted. When I asked why a man would not be with his wife at this time, she replied, "Because . . . he's a man and doesn't need to know."

I laughed.

"Yes!" she retorted. Then, recalling changes over the decades since she had first attended a birth, at the age of fifteen, in 1947, Doña Hermila intoned, "Most of the time the man is not there. Only when the woman wants him to be. In my mother's case, my father was never there. When my mother had her last one she was in bad shape, so my father was there. That was an emergency. Now times are changing. Now there are some husbands who are becoming more conscious, but traditionally there are communities with men who participate [in childbirth] and communities where they don't participate." She estimated that at the time we had first talked, in 2001, men were by then present at perhaps 60 or 70 percent of childbirths in indigenous communities.[18]

A recurring theme in my discussions with the indigenous healers and midwives was how they felt sorry for the women who had to deliver their babies in the hospitals, because men were not allowed into the delivery rooms. One principal reason was voiced by the Zapotec healer Rosario Gaspar, who is from the village of Santiago Laxopa, in the Sierra de Juárez, three hours north of Oaxaca City. She told me, "The poor women who go to hospitals! The ones who give birth in hospitals. Because men can't be there with them, so the poor thing is fighting through all her labor, alone, with doctors she does not know." Writing about midwives in Yucatán, Jordan states that "the woman's husband is expected to be present during labor and birth. They say he should 'see how a woman suffers.' This rule is quite strong and explicit and we heard of cases where the husband's absence was blamed for the stillbirth of a child" (1993 [1978]:33).

Doña Hermila was not sure it was a good thing to have men present during the birth process, but she was adamant that women in labor were frequently treated in abusive ways in hospitals:

> Doctors have no respect for the women, for the position to deliver, for [women's] bodies. "They take my clothes, I want to wear the clothes I brought," the women complain, to no avail. As one woman told me, "I felt like they were kidnapping me. Why? Because they put me in one place, with my clothes in another, and my mother in another. It was an assault on me." They told her to take off her clothes and put on a johnny, because the johnny was boiled. Then they "cleaned" her up by shaving her. This is rape, the rape of women. A little shaving, that's to prepare the women. And even though we are *empíricas* [meaning traditional doctors], we have clean clothes, we boil our clothes to sterilize them.

Childbirth is thus seen as biomedical aggression against the mother, and sterile technique as a weapon.

Said Mariana in our talk in Nochixtlán, "There are husbands who want to find a [male] *partero* and there are husbands who prefer a [female] *partera*."

"Do men participate in childbirth in the Mixteca?" I asked Mariana, Amparo, and Abigail.

"Well, when the husband is there, fine," replied Amparo. "And when he's not . . ."

"If the man is there, he holds her. But he doesn't deliver [receive] the baby," Abigail clarified.

I asked what they did with the placenta.

Mariana answered, "Well, it is our custom, what we do in every village when the placenta comes out, we roll it up. I take the placenta and I roll it up in a cloth. I sew up the cloth, and then I tell someone, 'Go hang it from that tree in the distance.'"

In contrast, Amparo described what she does with the placenta. "My custom is to take the placenta, throw it in a cloth or whatever, and then I burn it, get it clean, clean, just ashes. Then I put the ashes in a little bottle or bowl and I bury it. If the child gets sick, for example, from the umbilical cord or the eyes, then the bowl is dug up to see what's wrong, to see if a spider has gotten into the ashes. Then we see if it's clean and we clean the child's face."

Doña Meche, the Zapotec midwife from San Felipe Tejalapam, insisted that the placenta must be burned and that the ashes thrown in the river, not just anywhere. If the placenta is buried intact near the house, she told me, sometimes a bolt of lightning will strike the spot, a very dangerous situation indeed.

Through all my discussions with traditional healers and midwives in various regions of Oaxaca, one thing that became clear was that their work on reproductive health matters revolved overwhelmingly around women and infants. When I nudged them to talk about men, they had experiences and knowledge to recount, but they inevitably turned the conversation back to women in pregnancy, childbirth, and the *cuarentena*, the forty-day "quarantine" post-partum period during which, ideally, a woman recuperates from pregnancy and childbirth and is tended to by others. This period is also sometimes referred to as "the man's diet" or "the woman's diet." Doña Meche called the *cuarentena* the "globo de seguridad," the sphere of security.

Men seemed relevant mainly in relation to women's health. When I asked about restrictions on sexual activity following birth, Amparo cautioned that men "have to wait, even though sometimes they don't show respect toward the woman, that's what should happen," meaning men should wait a decent interval before they initiate sex again with their wives. Otherwise, "you've got another pregnancy."

"How long do you have to wait to have sexual relations again?" I asked, not realizing I would spark a raucous round of teasing by the women.

"I'd say seven or eight years . . ."

"No! Who could stand that if they can't even stand forty days?"

"But don't you see, now they [the men] have another [woman] and another?"

"Well, let them go around like that. As I say to my *compañeras*, 'Don't give them the wrong advice, but if your husband is straying, let him go, but take care of yourself. You're better to let him go.'"

"As if he's not coming back!"

"Who knows?!"

"Who said he's not coming back?!" At which point, all three women burst out laughing.

I asked, "And do the women want to wait so long?"

"Well, no!"

"Forty days?"

"Maybe a month or two. And what I tell the young women is that if you're going to have relations, have them. But take care of yourselves. When the moment comes, careful. At that moment, tell the guy to spill his liquid on the side. Like that! So it doesn't stay inside her, so she doesn't get pregnant."

"And men here do that?"

"Well, there are men who do that. There are men in my village who do that."[19]

When I asked various of the traditional indigenous midwives around the state about men's participation, or lack thereof, in childbirth, I initially had in mind to learn about the men's relationships to their children, beginning from the moment of birth. Was this an experience they sought or avoided, and what was the attitude of the midwives, in terms of welcoming or shunning the fathers? A recurring theme several midwives raised with me was not one I had expected: make men witness the agony of childbirth so they would feel remorse about having impregnated their wives and be more reluctant in the future to have sex with their wives without protection. Said Obdulia, the midwife who attended births in the Mazateca region:

> If the father shows up during birth, I let him in. I let him in so he can see the birth process. So he can realize the woman's suffering as it progresses. And as he observes, I say, "Come here so you can take into account the woman and so you don't get her pregnant again right away." Because a little one needs to grow up healthy, and as long as the woman is lactating she is not improving. During the pregnancy she loses iron, calcium, and loses her force, her energy. And if she is pregnant again after a year! She is going to be a malnourished woman if that happens. So I tell the men, "Look how women suffer when they have children." I tell them about ways to take care of themselves [with contraceptives]. Men, I tell them, can use condoms.[20]

"And do they use condoms?" I inquired.

"Really, the majority of men don't like them! They say, 'If we are going to eat candy with the paper still on, it's not going to taste like candy.' And they say that it doesn't feel the same."

Dalia spoke up. "For the woman, either. Because I've heard, I don't know myself and I am not going to know since I'm already old. But they say, I have heard, they say that women hurt themselves with these things. So the poor woman has desires to make love the way she wants it and that's not the way she wants it."

As to what constituted a proper "waiting period" before initiating sexual relations again, there were various opinions about a suitable interval to wait, but then the discussion returned to the question of desires, at which point Obdulia sighed and concluded, "Yeah, because the body demands it, demands it. The body, that's just the way it is."

THE LIMITS OF "MEDICAL PLURALISM"

Traditional healers, as we have seen, work in marginal areas, where, until fairly recently, if they didn't diagnose and cure people, no one did. By the early 2000s, services that had been offered in the past by traditional midwives and healers, sometimes through the auspices of the Instituto Nacional Indigenista (INI), were falling under the jurisdiction of primary state health care institutions like the Secretaria de Salud (SSA) and the Instituto Mexicano de Seguridad Social (IMSS). As a result, there was concern on the part of many traditional doctors that people from indigenous communities might be seeking their services less frequently when they were in need of medical attention.[21]

With respect to reproductive health in another region of Mexico with a high proportion of indigenous people—the Nahua area north of Oaxaca—Huber and Sandstrom note: "Midwives play an important role in introducing birth control and participating in public health campaigns. The salience of these roles is evident in the terms people use to refer to them: *parteras pastilleras* (birth-control-pill midwives), *parteras boticarias* (patent-medicine midwives), *parteras promotoras* (health-promotion midwives), *parteras adiestradas* or *parteras capacitadas* (trained midwives), and *parteras empíricas diplomadas* (qualified empirical midwives)" (2001b:171). Nonetheless, as Paola Sesia shows in her study of midwifery in Oaxaca:

"Midwives represent a subaltern model of care in the face of the official hegemonic health system," and biomedical practitioners manifest "a certain disdain for the supposed 'ignorance,' 'backwardness,' and 'superstitious baggage'" of midwives (1992b:18).[22] The very medical model that contrasts biomedicine with *medicina tradicional* is, of course, premised on the understanding that the two systems are largely incompatible.

In March 2001, when Decreto 345 became law in Oaxaca, thus legally placing Western biomedicine and traditional indigenous medicine on an even footing in the state even as the two systems were legally cataloged as distinct, those promoting the law sought to tamp down the most flagrant attempts at marginalization of indigenous doctors and healers. After Doña Hermila gave a talk on the radio, for example, a biomedical doctor called in and ridiculed her and traditional healing in general. The new law giving titular respect to indigenous medicine put her in a better position to challenge these insults. Several prominent members of the biomedical community, sometimes referred to as "modern doctors," were outraged at the passage of the bill and expressed their grave concern that it would turn the health care community in Oaxaca into a national laughingstock, subjecting Oaxaca to ridicule as an Indian state that could offer nothing better than Indian medicine.[23]

This kind of racism is apparent not only in the refusal to acknowledge the efficacious treatments available from traditional doctors, but in the very rejection of the central tenets in much of the practice of medicine by traditional midwives and healers. Holistic approaches to diagnosis and healing—for example, with respect to infertility—run counter to the either-the-woman-or-the-man dichotomy that is prevalent in biomedicine. Few biomedical practitioners in Oaxaca seem to feel that they have much to learn from traditional doctors. In a similar way, the history of ethnomedicine—"too narrowly confined to eliciting taxonomies of disease without considering their application in practice" (Lock 2001:479)—has limited the potential lessons to be learned from traditional medicine with respect to the meaning and social context of healing. And as Nancy Scheper-Hughes insists, "Some degree of biomedical, and certainly medical anthropological, tolerance toward heterodox therapies as valid alternatives to scientific medicine in certain instances is certainly in order"

(1990:194). Unfortunately, the gloried past of Mexico's indigenous peoples does not carry down to the recognition of many beliefs and practices worth celebrating—much less emulating—among contemporary Indians.

Although it is undoubtedly true, in a sense, that the practice of *usos y costumbres* associated with Oaxaca's indigenous peoples is in part a relic from Mexico's colonial past (see Bartra 1999:64), what Michael Higgins (personal communication) calls a remapping of ethnic claims is also relevant as a way to identify parts of the past in present-day Oaxaca. Higgins is referring, in particular, to the multiple levels of ethnic representation that have emerged in Oaxaca in recent decades. In my conversations in vasectomy clinics and in the state-run AIDS clinic in Oaxaca City, for example, I was struck by the casual mention the men would make to a father or uncle who spoke Mixe, or a grandfather who spoke Mixteco, or a wife who speaks Zapoteco ("From Tehuantepec!" one man clarified), or in another instance to the fact that both the man and his wife understood Zapoteco (in this case, meaning the dialectic variant of the mountain Sierra region), though only she could speak it well. Men and women would similarly refer to their "pueblos" in Mazatec, Mixe, Zapotec, Huave, Trique, Mixteco, or other regions of the state identified with particular past and present *usos y costumbres,* including with respect to medical diagnosis and healing.[24] Ethnicity as identity and self-described being is most assuredly part of Oaxaca's past—precolonial, colonial, and post-Independence. It is also, in familiar and dramatically novel ways, part of the present and future of Oaxaca.

In late July 2004, I traveled to the Isthmus of Tehuantepec with Nacho Bernal, the doctor and medical anthropologist who worked for the government agency responsible for defending the rights of indigenous peoples. We were headed to see a group of Huave midwives and healers in the town of San Mateo del Mar. As we drove into San Mateo, the wind was blowing sand across what looked to me like a desolate and desperate community; I knew there were poorer villages in Oaxaca, but this was the most destitute one I had encountered. Reed walls enclosed the homes that were topped with tin roofs. We heard announcements being broadcast over loudspeakers, a change from the days when drums would be used to send communitywide messages.

At the Organización de Médicos Tradicionales Huaves, on Calle Guerrero, we were met by thirteen *curanderos* and midwives, nine women and four men, including one man who professed to be ninety-eight years old. Nacho had been invited by the organization to lead a workshop on violence, and he brought with him several poster boards depicting "typical scenes" that would be utilized to prompt discussion. One scene that caught the attention of several women there showed a health promoter on one side of a desk talking with a young couple on the other side of the desk. The health promoter was holding up various birth control devices.

I assumed the discussion about this image would revolve around nothing more sensational than contraception. Instead, to my surprise, an older woman who was a leader in the group explained to Nacho and me that this interaction reminded her of the Huave women who had had IUDs placed inside of them without either their consent or even their knowledge. Several years later, three of these women had started bleeding as a result of the devices, without understanding why and not realizing the reason they could not get pregnant. Needless to say, the women had not had their IUDs changed periodically, as they should have, and they had remained ignorant about what was causing their bleeding until they had gone to a nearby city for help. (There were repeated complaints that the young doctors who were sent to staff the local clinic in San Mateo were next to useless; if they could even be found, they were often found carousing with the local women and/or wandering around drinking alcohol in the street.) Writing about women's reproductive health in Mexico overall, Ortiz, Amuchástegui, and Rivas (1998:163) concluded that " 'informed consent' is limited at best," all the more reason that international organizations like the World Health Organization and the United Nations Commission on Human Rights have decried the sterilization of women, without appropriate consent, immediately after they have given birth and when they are under great stress (see Castro 2004).

The concept of *consentimiento informado* (informed consent) is even more perilous for monolingual speakers of indigenous languages than it is for monolingual Spanish-speaking populations, in that signing forms in Spanish becomes an even less meaningful exercise for these women and men. As long as a piece of paper is signed, formally signifying informed consent, the state is duly absolved of responsibility. The fact that signatures are obtained in this way, without any actual understanding of a particular procedure, and that patients are asked to sign at a moment of trauma or high tension, is an example of what Sankar calls the "idealized model of communication that ignores social context" (2004:429).

In San Mateo del Mar, under an almond tree that was bearing fruit, we lunched on the local delicacy—gray mullet *lisa* baked in a cornmeal batter. I listened as the women and men complained that there was less and less work for *médicos tradicionales,* either midwives or *curanderos.* Yet in Oaxaca, where no vocation, including traditional indigenous medicine, is ever very far away from the tourist market, a temporary solution may have been discovered. In the capital city and to a lesser extent in surrounding villages, indigenous medical tourism has now materialized. The dollars, euros, and yen earned by some indigenous midwives, for example, have allowed them to continue providing services to women and men who are too poor to pay for them. One organization, the nondenominational Congregación Mariana Trinitaria,[25] was running ads in Oaxaca announcing its services and tapping into the wellspring of positive attitudes on the part of foreigners toward the medicinal powers of indigenous healing:

> For centuries we have trusted our health and well-being to . . .
> TRADITIONAL MEXICAN MEDICINE
> Therapeutic massage
> Anti-Stress Massage
> Indigenous steam [presumably, the *baño temazcal,* or steam bath]
> Aromatherapy
> Energy renovation
> Bodily harmonization
> Psychological stimulation
> Emotional therapy

POSTSCRIPT: THE TRUE STORY OF "COCOS A LA VIAGRA"

Driving north on the Pan-American Highway, just outside the Oaxaca City limits, one sees an enormous field where on Sundays people bring

Roadside stand in Oaxaca City offering concoction of coconut *(coco)*, shrimp, and octopus said to be an aphrodisiac, 2005.

cars that they want to sell. Thousands of people stop to inspect and haggle over used vehicles there each week. For those with an entrepreneurial spirit, it is a great location to sell food as well as cars. Perhaps because most of the potential car buyers are men, in 2004 a new food stand that targeted a certain kind of male consumer went up in the back of an enterprising vendor's pickup.

The photograph seen here and on the cover of this book shows that food stand, where I stopped one afternoon to chat with the proprietor. Deciding to get right to the point, I asked him, "Why 'a la Viagra'?" His first response was "It's a nice name." (Viagra is sometimes jokingly referred to as "viejas agredicidas," grateful old ladies.)[26] When I pressed him, he told me that the concoction he sold, consisting of *cocos* (coconuts) mixed with octopus and shrimp, was a well-known "stimulant."

Medical pluralism *oaxaqueño* at its finest was on display in this very public advertisement. The promise of the modern, multinational pharmaceutical company blended effortlessly with local, traditional prescription-recipes for good erections and, presumably, good manly sexual healing.

EIGHT From Boardrooms to Bedrooms

The Utopia of this century—that which has been desired above
all else. and desired most deeply—has been the modernization
of body and soul.

Carlos Monsiváis (1997:136)

In a mountain village of Oaxaca, there is a story told of an elderly man
who, with his wife, regularly attended Mass in the local church. One particular Sunday, the priest's sermon dealt with questions of health, affliction, and healing. Because they were elderly, it made sense that the
couple followed carefully as the padre encouraged his parishioners, "If
you have faith, you will be saved. You must place your hand on the affected part of your body and then you will see there a miracle." Now, it
just so happened that the old man was himself tormented by a most
dreadful misfortune—a stubbornly flaccid member, to be specific—and
when he heard these words he felt a rush of relief flow through him.
Then, discreetly and delicately, he lowered his left hand and put it between his legs. Out of the corner of her eye the old woman watched as her

husband did this, and she sighed. Then, turning to him, she gently whispered in his ear, "Old man, the priest said miracle . . . not resurrection."

PETATES AND PUBLIC BAÑOS

That many taken-for-granted culturalist assumptions about male sexuality are widespread and little questioned in Oaxaca City is unremarkable. Nor is it surprising that so many medical practitioners, such as doctors, nurses, health psychologists, and social workers, concur with commonsense culturalist beliefs about Mexican men's sexuality—for example, that men have primordial sexual urges and needs that are different or more intense than those of women. It would be unusual if these health personnel, who grew up with the same cultural lifeways, felt otherwise. Thus, public medicine that is devoted to reproductive health in Oaxaca is guided as much as anything by the cultural presumption that men's sexual behavior is regulated by unique bodily processes and a distinctive sexual culture.

It is also noteworthy that of the dozens of medical practitioners I interviewed in the course of this project on male sexuality, birth control, and AIDS in Oaxaca, the only group that consistently challenged the underlying dichotomy of male/female sexualities were the traditional doctors, midwives, and healers. Despite repeated attempts on my part to elicit comments from *médicos tradicionales* about innate male sexual proclivities, on the straw mat *petates* found in rural homes until recent decades or in the public *baños* (bathrooms, said to be sites of clandestine male prostitution in Oaxaca City),[1] my attempts to find confirmation of this male/female sexual dichotomy were repeatedly rebuffed, as the midwives and healers insisted that individual variation in sexual desire and activity is the only sensible analysis that should inform caring treatment for afflictions like impotence and infertility.

I had gone to Oaxaca in search of unique and familiar truths about men's reproductive health and sexuality. Glimpses of the exotic and mundane were all around as I talked with women as they plucked the feathers from turkeys, and with young men and women who told me they had eloped in a *robo* to avoid arranged marriages. I heard the mayor of one town boast that he used to throw people in the local *bote* (jail) when they did not carry out their religious/community obligations; now he locked up parents who would not let their daughters go to school. And as evidence of the often futile quest for exotica, when a Zapotec woman was asked in a market stall in the town of Tlacolula if her beautiful skirt and blouse came from a nearby village, she replied matter-of-factly, "No, the fabric comes from the United States." In another mountain village in the Mixteca region, I learned of the perils of exaggerating the degree of social isolation that might exist in these remote regions, as I noted that the shelf of a schoolteacher there held books in Spanish by Paolo Freire, Claude Lévi-Strauss, Jean Piaget, Oscar Lewis, Karl Marx, George Foster, Lourdes Arizpe, and Ruth Benedict. Meanwhile, in the street outside the teacher's home, boys played soccer with a milk carton they had inflated with air, a sign of the intense and pervasive poverty of this region devastated by out-migration, soil erosion, class cleavages, and racism.

In a manner similar to the remedicalization of sexuality more generally in health care work, as a result of AIDS (see Parker, Barbosa, and Aggleton et al. 2000), in family planning campaigns in Oaxaca there have been only sporadic and half-hearted campaigns to engage men in active partnership with women. And even these attempts are, in a classic self-fulfilling prophecy, considered by many doctors and health administrators to be doomed to fail. Men are said to be "naturally" less inclined to participate in contraceptive efforts, because most men are concerned with having more sex and care little about limiting their procreative capacities. What is more, I was told with some frequency, men may be unreachable and unreliable as users of birth control for the simple fact that men cannot get pregnant. That is also why some believe there is a greater variety and availability of contraception for women, as if contraception were all or even mainly a matter of bodily capacity and constraint.

Claims about the preternatural powers of culture were also evident in AIDS care in Oaxaca, where widespread culturalist assumptions about the ubiquity of male–male sexual relations among Mexicans have substituted for substantial epidemiological studies showing conclusively the vectors of transmission of the virus. Men who have sex with men are classified in Oaxaca as the key risk group responsible for AIDS in the state. Whenever I asked health workers at COESIDA how they could be so sure that all the men in the clinic had been infected through sex with other men, and what was the basis of their claim that substantial numbers of men in Mexico had sex with other men, I was told that this knowledge came from just living in Oaxacan society. Sometimes people told me about "heterosexualidad flexible," an expression used by the urban middle class in Oaxaca to refer to men who have sex with other men and abjure the label "homosexual," or even "bisexual." Mainly I was informed that "men lie about sex" and refuse to acknowledge their homosexual experiences.

When I asked one assistant at the COESIDA why he thought men lied in this way, he responded, "Because it's a Catholic country." I must have looked puzzled when I countered that plenty of men and women who are Catholics tell the truth about committing sins like adultery and using contraception. I asked him again how he could be so sure that men lied about the particular sin of having had sex with other men, and he responded with an exasperated groan, "Experience and knowledge, Mateo!" One simply knows things, or one does not. If you are unfamiliar with the cultural lifeways, do not expect to understand. Trust those who say they do.

We must not conflate male sexuality with male reproduction. Biologistic notions of primal male urges and facile models of erectile functioning have little place in a serious analysis of male sexuality. In my dozens of discussions with men who had chosen to get sterilized, and with the women in their lives, it became obvious that a key factor for most, though not all, was what they termed the suffering of the women. In one way or another, numerous husbands and wives spoke of women having been the ones responsible, for years or even decades, for birth control, of the difficulties many women had experienced during their pregnancies and in childbirth, and of how it was now the men's turn to prevent pregnancy and to suffer a little for sexual relations. The men who got vasectomies were unusual in the sense that they were among a tiny fraction of men in Oaxaca, and in Mexico overall, to do so. But they were just as much the products of Mexican culture as any other men. They were not cultural deviants or outliers of the dominant macho culture: many sterilized men in Oaxaca noted that they considered the operation the incarnation of good manly behavior.[2]

Similarly, blaming the men who migrate to the United States and return infected for causing AIDS in Oaxaca perpetuates the medical profiling of populations for the disease (Briggs and Mantini-Briggs 2003) and avoids grappling with the larger political economy underlying the spread of AIDS. Labeling Mexican migrant men who have sex with other men as the primary risk group makes the causes of the disease individual and cultural. Why do millions of Mexicans have to go to the United States to find gainful employment? Why are multinational pharmaceutical companies unwilling to provide antiretroviral medications at greatly reduced prices to those in need? Attributing the spread of AIDS to Mexican migrant men who have sex with other men also ignores other possibilities— for example, that men might become infected as a result of sex with female prostitutes, including when they come into contact with semen from their "milk brothers," or that men might be sharing infected needles to inject antibiotics and vitamins. We cannot understand why there is AIDS in Oaxaca by using a framework of autonomous local cultures, politics, and funding; AIDS and AIDS care in Oaxaca are contingent issues dependent in good measure on decisions made in the government offices and pharmaceutical boardrooms of Mexico City, Washington, D.C., London, Basel, and Geneva. These boardroom decisions have direct repercussions on the wages of love and on a range of sexual cravings, conduct, health, responsibilities, and outcomes in the bedrooms of Oaxaca.

WOMEN AND MALE SEXUALITY

The issue that first prompted me to study men's reproductive health and sexuality in Oaxaca had nothing to do with vasectomies or AIDS. I wanted to look closely at the negotiations that take place within heterosexual couples about an important and intimate topic; yet, though I realized from the beginning that decision making about contraception and sexuality was ultimately connected with larger social issues, I think in retrospect that I underestimated the extent to which this was true. Raising children, earning and spending money, domestic violence, alcohol consumption, relations with in-laws, living situations, and sex and birth control were all possible topics I considered. A central issue I wanted to explore was my belief that adult women have had a greater influence on adult men than has been previously recognized in anthropological and feminist studies; I wanted to document and understand how these men and women discussed, debated, and decided on important issues in their lives. But I needed to choose a particular area of interaction between women and men to be able to chronicle the coaxing, flattering, persuading, and demanding that I viewed as essential aspects of the daily conversations and silences between men and women in the choices they made in their lives.[3] By studying the negotiations that take place over an inherently personal topic like sexuality, I hoped to gain purchase on the powerful effect of women on the beliefs, actions, and lives of their men. In addition, as most previous studies on reproduction had focused on women, by concentrating on men, this one could speak about the missing players in earlier accounts of the reproductive process, all the while maintaining a broader orientation centered on the study of gender differences and inequalities and on the efforts by women and men to transform gender relations grounded in power differences.

A decade earlier, in Mexico City, I had studied domestic violence by talking with wives and husbands about how they had overcome this awful part of their lives. In a more general way, I had also traced other factors that had influenced them to change, for example, announcements on the radio that condemned wife-beating, confrontations with neighbors and family members over such beatings, and drinking and abstaining from alcohol. In Oaxaca, I thought that studying decision making within couples with respect to birth control might be a good window through which to chart the influence of adult women on adult men (as well as the other way around) that had been so understudied in the scholarly and popular literatures on gender relations.

In part, I always knew that this quest to study male/female negotiations in an isolated microcosm like marriage was doomed to fail. The reasons were simple: one, such negotiations occur over a period of years, sometimes decades, and cannot be adequately captured in the slice-of-time interviewing and observation that form a key component of the ethnographer's toolkit. My discussions with couples at one moment in their lives could not substitute for a comprehensive, long-term view of such negotiating. Two, and more unhappily, with regard to the choices available to couples seeking contraception, there was little to negotiate: other than condoms, and the withdrawal and rhythm methods, there were no contraceptive techniques that depended mainly or largely on men's participation. In other words, as I have tried to make clear throughout this study, studying couples as if they lived in isolation from the larger decisions made by the pharmaceutical companies, government health institutions, the Catholic church, and the planned parenthood federations—to name a few "outside" influences—is foolhardy at best. The global political economy of reproductive health and sexuality is central to every decision made by couples in every home in Oaxaca regarding matters like birth control, regardless of how personal and intimate the choice may seem to the men and women themselves.

Similarly, so-called Mexican beliefs regarding women's need to protect themselves from men's uncontrollable sexual urges (and from being impregnated by sperm) should not be viewed primarily as individual tests of temptation and fortitude, but rather as one element in a social panoply grounded in patriarchal institutions that promote the dichotomy of man-as-predator and of woman-as-preyed-upon and that exhibit an extraordinary grip on the popular imagination. It might be assumed that the supposedly widespread belief that men have stronger sexual drives than women (see Liguori and Lamas 2003:88) is in turn grounded in solid, unimpeachable scientific evidence. Instead, I would argue that the emphasis, for example, on rapacious men offered in the public health literature devoted to sexuality often suffers from self-limiting topics of inquiry that reflect previous biases about inherently binary male/female sexualities. Although not unique, López Juárez (2003) is unusual when he writes of women who are concerned about men's problems with sexual performance (such as premature ejaculation) and when he frames his argument to show how loving concern between men and women can also be central to discussions about sexuality. If this point seems ridiculously obvious, that just makes the dearth of such conceptual frameworks in the study of heterosexual sexuality all the more remarkable.

With highly effective forms of contraception for women widely available throughout the world, women became the central target of planned parenthood campaigns in the last several decades. As decisions about birth control increasingly occurred in a female contraceptive culture, men have been intentionally and inadvertently marginalized from responsibility for preventing pregnancy. It seems to me more reasonable to explain the low prevalence rates for male users of contraception this way than to assume it is a reflection of some bad cultural trait, like machismo, that exists in an especially unbridled form in Oaxaca and Mexico.

The main outcome of an emergent female contraceptive culture, of course, has not been the exclusion of men from contributing in more ways to the prevention of pregnancies. Through the development of technologies like the pill and the IUD, through national and international family planning efforts, and through the medicalization of women's reproductive health and sexuality in general by health and even financial institutions, the management of women's bodies has become an even more central feature of social life throughout the world in the last several decades.[4] My emphasis in this book on the implications of the female contraceptive culture for men is not meant to supersede, in an overall sense, the implications of this development on women. Neither has my purpose been to offer stories of men in isolation from women.

This study has sought, in part, to examine men's experiences in a contemporary female contraceptive culture in Oaxaca, Mexico. Certainly, the decisions made in the boardrooms of Mexico's health institutions—IMSS, ISSSTE, the Secretaría de Salud—are responsible for how educated the general public in Oaxaca is about vasectomy. More than one doctor in Oaxaca complained to me that, following an initial spurt of activity in 1994, when specialists were sent from Mexico City to the provinces to train people in the procedure, institutional support for the operation had steadily declined in the state. In an analogous fashion, decisions made by the Mexican government to pay top dollar (often literally) to the international pharmaceutical companies for antiretrovirals are far more significant than any resolutions made locally, either by patients or local health care workers, regarding adherence to taking medications, lifestyle issues like alcohol consumption, and ongoing sexual relationships.

Understanding the role of the greater social context, political economies, and the reproductive world order is crucial for understanding the
intricacies of decision making within couples. But this assertion should
not be construed to mean that discussions by couples are ineffectual or ex-
traneous. Local mores and individual appetites are critical to decisions.
Writing about the central Mexican town of Ocuituco, Castro's (2001:153)
distinction between women's normalized sexuality that must be controlled and repressed by men and men's naturalized sexuality that is
uncontrollable and irrepressible is based—perhaps a bit too literally—
on interpretations of men's and women's comments about each other.
Browner and Perdue similarly show how "fears of community censure"
(1988:94) led women in San Francisco, Oaxaca, initially to report that they
knew of no way to limit their fertility, whereas after further discussions
with these two female researchers most of the same women acknowledged
that various techniques did exist.[5] The evidence of "classic manly privilege," as well as the "female invocation" of male dominance (to recall
Rapp 2000:99), was evident throughout my research with the men who
opted for vasectomy and the women who encouraged and benefited from
male sterilization.

The point is not to minimize the importance of discussions, debates,
and decisions on the part of couples, any more than one should discount
the severe effects of sexist thinking on gender relations in Mexico or elsewhere. Rather, the goal should be to develop analyses that sufficiently account for the multiple layers of influence that are brought to bear on reproductive decisions that may appear to emanate from couples alone.
And the goal should be to reveal the underlying assumptions about innate male sexuality that are, in many cases, little more than rehashed versions of earlier monochromatic theories of fixed sexual drives, repression,
and release (for a brilliant critique of these theories, see Segal 1994).

THE LINGERING HANDSHAKE

It is often difficult to decipher the meanings behind people's words that
express fear, manipulation, curiosity, domination, and any other state of

being and emotion. This is also true about gestures. To explain how he came to be infected with the AIDS virus, Primitivo Sánchez, the man described in chapter 3 who worked as a short-order cook at a downtown greasy spoon, related to me his account of having sold his blood in an illegal market in Oaxaca, of having had sex with various female prostitutes over the years without using a condom, and then, in still greater detail, of having sold his own body to other men who would pay him to perform oral and anal sex with them. From the time he was a teenager until I met him, in 2001, when he was forty-eight years old, Primitivo explained to me, whenever he had been especially desperate for money to support his family, he would find men in the public *baños* in the main downtown market and grab a stall in which to exchange money and favors.

In the middle of one of Primitivo's stories one morning at the COESIDA clinic, we were interrupted by a nurse. It was time to take his blood, so our conversation would have to continue another day. I extended my hand to thank him for his candor in narrating the painful events from his sexual life history. Primitivo took my hand in his, but instead of shaking and releasing quickly, as is normal in Oaxaca, he would not let go. He did not look at me, either. But he continued to gently hold my hand in his. Primitivo seemed to be asking me, through this gesture, if I wanted to do what the other men had done with him—I assumed in exchange for money. The lingering handshake confused me and then distressed me: Had I done something to encourage such an encounter? Primitivo's lingering handshake also served to remind me that, like it or not, my own sexuality—or at least others' perceptions of my sexuality—was an unavoidable and ever present feature of the verbal, visual, and corporeal interactions I had with the dozens of men and women I interviewed in Oaxaca.

Sometimes when I arrived at the COESIDA AIDS clinic, Mario, one of the aides there, liked to play an analogous homoerotic game with me. Never making clear his intentions, Mario began one afternoon by asking if I had ever had oral sex with another man. When I said I had not, he challenged me: "How can you know anything about AIDS in Oaxaca if you have never had oral sex with a man?" Married, and with two children of his own, Mario told me he became involved with AIDS care after his brother died from the disease.

"Have you had sex of any kind with other men?" Mario asked me.

I said, "No," and I asked if he had.

"No. But even if I had I wouldn't tell you."

All of which raised for me a foundational enigma in research on sex and sexuality: How do you know if the people you talk with are lying? And I do not just mean intentionally lying, although that is an important concern. What about faulty memory, contradictory memories, conflated experiences, and sincere confusion between repressed feelings and realized actions? It would seem that of all the many kinds of human endeavor, sexuality is the one most fraught with double entendres and among the most difficult to describe and measure with precision. It may in fact be the case that there are numerous crucial aspects of male sexuality—such as the percentage of men who have sex with other men, the frequency of sexual activity, and sexual motivations and fears and desires—that we will never be able to measure in the same way as we measure other aspects of sexuality, such as prevalence rates for contraceptive use, or adherence to antiretrovirals, or the fertility of women between the ages of fifteen and forty-nine.

In part, we are confronted with the limits of self-reporting. In his review of books that were being championed in some social science quarters as representing meticulous and unimpeachable studies of sexuality in the United States, the geneticist Richard Lewontin wrote about "the fundamental methodological difficulty that faces every historian, biographer, psychotherapist, and reader of autobiography, the problem of self-report. How are we to know what is true if we must depend on what interested parties tell us?" (1995:24). If we are not present, how can we know what happens where and when people engage in sexual relations—assuming, as we cannot, that these could always be defined with any specificity? We must rely on what the participants themselves report to us. Important aspects of sex and sexuality cannot be studied in the same verifiable way that other topics, like birthrates, can be. How can one man's sexual pleasure, for instance, be reliably calibrated and compared to another's?[6] Lewontin concluded his critique of the pseudo-science of sexology and, by extension, the pretentious claims by certain researchers to uphold scientific rigor on topics like sex with the following observation: "By pretending to a kind of knowledge that it cannot achieve, social science can only engender the scorn of natural scientists and the cynicism of humanists" (29).

In a paper on "lying informants," based on research in Ghana, Wolf Bleek stated simply that "survey research cannot handle delicate issues" (1987:314). After extensive periods of ethnographic fieldwork, Bleek concluded, "Anthropological knowledge is predominantly based on what people *say* they do, not on what researchers *see* them doing" (315).[7] To an extent, one may overcome people's fiddling with the truth through indirect means. Even if there are many things we can never know about men's sexuality, and even if standard statistically driven interview schedules are of limited utility, as Lewontin argues, we can nonetheless learn from people, including by establishing personal connections between ourselves and those we are studying. I did this especially with respect to vasectomy, as I was able to speak not only as an anthropologist but could also claim insider status as someone with authoritative knowledge, based on my own experience with the operation. So I presented myself as a "usuario" of vasectomy when I eased into my role as emotional anesthesiologist during the vasectomy procedures. In certain ways, the clinical setting of the vasectomy clinics made conversation about this and other intimate topics easier, because it was impersonal. But, just in case, I also sought to make evident and available the bonds that men who were about to get sterilized might feel to exist between us.

When I repositioned the lamp that was used to heat up a man's scrotum, when I noticed that a patient was still in pain in the middle of the procedure and I was asked by one of the doctors to hold a tiny bottle of Lidocaine upside down while they stuck in a needle and drew out more of the painkiller, or when I retrieved a packet with thread for stitches, opened it, and dropped the contents out, I was a participant, sure, but more as an available bystander than as a man who also was sterile. At other moments, outside of the clinical setting, I was able to learn about sexual ethics and, perhaps, practices in more indirect ways. This certainly occurred in the Ethnobotanical Garden, where I worked with two dozen men and was able to wait for them to raise issues of sex, birth control, and AIDS without much prompting from me. And I gained insight into sexual beliefs in unexpected places.

After I took photographs of the gas station attendant during his vasectomy, I brought them by a photo shop to make copies, as the man had requested. The particular photo shop I used was near Hospital Civil, and not surprisingly they often developed film of the operations conducted there. When I stopped by to retrieve this particular set of prints, the young man who operated the developing machine asked, "Were these photos of a castration?" I assured him they were not, but instead of a vasectomy. Several weeks later, I went by to drop off more film and the same young man asked me to tell another clerk about the vasectomy shots. She was dubious. When I confirmed this to have been the case, she seemed upset. She told me she was against vasectomy. "Why?" I asked her. "Díos nos manda completos," she replied. God sends us into the world complete, and it is wrong to change one's God-given body.

In the course of my study of sex, birth control, and AIDS in Oaxaca, I had my hand grasped by one man in a gesture I took for sexual solicitation, I was rebuked by a photo shop clerk for contributing to the destruction of God's handiwork on the male body, and I was the target of half-in-jest humiliation for my lack of sexual experience with other men. My relationship with the dozens of people I talked with, lived near, visited, and learned from in Oaxaca was as convoluted and confusing at times as all other human relationships. I imposed myself on some people's lives, and in so doing I became a presence that was not necessarily welcomed. But I was also the object of curiosity and appreciation and, I hope, some delight. People in Oaxaca were also enticed by my presence and research. I was regularly chastised for *not* having stopped by more often in the Eth-nobotanical Garden.

In the course of my study, I also came to the conclusion that I might have at times used my class privilege, albeit inadvertently, to persuade men to be interviewed: no one I sought to interview during their vasectomy refused me, and I suspect that their acquiescence was not always an indication of their wholehearted appreciation of my project. At the same time, class privilege prompted some men from the middle class to be more forthcoming with me about their own class and racial prejudices. Doctors made openly racist pronouncements to me about the irrational Indians who still used midwives, those whom Sesia reports are routinely labeled by biomedical doctors as "ignorant" and "a mess of superstitions"

(1992b:18). A professional man exonerated himself from the possibility that he could spread any disease to another with the explanation, "In my case I am a healthy man, from the middle class, right? I eat three times a day. I bathe every day. I have good personal hygiene." Lingering hand-shakes and the charmed sanitary habits of the middle class provide us with windows into sexual predilection and predation in Oaxaca.[8]

LATE-MODERN LOVE: INFECTING AND INFECTED WOMEN

As noted in earlier chapters, if the largest population of HIV+ persons in Oaxaca in the early 2000s were men who had spent time living and work-ing as migrant laborers in the United States, then the second largest group were the women who became infected after having unprotected sex with these migrant men after they had returned to the state. I did not especially seek out these women, but I eventually talked with dozens of them, in-cluding many widows whose inheritance from their dead husbands in-cluded their own HIV+ status. I expected these women to be far more bit-ter than was the case. They were literally dying from having had sex with men who were infected. Why had the men not told them they were in-fected? If the men did not know, why not? I was startled time and again by the sympathetic, empathetic, decent, generous, and loving expressions of forgiveness of these women. There was remarkably little anger and re-sentment expressed by these women against the men who had planted the virus deep inside their bodies, a virus that would in most cases kill them and perhaps the children they bore after becoming infected. The comments of HIV+ women bear witness to the broader negotiation that takes place between men and women in the time of AIDS in Oaxaca, to their ways of justifying and explaining and resolving even the most dreadful events in their lives as couples.

One woman in her late twenties, María, described to me a conversation she had with her husband before he died from the virus. "And I told him, 'You know what, you need to be honest. I am not blaming you. I don't hate you. I don't bear a grudge.' Because I am partly to blame for letting him [have sex with me and not use a condom]." María's abject resignation—"What good does it do to blame him?"—was grounded in the belief that "to talk about AIDS is to talk about death." While María's husband was working up north in Sinaloa for a couple of years, their daughter wrote a paper for school on AIDS. The pamphlet her daughter used to learn about the virus described people very different than María. She could not see herself among those classified as "promiscuous, prostitutes, or homosexuals." These labels did not apply to her in the least. They were the ones who needed to use a condom, not her. So when her husband balked at putting one on after his two-year absence, she felt a little silly insisting he do so.

Every one of the women and men in couples I met at the state-run AIDS clinic in Oaxaca told me that, first, the man had become infected and, then, he had infected the woman without knowing he was already carrying the virus. As there was nothing that could be done to reverse this fact, the women's attention usually turned to finding ways to cope with the illness rather than dwelling on what they saw as pointless recrimination. Coping with the social and physical ostracism of family members and neighbors who were frightened by the couple's HIV status was often a consuming problem they faced. Some women had been pleasantly surprised that their own families and their in-laws had been more generous and supportive than they initially expected, though many had their worst fears realized time and again. Josefina, a widow in her mid-twenties, confided that she had no income after her husband died and therefore she and their two small children had to continue to live with her in-laws. Her mother-in-law tormented Josefina and blamed her for having infected and killed the son. When Josefina began crying, during our talk at the COESIDA clinic, I reached into my backpack for a small roll of toilet paper and offered some to Josefina. "They are just waiting for me to die," she sobbed as she accepted a tissue.

Josefina and María both attended a special group meeting of women with HIV at COESIDA. There were particular experiences shared by women, they explained to me, that could best be addressed only in a gender-segregated discussion session. Men's presence tended to stifle the women for various reasons, including because of the rancorous disputes that had regularly erupted between homosexual and heterosexual men on the few occasions that male-only clinic discussion groups had been convened.

As a result of the women's willingness to forgive their husbands, living and departed—"He just didn't know what he had or that he could infect me"—my own prejudices were repeatedly challenged. Whereas I could only imagine the rage with which I would have reacted to the news that my spouse had infected me and that I would probably die from the virus, these HIV+ widows and wives dared me to look at their problem in a different, less individualistic manner. At first I attributed their generosity toward their husbands to naïve fatalism with a dash of self-sacrificing resignation. Yet where does fatalism leave off and love begin? And where does one draw the boundaries of acceptable love?[9]

From these women I learned about the perils of transferring responsibility to their men, who were hardly the most culpable parties in a social pandemic. Mexican men in the prime of their lives—and of their productive capacities—were forced to leave their homeland to seek their fortunes in the United States; Mexican men who became poisoned there by the AIDS virus and were no longer able to work returned to their erstwhile homes in Oaxaca to seek care from their womenfolk, and, in the majority of cases, to die in wretched misery. Although no woman sought to link these issues of international migratory circuits that drove so many of their husbands away to the North to seek work so they could support their families back home in Oaxaca, they were loath to castigate their men, whose biggest sin had proven to be an inability to cope with the loneliness of long-term separation from their loved ones back home.

If most of the HIV+ women I talked with did not explicitly blame their husbands, I came to believe, this was not necessarily wrong or because they were so thoroughly deceived. On a deeper level, there was inherent in their forgiveness a critique of the analysis that holds individuals primarily responsible for AIDS.

From these women I learned about love and generosity in our late-modern times.

Notes

CHAPTER ONE. TAMING MEN'S NATURAL DESIRES IN OAXACA

1. For a dazzling treatise on the male body, sexuality, and the relation of women to all this, see Bordo (1999).

2. Among the classic studies in this genre is Chodorow (1978). See also Chodorow (1994, 1999) for further theoretical development of a psychoanalytic analysis of the relationship between gender and sexuality.

3. See Gutmann (1997, 2006 [1996]). In a broad sense, then, this study also seeks to contribute to new anthropological agendas in demography, family systems, parenthood, fertility, and social reproduction (see Kertzer and Fricke 1997).

4. On reproduction and the global order, see especially Ginsburg and Rapp (1995); Browner and Sargent (1996); and Adams and Pigg (2005). See also the prolegomenon on "the mindful body" by Scheper-Hughes and Lock (1987).

5. But see Inhorn's subsequent work (2002, 2003, 2004), including its most

laudable emphasis on the impact of male infertility ("weak worms") on perceptions of masculinity in Egypt and Lebanon, on women married to infertile men, and on marital problems. It is far less clear why authors of a recent textbook on "gender and anthropology" (Mascia-Lees and Black 2000) found virtually nothing to say about men and masculinities. As I argue throughout the present study, if we are to understand not only issues of gender, in their fullest sense, but also fundamental questions of engendered power inequalities, we should stop using the term "gender" when we just mean "women."

6. Rayna Rapp writes that "problematic reproduction [for example, resulting from infertility] has played an increasingly important role" in studies of reproduction generally (2001:469).

7. INEGI 2003: "Promedio de escolaridad de la población de 15 años y más por entidad federativa según sexo, 2000."

8. INEGI 2003: "Esperanza de vida por entidad federativa según sexo, 2001."

9. INEGI 2003: "Ingreso mediano por hora trabajada de la población ocupada por entidad federativa y sexo, 2001." Also of note, average hourly wages for women in Oaxaca that year were 11.3 pesos, and for men only 9.1 pesos, though to be sure fewer women than men worked for wages.

10. I lived in Oaxaca for a full year in 2001–02, and then returned during the summers of 2003, 2004, and 2005.

11. In response to a glum e-mail from me at this time, in which I complained about the research not going as I had hoped, Stanley Brandes responded: "Loosen up! Look around! Do what you really want to do! You will eventually get back to your planned project, but indirectly and in a more interesting way, perhaps." My thanks to him again for this refreshing message.

12. See also González-López (2005:72, 229), who expresses shock and dismay that my male friends and neighbors in Mexico City did not confess to me their experiences with prostitutes. As a result of my research in Oaxaca, I became more inclined than ever to conclude that there may be regional differences within Mexico on this score.

13. At first I was confused about why my nickname was the feminine version of fox, zorra, as opposed to the masculine zorro. The use of zorra for males and females appears to be a matter of dialect and marks the speaker as being from the working class. That is, the men from the Garden all told me that the term zorro did not exist (except in the movies), whereas my anthropologist friends, also from Oaxaca, informed me that they do use zorro as well as zorra.

14. Technically, a "dialect" is a variant on a language that is intelligible to other speakers of the language. As such, to call a language a dialect is, in effect, to disparage its significance as an independent form of communication. Nonetheless, throughout Mexico the term dialecto is commonly used by non-

anthropologists, including native speakers of these languages/*dialectos*, to refer to indigenous languages.

15. See, e.g., Murphy and Stepik (1991); Higgins and Coen (2000).

16. For recent debates on the effect of remittances to Oaxaca and other parts of rural Mexico, see Binford (2003); Cohen, Jones, and Conway (2005); and Van-Wey, Tucker, and McConnell (2005).

17. Reflecting the impact of the spread of new clinics in rural areas of Mexico in the late 1980s and early 1990s, Behar quotes her friend Esperanza exclaiming, "Now we're in heaven, as they say, because we have the medical center" (1993:67). For an overview on the changes in health care in Mexico beginning in the 1990s, see Bronfman and Castro (1999); Gómez-Dantés (2000); and Chant with Craske (2003: chapter 5).

18. On privatization, decentralization, and neoliberal health reforms in general, see Birn (1999); and Homedes and Ugalde (2005a, 2005b). For a paper on decentralization of maternal health policy in Mexico, see Mills (2006).

19. Cited in Foster (2003:498).

20. See also Scheper-Hughes (1997) for a critique of research that claims to combine mixed methodologies.

CHAPTER TWO. THE MISSING GAMETE

Chapter subtitle: Apologies and thanks to Eduardo Galeano (1982) for cribbing the subtitle of his essay "Literatura y cultura popular en América Latina: Diez errores o mentiras frecuentes."

1. See Beauvoir (1970 [1949]:29). And, of course, she went on to argue that such biological facts "are insufficient for setting up a hierarchy of the sexes; they fail to explain why woman is the Other; they do not condemn her to remain in this subordinate role forever" (29).

2. See, e.g., Anne Fausto-Sterling's *Sexing the Body* (2000).

3. On the relation of feminism to masculinity studies, see the fine collection by Gardiner (2002).

4. I do not count advice columns in "men's magazines" as a scholarly venue.

5. See also Connell (1987, 1995); and Scheper-Hughes (1994a, 1994b).

6. To be sure, in the present discussion of men's sexuality and reproduction, the case of the *hijras* may be inherently problematic, because *hijras* not only do not define themselves as heterosexual but they see themselves as neither men nor women. Nonetheless, of those who were born male, some undergo castration, and it is this process, discussed by Nanda and others, like Cohen (1995), in relation to sexuality, sexual desire, and sexual pleasure, that is relevant here. See also

Higgins and Coen (2000) on similar issues raised by transvestite prostitutes in Oaxaca.

7.   Freud (1962 [1905]), of course, coined the term "polymorphously perverse disposition" to reveal, among other things, that human sexuality does not begin with puberty, but can be found throughout infantile experience as well.

8.   See also Greenhalgh's (1990, 1996) discussion of population studies.

9.   In addition to Ginsburg and Rapp (1995), see especially Browner (2000); Browner and Sargent (1996); and Clarke (1998).

10.   For extensive bibliographies regarding studies of fatherhood in the social sciences, see Townsend (2002); and Marsiglio and Pleck (2005).

11.   And if we cannot treat heterosexuality as a singular entity, what of heteronormativity? Can we speak of heteronormativit*ies*?

12.   Carrillo's (2002) study is unusual because he deftly explores sexuality among men and women, straights and gays, in Guadalajara, Mexico, in the time of AIDS. In my own work, I have possibly too often focused on men, though I have always tried to incorporate as central to the study of masculinities the ideas and experiences of women in their relationships with men. See, e.g., Gutmann (1997, 2003a, 2004, 2006 [1996]).

13.   The activities of men in certain tribal societies during their wives' pregnancies and the births of their children—known in the anthropological literature as "couvade"—has received periodic and limited attention; see, e.g., Munroe, Munroe, and Whiting (1973); and Paige and Paige (1981).

14.   On anthropological studies of infertility more generally, see also Inhorn and Van Balen (2002). For the best anthropological demography collection to date on men and fertility, see Bledsoe, Lerner, and Guyer (2000).

15.   Another possible exception is the circumcision literature. See, e.g., the discussion of circumcision in Bloch (1986); Heald (1999); and Bilu (2000).

16.   For an overview of studies of masculinity in Latin America, see Valdés and Olavarría (1997, 1998); and Gutmann and Viveros (2005). Within the rich literature on homosexuals and men who have sex with men (MSMs) in Latin America (including Latinos in the United States), see Alonso and Koreck (1999); Carrier (1995); Carrillo (1999, 2002, 2003a, 2003b); Green (2000); Higgins and Coen (2000); Kulick (1998); Lancaster (1992, 1998); Núñez Noriega (1994, 2001); Parker (1999, 2003); Parker and Cáceres (1999); and Prieur (1998). Scholars who have focused more on heterosexual men and reproduction in this region are almost all themselves from Latin America; see especially Amuchástegui (2001); Figueroa (1998a, 1998b, 1998c, 2003); Fuller (2001); García and de Oliveira (2004, 2005); Leal (1995, 1998); Lerner (1998); Minello (2002); Olavarría (2002); Olavarría and Moletto (2002); Olavarría and Parrini (2000); Szasz (1998a, 1998b); Szasz and Lerner (1998); and Viveros (1998a, 1998b, 2002).

17. And when it is—a condition known as priapism—this is cause for immediate medical attention.

18. It would be interesting to know if men's depictions and rationalizations of their presence at strip clubs would be different when reported to other men, or even to women who were not themselves strippers, like Frank, including with respect to feelings of control over women.

19. Though, as Laqueur (1990) has famously shown, for a long time in Europe it was believed that in order to conceive, women too had to have orgasms.

20. For a pioneering collection on the anthropology of contraception, see Russell, Sobo, and Thompson (2000).

21. Regarding research for a male hormone pill, see Oudshoorn (1994, 2003, 2004). At this juncture, some researchers have concluded that the development of male contraception that does not simultaneously help prevent sexually transmitted infections (STIs) would be irresponsible. On the science and politics of male reproduction, see also Daniels (2006).

22. For more on research regarding male contraception, see Marsiglio (1998:75–85).

23. And on the "erosion" of machismo in Mexico, see Barbieri (1990).

24. See Marston (2004) on "gendered communication" and sex education among youth in Mexico. For a paper reporting on hands-on experience involving men in reproductive health in the United States, see Armstrong et al. (1999).

25. For a recent collection critiquing evolutionary psychology models of rape, see Travis (2003); and especially articles by Kimmel (2003) and Martin (2003). For a discussion of the Darwinian origins of modern thinking about men's sexual nature, see Lancaster (2003:86–90).

26. The work of Jennifer Hirsch (2003) begins to chart new directions in this respect.

27. Though see Hirsch and Wardlow (2006).

28. For exceptions, see Hart (1994) and Brennan (2004).

CHAPTER THREE. NEW LABYRINTHS OF SOLITUDE

1. For an anthropological analysis of the global roots of AIDS, see especially Parker (2000, 2001, 2002); and Schoeph (2001). For public health studies on AIDS and Mexican migrants, see especially Sepulveda (1992); Bronfman and Minello (1995); Bronfman et al. (1995); Bronfman et al. (2002); and Bronfman, Leyva, and Negroni (2004). For case studies of AIDS in Mexico, see Wilson (1995); and Carrillo (2002). For an excellent biography of a "transmigrant" from Oaxaca to the United States, see Besserer (1999).

2. COESIDA Oaxaca (Consejo Estatal para la Prevención y Control del

SIDA) was part of the national AIDS program known until 2001 as CONASIDA (Comisión Nacional para la Prevención y Control del SIDA) and since then called CENSIDA (Consejo Estatal para la Prevención y Control del SIDA). In chapter 4, I discuss AIDS care in Oaxaca, including at COESIDA.

3. Since 1996, this situation has improved with the work of researchers like Carrillo (2002), Hirsch (2003), and González-López (2005), but still far too little is known about the sex lives of Mexican migrant men and the transmission of HIV.

4. For a recent study of prostitute women in Tijuana, see Castillo and Delgado (1999).

5. Another widow acknowledged to me in an interview at the AIDS clinic that although she still had her own sexual *necesidades* (needs), in her present circumstances she had to try to deny them.

6. "Men do it out of loneliness," one man told González-López (2005) about sex with other men. In this pioneering study of Mexican migrants' sexualities, one of González-López's chief conclusions is that linear analyses of sexual practices "before" and "after" migration are to be avoided, among other things, because they are premised on static notions of change in Mexico itself.

7. In a similar fashion, health researchers in the United States frequently make uninformed allegations about life on the other side of the border, in Mexico (see Gutmann 1999, 2004). For an excellent recent collection on gender and U.S. immigration, see Hondagneu-Sotelo (2003).

8. Filemon was confused on this point. There is no state of Toluca; it is a city in the state of Mexico.

9. Although by law no one may be tested for his HIV status, the Mexican Army routinely takes the blood of new recruits and expels them from the service if they are found to be positive for HIV.

10. The main identified vectors for transmission of HIV are infected hypodermic needles, blood transfusions, mother's milk, semen and vaginal fluids, and in vitro transmission through a mother's blood.

CHAPTER FOUR. FRISKY AND RISKY MEN

Heading with apologies to Charles Mingus for his "Wednesday Night Prayer Meeting." This chapter has benefited from comments of Gareth Jones.

1. In this case, one of the man's sons dropped by the clinic two weeks after the decision to inform the pharmacy workers that there was no longer any need to provide his father with any medications, even to make his remaining time more tolerable; the man had decided to die and wished to be left alone to go as quickly as possible. The son did not want them using scarce funds on his father any longer.

2. This situation is hardly unique. Kidder, for example, reports a similar frustration on the part of doctors trying to cope with an outbreak of multidrug-resistant tuberculosis (MDR-TB) in Russia's prisons: "So most of these one hundred thousand inmates will probably die without ever knowing whether they have MDR-TB or not" (2004:161).

3. For a study of bisexuality and AIDS in Mexico, see Liguori, González, and Aggleton (1996).

4. Stigma and discrimination related to HIV/AIDS in Mexico, as elsewhere, continue to be an enormous factor in prevention and treatment efforts, at local as well as federal levels.

5. Writing about an Alcoholics Anonymous group in Mexico City (where "a hyper-masculine atmosphere prevails"), Stanley Brandes recounts the story of one man who "even boasted in private to me that he has had sex with fourteen men, specifying at the same time that it was he who was always the partner to penetrate" (2002:127).

6. On the uses and abuses of the term *culture* in AIDS care, see especially Farmer 1992, 1994, 2003. The literature on AIDS in Africa and on *traileros* in Central America is rife with references to (or innuendo regarding) promiscuity and excessive and dirty sex (see, e.g., Campbell 1997; Bronfman 1998; Bronfman, Leyva, and Negroni 2004).

7. On the limits of educational campaigns in AIDS prevention, see Patton (1996).

8. *Mampu* (*mampo* in other parts of the Isthmus) does not translate perfectly as "sissy," but this is a decent approximation. It is a very derogatory way of referring to men who have sex with other men. Thanks to Manny Campbell for clarification of this word. My friends Melania and Modesta, who are also from the Isthmus of Tehuantepec, and who, unlike Cubano, speak fluent Zapoteco, insist that *muxe'* does not come from *mujer* (woman) or mean *puto* (faggot); according to them, the word is similar in usage to *cobarde* (coward) and *gallina* (chicken), and therefore women too can be *muxe'*.

9. In addition to Miano (2002), for questions of gender and sexuality in the Isthmus, see especially Chiñas (1983) and Campbell (2001). On gender and health in Mexico, see also Finkler (1994a).

10. Section heading with apologies to Michel Foucault (1963 [1994]).

11. On the shadow state, see Nugent (1999). I borrow the term from Nugent, though I am using it in a somewhat different way. The similarity is to call attention to a parallel governing structure behind the scenes; the difference is that the shadow state in early-twentieth-century Peru that Nugent examines was illegal, whereas it is not clear whether the United States could be juridically charged with illegal actions with respect to Mexicans becoming infected with the AIDS virus and then being denied medical treatment.

12.   What had once been a thriving pharmaceutical industry in Mexico, albeit one with strong ties to the research and development arms of companies in the United States, Germany, and Switzerland, was by 2005, for all intents and purposes, nonexistent. See Gereffi (1983) for the earlier history; see the pamphlet by Rivas and Molina (n.d.) on contemporary pharmaceutical politics and AIDS in Brazil and Mexico; and Petryna, Lakoff, and Kleinman (2006) on the anthropology of global pharmaceuticals.

13.   On recent discussions regarding remittances, see Binford (2003) and Cohen, Jones, and Conway (2005).

14.   The issue of U.S. culpability is pressing, including the reasons why the course of AIDS may be more accelerated for these migrants. As a state AIDS official in Oaxaca remarked in 2002, with respect to the trajectory that Oaxacans more typically faced with the disease: "If you see the statistics, they have a short second stage. Between infection and death, it can be two years, maybe three or four. It is far from the famous 10 years that is the average in the U.S." (cited in d'Adesky 2002:6).

CHAPTER FIVE. PLANNING MEN OUT OF FAMILY PLANNING

1.   Though see Greene and Biddlecom (2000); Bledsoe, Lerner, and Guyer (2000); and Dudgeon and Inhorn (2003, 2004).

2.   Although at one time Mexico was the leading producer of steroids used in birth control pills, with exports to over twenty countries (McCoy 1974:386), by the 1990s the national drug industry in Mexico was almost nonexistent and foreign pharmaceutical companies dominated the markets of drugs available from private pharmacists and government physicians in Mexico. (On the history of the pharmaceutical industry in Mexico through the early 1980s, see Gereffi 1983.) In addition, and regardless of the state of the Mexican pharmaceutical industry, by the 1990s most large international pharmaceuticals had withdrawn from contraceptive research (Ford Foundation 1991:5).

3.   See, for example, *Our Bodies, Ourselves,* first published in 1973 by the Boston Women's Health Book Collective. English-language versions of this text were passed around among feminist activists and scholars in Mexico in the 1970s.

4.   One Mexican researcher, Juan Guillermo Figueroa, has argued for men's reproductive health rights (see Figueroa 1998b). Figueroa's work in turn reflects some of the productive tensions evident in "men's studies" in Mexico since the inception, in the early 1990s, of the Laboratorio de la Masculinidad by scholar-activists such as Daniel Cazés and Francisco Cervantes. Cervantes went on to found CORIAC, a group that works to prevent male violence against women.

Others in Mexico who participated, to one degree or another, in early scholarly and activist efforts regarding men, men's health, and men's sexuality include Ana Amuchástegui, Benno de Keijzer, Brígida García, Susana Lerner, Eduardo Liendro, Ana Luisa Liguori, Nelson Minello, Guillermo Núñez, Orlandina de Oliveira, Irma Saucedo, Claudio Stern, and Ivonne Szasz. For emblematic feminist statements on global reproductive and sexual rights, see Corrêa and Petchesky (1994); Petchesky and Judd (1998); and Petchesky (1999).

5.   The birth rate is defined as the ratio of total live births to total population in a specified community or area over a specified period of time. The birth rate is often expressed as the number of live births per 1,000 of the population per year.

6.   General features and key highlights in the history of family planning in Mexico are described in McCoy (1974); Mora Bravo (1984); Alba and Potter (1986); Zavala de Cosío (1992); Cabrera (1994); Brambila (1998); González (1999); Pérez Vázquez (1999); and Palma and Rivera (2000). So as not to clutter the text, I specifically cite only quotes and points about which there may exist no general consensus.

7.   Among those ignored were, especially, the Centro de Estudios Económicos y Demográficos (CEED, later the Centro de Estudios Demográficos y de Desarrollo Urbano), at the Colegio de México, and such private organizations as the Asociación para el Bienestar de la Familia; the Asociación Pro-Salud Maternal; and the Fundación para Estudios de Población, which in 1965 became the Fundación Mexicana para la Planeación Familiar (Mexfam). The CEED was created in 1964 with funds from the Ford and Rockefeller foundations.

8.   These included the International Planned Parenthood Federation (IPPF), the Ford Foundation, the Population Council, and the United Nations Population Fund (UNFPA).

9.   "Toda persona tiene derecho a decidir de manera libre, responsable e informada sobre el número y espaciamiento de sus hijos" (http://info4.juridi cas.unam.mx/ijure/fed/9/5.htm?s%20=, accessed 13 January 2005). The translation "their children" is from the Spanish "sus hijos." Normally this phrase is rendered "his or her children." Nonetheless, because there is no gendered connotation in the Spanish, and despite the singular–plural incongruence, I believe this translation is closer in meaning to the original.

10.   On the classic case of sterilization in Puerto Rico, see Briggs (2002:142–61) and Lopez (1998).

11.   My thanks to Ana Luisa Liguori for sharing this paper with me.

12.   Brambila (1998:174) exaggerates Mexican exceptionalism with respect to the Catholic church tacitly giving its blessings to parishioners using contraception. He notes the separation of church and state and the muzzling of priests in Mexico as major contributing factors leading to a decline in population growth in Mexico. Yet other Latin American countries also saw dramatic rises in contracep-

tive prevalence and drops in fertility, indicating that these were not explanatory factors in Mexico alone. For a recent reconsideration of Catholic church values and sexuality, see Mejía (2001).

13.   Often translated as Secretary of the Interior, this post represents the second most powerful national political office in Mexico.

14.   See also McNamara's (1984) later (though hardly updated) statement on "the population problem."

15.   Comprehensive histories of the reproductive health sciences may be found in Symonds and Carder (1973); Clarke (1998); and Rapp (2001). Amuchástegui (2001) writes on the effect of scientific knowledge on sex experiences and on the history of sexuality in Mexico.

16.   For a general essay on men's involvement in family planning, from a leader in the field, see Helzner (1996).

17.   Sometimes mockingly known as the Imposible Solicitar Servicio Solo Tramitamos Entierros (Impossible to Get Service We Only Process the Buried).

18.   On the history of Mexfam and its precursor, the Fundación para Estudios de Población, see Pérez Vásquez (1999).

19.   This point has also been made to me repeatedly by feminist activists from organizations helping battered women in Mexico City and Oaxaca.

20.   See González Montes (1999) and Bliss (2003b) on the history of NGOs and reproductive health generally in Mexico.

21.   With reference to male sterilizations, in an undated book on "fertilization and contraception" that I estimate was published sometime in the 1950s, the author, one "Dr. Frey," concludes: "But it is unusual that men voluntarily agree to this kind of operation, that is actually innocuous and simple, except in a few cases of men condescending to women who are fearful of getting sterilized, or in special situations in which men fear they might produce physically defective children, and with selfish men who want love without inconveniences and who consider children inconvenient" (see Frey, n.d.:146).

22.   The most recent reliable surveys conducted by the official Mexican government agencies (e.g., INEGI and Conapo) charged with gathering demographic information regarding contraceptive use are from 1997.

23.   Although I occasionally heard of youth who engaged in anal intercourse as a form of birth control, I never heard from youth about this practice, nor did anyone mention it as a method they had practiced. On the contrary, when I asked men and women about anal intercourse, I was told repeatedly that they had never had this kind of sexual relation.

CHAPTER SIX. SCORING MEN

This chapter has benefited especially from comments made early in the research by colleagues at the Colegio de México seminar on men's reproductive health, and especially Ana Amuchástegui, Juan Guillermo Figueroa, and Ivonne Szasz, as well as from later reviewers' comments on a paper published as Gutmann (2005).

1. See chapter 1 (17–18) for a description of the clinics where I interviewed men who were getting vasectomies.

2. Following his wife's tubal ligation, I saw a man taking photographs of her as she left the operating room, although I am not sure she would have wanted a permanent record of herself in such a disheveled state. I was often struck by how easy it was for me to have access to both male and female sterilization procedures. I always asked the men's and women's permission, but undoubtedly there were elements of class privilege at play in all these situations, since working-class people more quickly acquiesced to my requests than was the case with those from more well-to-do strata.

3. The work of Mara Viveros (2002) on Colombia is of inestimable importance in the study of vasectomy and men's reproductive health generally in Latin America.

4. Country figures on sterilization are from EngenderHealth (2002). Although the actual numbers of people who have been sterilized are undoubtedly somewhat different, these figures provide the essential portrait indicating that women vastly outnumber men in this regard.

5. On broader attempts to introduce men into studies of men and reproductive health, see also Dudgeon and Inhorn (2003) and Russell and Thompson (2000). Of the three key areas of demography—fertility, mortality, and migration—the latter two have always included men and women in significant ways. As for the former, until recently some scholars have remained reasonably puzzled as to whether we can even measure male fertility. See Townsend's (2000) ideas toward solving this riddle.

6. Interestingly, one doctor claimed that he knew of only one male doctor who performed the surgery who had himself had a vasectomy.

7. See Gutmann (2003a). On youth and sexuality, see also Cáceres (1998); Gutmann (2003b); Cabral Soto et al. (2000).

8. Stanley Brandes writes of masturbation as it is discussed by men in an Alcoholics Anonymous group in Mexico City, including as part of the pursuit of pleasure as "a necessary quality for any fully developed male" (2002:124).

9. See also the discussion of contraception and modernity in Russell and Thompson (2000). It is perhaps indicative of the lack of attention to men and con-

traception by the leading practitioners of "men and masculinities studies" that in a recent sampling of the indexes of collected volumes in English on men and masculinities, only Whitehead and Barrett (2001) included several entries under "birth control" and "contraception." Kimmel, Hearn, and Connell (2005) had one entry; and the others volumes consulted—Adams and Savran (2002), Brod and Kaufman (1994), and Gardiner (2002)—had none.

10.   See Markens, Browner, and Preloran (2003) for a study on how Latino couples in the Los Angeles area seek to share parenting responsibilities while maintaining a woman's ultimate control over her body and decisions associated with it.

11.   Hirsch (2003) points out that Mexican women routinely receive better overall reproductive health care in Mexico than in the United States.

12.   This point is also made in earlier studies, such as Castro Morales's (1998) sensitive examination of negotiations within couples regarding sterilization. On vasectomies in Mexico, see also Givaudan, Pick, and Fuertes (1999).

13.   In the same vein, Olavarría (2002:17) notes various expressions used in Chile to link the penis with untamed male sexuality: *el caballo encabritado* (the rearing stallion), *el niño travieso* (the naughty boy), and *el otro que tiene hambre* (the other, hungry one).

14.   Sapolsky (1997) argues that testosterone levels predict nothing about male aggression, and that more often than not behavioral differences in violence drive hormonal changes and not the other way around.

15.   See Dudgeon and Inhorn (2003, 2004); Parker (1999).

16.   See, e.g., de Keijzer (2001); Figueroa (1998a); Higgins and Coen (2000); Lamas (1996); Lancaster (1992); and Núñez (1994, 2001).

17.   For a paper on the spread of information about reproductive health through mass communication in Mexico, see Camarena Córdova (2001).

CHAPTER SEVEN. TRADITIONAL SEXUAL HEALING OF MEN

With apologies to Marvin Gaye for the chapter title and to two generous colleagues who suggested I move this chapter to earlier in the book. I have reluctantly resisted this advice because it seemed a too traditional-to-modern ordering of understanding. Thus, in an effort to tweak convention, I present the "traditional" healing not as precursor to modern forms of diagnosis and treatment, but in a more post-traditional framework that seeks to emphasize the simultaneity of these varied medical systems and practitioners in the early 2000s.

1.   See my discussion of the harmful effects of conceptual dichotomization on gender studies in Latin America in Gutmann (2003a). In light of the nondi-

chotomous gender framework among indigenous healers in Oaxaca, it is interesting to consider the generalization offered by Emily Martin that the "attempt to
ground differences between the genders in biology grew out of the crumbling of
old ideas about the existing order of politics and society as laid down by the order
of nature" (1987:33). Could nature itself be more diverse than that found simply
in Europe? See also Laqueur (1990).

2.   It is instructive to compare the emphasis on couples with recent work on
the couvade, the institution of birth observance involving prenatal dietary and activity restrictions. Often described as a male response to female pregnancy and
childbirth—and a way for men to feel that they, too, are participating in a more
corporal fashion in the proceedings—Rival, in particular, notes that "the couvade
is not a male rite but a rite of a couple" (1998:622–23). That is, with the couvade,
men's participation in dietary restrictions and such represents as much the couple
as a couple physically joined together subsequent to coitus in order to give birth
to a child.

3.   I generally avoid the word *traditional*—for example, in expressions like
"traditional gender roles"—because it means so many different things to different people and can erroneously imply that some cultural features are timeless.
The expression *medicina tradicional,* in contrast to *medicina moderna* or *alopática,* is
commonly employed in Oaxaca, however, and therefore I am happy to adopt that
term here.

4.   Lomnitz (2001:141, 301 n. 21) extends the notion of contact zones, coined
by Mary Louise Pratt (1992), to refer to transnational spaces of national identity
formation. Stephen's (2005) work on questions of community and transnational-
ism among Oaxacan migrants also illustrates the special porosity of ethnicity. Far
from disappearing, with migration to cities and across international borders, ethnic identities among Oaxacans are rearticulated. In some ways, this process is
analogous to what Oscar Lewis (1952) documented in a famous paper many
decades ago: among rural migrants to Mexico City there existed "urbanization
without breakdown," as family and religious ties proved to be of enduring and
newfound significance.

5.   INI was the National Indigenous Institute. CDI stands for the National
Commission for the Development of the Indian Peoples; *pueblos* has a double
meaning in Spanish, and in addition to meaning "peoples" can also refer to "villages." With respect to traditional midwifery and healing in Oaxaca, in addition
to Nacho Bernal I also benefited from discussions with Paola Sesia and Alejandro
de Ávila.

6.   Consejo Estatal de Médicos Indígenas Tradicionales de Oaxaca. On indigenous organizations in Oaxaca generally, see Hernández-Díaz (2001).

7.   According to Steffan Igor Ayora Diaz and Gabriela Vargas Cetina (personal communication), what had occurred in Chiapas was that, among various
competing indigenous groups of healers, the ethnobotanist and his collaborators

had worked well with some and had fallen out of favor with others. For more on bioprospecting and this specific controversy, see Hayden (2006), Greene (2004), Nigh (2002), and Rosenthal (2006). For more on indigenous doctors in Chiapas, see Ayora Diaz (2002).

8.   In fifteen years of ethnographic fieldwork in Mexico, I had never paid anyone for an interview before the summer of 2004. Although the practice of paying interviewees (or "informants," in some methodological lingos) is common in certain allied academic disciplines, it is not common practice in anthropology. Indeed, it runs against the grain of establishing ethnographic friendships and rapport. Nevertheless, after most of my conversations with traditional doctors that summer, I gave a donation, usually 100 to 200 pesos (approximately $10 to $20 U.S. at the time), and I expressed the wish that I wanted to contribute to the curing and caring efforts of the people I interviewed, to support their travel to distant and remote villages, and to buy plants and towels and lamps and other materials they used in their healing. It seemed like the right thing to do.

9.   For different views on indigenous autonomy, see Bartra (1999); Bartolomé and Barabas (1998); and Barabas (2003).

10.   Development Center for Traditional Indigenous Medicine, Chocho-Mixteco.

11.   On the use of the term *dialectos,* see chapter 1, note 14.

12.   The Organización "Xee Tatnaa" was chronically in need of cash, although it had received a gift from Médicos Sin Fronteras (Doctors without Borders) for some basic cooking supplies.

13.   For earlier work on medicinal plants and reproductive health in Oaxaca, see Browner (1985a, 1985b, 1991); and Browner and Perdue (1988).

14.   *Brujo* is often translated as "witch," but given the pejorative connotation of this term for most English-speaking people, it lacks the subtlety of the Spanish original. "Medicine man" (or woman) rings closer to how many of my friends at the garden used the terms *brujo* and *bruja,* though to be sure, sometimes the terms are used in a similarly disparaging way. Indeed, while I was looking around for the traditional healers' clinic in the town of Valle Nacional, a boy of around twelve years old responded to my request for directions, "¿De los brujos?"

15.   The double meaning of "come" here is present in the Spanish as well: "a fuerza tiene que venir con ella."

16.   See note 14 on the term *brujo.* Another reason for the nickname no doubt relates to the fact that Claudio as well as Virgilio and Martina are Jehovah's Witnesses; healing for them must be achieved in the context of God's will as expressed through their reading of the Bible. At the garden, Poncho once asked me what I was learning about the role of the saints in traditional healing methods. He

then commented disparagingly about Claudio, "We are Catholics. We pray to saints, not like Bruja." Claudio tried to convert me on several occasions, including when we went to services at his church near his house. I never saw him try to convert other men at the garden.

17.   For a remarkable ethnography on male infertility, see also Castañeda's (2005) doctoral thesis, "Hipooligoastenoteratozoopermia: Representaciones y prácticas de médicos y parejas pacientes en torno a la infertilidad masculina."

18.   In a subsequent interview, in July 2004, Doña Hermila gave the number of men who are in attendance when their wives give birth as only 20 percent, and she suggested that many men do not like the sight of blood.

19.   See Jennifer Hirsch's (2003:259–63) discussion of generational differences regarding the significance of the withdrawal method (coitus interruptus) among Mexicans in Jalisco and Georgia. On coitus interruptus, in general, and other cultural contexts, see also Santow (1993) and Schneider and Schneider (1996).

20.   In addition to Brigitte Jordan's (1993 [1978]) classic cross-cultural study of childbirth, several decades earlier, also in Yucatán, Robert Redfield and Alfonso Rojas noted, "At the time of delivery the mother is secluded from everyone except the midwife and her husband. It is regarded as positively advisable that the father of the child should remain and assist" (1971 [1934]:181). Vogt reported that in Zinacantan, Chiapas, in the 1960s, "A woman's husband should assist at the birth, and she may also be aided by her husband's mother, father, sisters, and brothers. The woman kneels on a petate [straw mat] on the floor, while her husband stands behind her pulling her sash tight. One of the other male relatives sits on a chair facing her, seizing her by the shoulders to support her during each labor pain" (1969:181).

21.   For background on medical pluralism and reviews of indigenous healing in Latin America, see Aguirre Beltrán (1963, 1986); Anzures y Bolaños (1983); Baer (2003); Birn (2005); Huber and Sandstrom (2001a); Koss-Chioino, Leatherman, and Greenway (2003); Zulawski (1999). For a pioneering historical work on men's sexuality and reproductive health among indigenous peoples in Mexico, especially among the Maya, see both the Spanish and English versions of Ruz (1998, 2000). See also Finkler (1994b).

22.   See also Sesia (1992a, 1997) on traditional medicine in Oaxaca, and Pigg (1995) on the relationship between "traditional medical practitioners," including "traditional birth attendants," and international health development training programs.

23.   For a study on "medicalizing ethnicity," albeit in a very different context, see Santiago-Irizarry's (2001) study of the construction of Latino identity in a psychiatric setting in New York City.

24.   Many terms are used to refer to rural communities, including *pueblo, agen-*

cia, ranchito, municipio, cabecera. Although there exist precise legal definitions for each of these terms, in practice many people from these communities use the terms interchangeably. Often, so as not to offend someone who may have a vested interest in whether a community is recognized as a larger or smaller entity, others will call it a simply a *población.*

    25. www.cmt.org.mx (accessed 5 February 2007).

    26. My thanks to Gloria González-López for this quip.

CHAPTER EIGHT. FROM BOARDROOMS TO BEDROOMS

    1. Not surprisingly, many male prostitutes in Oaxaca City, as well as other cities in Mexico, are indigenous youth. For a study of male prostitutes in Mexico City, see Liguori and Aggleton (1998).

    2. Nor does it make sense to argue that countries like Britain and China, with higher vasectomy rates, are inherently and in some measurable sense less "macho" than Mexico. Instead, government policies, educational campaigns, and tipping points of critical mass are the keys to understanding differential rates of male sterilization in the world.

    3. One classic exception to this absence of studies of heterosexual men and their relationship with women is Brandes (1980). Among the many insights captured in that study of "the metaphors of masculinity" in southern Spain, Brandes cites men's "basically defensive posture when describing their attitudes toward women" (76).

    4. Numerous other examples of the same pattern of foreign domination of domestic health care policies could be cited. See, for example, Morgan's (1993) thorough presentation of how the success and failure of health programs in Costa Rica depend more on international economic and political interests than on anything local communities decide.

    5. See also Browner's (1986a, 1986b) classic articles on reproduction and gender roles in a village in Oaxaca she calls San Francisco.

    6. This point is related to the discovery by Bourgois (2002) that drug addicts often report what they think epidemiologists want to hear—about not sharing infected needles, for example—one more reason that ethnographic fieldwork techniques are crucial checks on surveys that depend largely on self-reporting.

    7. My thanks to Dan Smith for referring me to Bleek's essay. Eric Wolf also succinctly wrote on this issue, in reference to criticism that the ethnographic work of Oscar Lewis in Mexico was too subjective. Wolf stated, "I would bet that no matter how hard we try to observe non-verbal behavior, the bulk of our field notes will be made up of verbal statements" (1967:495).

8.   For more on sex and the sexuality of the researcher in fieldwork, see Bell, Caplan, and Karim (1993); Kulick and Willson (1995); and Markowitz and Ashkenazi (1999).

9.   And see Segal's just complaint about the most "conspicuous absence" in all sexological writing: "its inability to theorize desire" (1994:113).

Bibliography

Acevedo, Marta. 1982. *El 10 de mayo*. Mexico City: SEP.

Adams, Rachel, and David Savran, eds. 2002. *The Masculinity Studies Reader*. Malden, MA: Blackwell.

Adams, Vincanne, and Stacy L. Pigg, eds. 2005. *Sex in Development: Science, Sexuality, and Morality in Global Perspective*. Durham, NC: Duke University Press.

Aguirre Beltrán, Gonzalo. 1963. *Medicina y magia: El proceso de aculturación en la estructura colonial*. Mexico City: Instituto Nacional Indigenista.

———. 1986. *Antropología médica*. Mexico City: CIESAS.

Alba, Francisco, and Joseph E. Potter. 1986. "Population and Development in Mexico since 1940: An Interpretation." *Population and Development Review* 12(1): 47–75.

Alonso, Ana Maria, and Maria Teresa Koreck. 1999. "Silences: 'Hispanics,' AIDS, and Sexual Practices." In *Culture, Society and Sexuality: A Reader*, edited by Richard Parker and Peter Aggleton, 267–83. London: UCL Press.

Amuchástegui, Ana. 1998. "Virginity in Mexico: The Role of Competing Discourses of Sexuality in Personal Experience." *Reproductive Health Matters* 6(12): 105–15.

———. 2001. *Virginidad e iniciación sexual en México: Experiencias y significados.* Mexico City: EDAMEX/Population Council.

Anaya Muñoz, Alejandro. 2004. "Explaining the Politics of Recognition of Ethnic Diversity and Indigenous People's Rights in Oaxaca, Mexico." *Bulletin of Latin American Research* 23(4): 414–33.

Anzures y Bolaños, María del Carmen. 1983. *La medicina tradicional en México: Proceso histórico, sincretismos y conflictos.* Mexico City: Universidad Nacional Autónoma de México.

Aristophanes. 411 B.C. [1994]. *Lysistrata.* New York: Grove.

Arizpe, Lourdes. 1990. "Forward: Democracy for a Small Two-Gender Planet." In *Women and Social Change in Latin America*, edited by Elizabeth Jelin, xiv–xx. London: Zed.

Armstrong, Bruce, Alwyn T. Cohall, Roger D. Vaughan, McColvin Scott, Lorraine Tiezzi, and James F. McCarthy. 1999. "Involving Men in Reproductive Health: The Young Men's Clinic." *American Journal of Public Health* 89(6): 902–5.

Ayala, Armida, Joseph Carrier, and J. Raul Magaña. 1996. "The Underground World of Latina Sex Workers in Cantinas." In *AIDS Crossing Borders: The Spread of HIV among Migrant Latinos*, edited by Shiraz I. Mishra, Ross F. Conner, and J. Raul Magaña, 95–112. Boulder, CO: Westview.

Ayora Diaz, Steffan Igor. 2002. *Globalización, conocimiento y poder: Médicos locales y sus luchas por el reconocimiento en Chiapas.* Mexico City: Plaza y Valdés.

Baer, Hans A. 2003. "Contributions to a Critical Analysis of Medical Pluralism: An Examination of the Work of Libbet Crandon-Malamud." In *Medical Pluralism in the Andes*, edited by Joan D. Koss-Chioino, Thomas Leatherman, and Christine Greenway, 42–60. London: Routledge.

Bandarage, Asoka. 1997. *Women, Population and Global Crisis: A Political-Economic Analysis.* London: Zed.

Barabas, Alicia. 2003. "Autonomías indígenas en México: Utopías Posibles?" In *Identidade, fragmentação na América Latina*, edited by Parry Scott and George Zarur, 67–86. Recife: Editorial Universitária da UFPE.

Barbieri, Teresita de. 1990. "Sobre géneros, prácticas y valores: Notas acerca de posibles erosiones del machismo en México." In *Normas y prácticas morales y cívicas en la vida cotidiana*, edited by Juan Manuel Ramírez Sáiz, 83–105. Mexico City: UNAM/Porrúa.

Barbosa, Regina Maria, and Tania Di Giacomo do Lago. 1997. "AIDS e direitos reprodutivos: Para além da transmissão vertical." In *Políticas, Instituições e AIDS: Enfrentando a Epidemia no Brasil*, edited by Richard Parker, 163–75. Rio de Janeiro: Jorge Zahar Editor.

Barbosa, Regina Maria, and Wilza Viera Villela. 1997. "A Trajetória Feminia da AIDS." In *Quebrando o silêncio: Mulheres e AIDS no Brasil,* edited by Richard Parker and Jane Galvão, 17–32. Rio de Janeiro: Relume-Dumará Editores.

Bartolomé, Miguel, and Alicia M. Barabas, eds. 1998. *Autonomías étnicas y estados nacionales.* Mexico City: CONACULTA, INAH.

Bartra, Roger. 1999. *La sangre y la tinta: Ensayos sobre la condición postmexicana.* Mexico City: Oceano.

Bernstein, Nina. 2006. "Recourse Grows Slim for Immigrants Who Fall Ill." *New York Times,* 3 March.

Beauvoir, Simone de. 1970 [1949]. *The Second Sex.* Translated by H. M. Parshley. New York: Bantam Books.

Behar, Ruth. 1993. *Translated Woman: Crossing the Border with Esperanza's Story.* Boston: Beacon.

Bell, Diane, Pat Caplan, and Wazir Jahan Karim, eds. 1993. *Gendered Fields: Women, Men, and Ethnography.* New York: Routledge.

Bellis, David J. 2003. *Hotel Ritz—Comparing Mexican and U.S. Street Prostitutes: Factors in HIV/AIDS Transmission.* New York: Hayworth.

Besserer, Federico. 1999. *Moisés Cruz: Historia de un transmigrante.* Culiacán Rosales, Sinaloa: Universidad Autónoma de Sinaloa / Universidad Autónoma Metropolitana–Iztapalapa.

———. 2000. "Sentimientos (in)apropriados de las mujeres migrants: Hacia una nueva ciudadanía." In *Migración y relaciones de género en México,* edited by Dalia Barrera Bassols and Cristina Oehmichen Bazán, 371–88. Mexico City: Grupo Interdisciplinario sobre Mujer, Trabajo y Pobreza and Universidad Nacional Autónoma de México.

Biehl, João. 2004. "The Activist State: Global Pharmaceuticals, AIDS, and Citizenship in Brazil." *Social Text* 22(3): 105–32.

Bilu, Yoram. 2000. "Circumcision, the First Haircut, and the Torah: Ritual and Male Identity among the Ultraorthodox Community of Israel." In *Imagined Masculinities: Male Identity and Culture in the Modern Middle East,* edited by Mai Ghoussoub and Emma Sinclair-Webb, 33–64. London: Saqi Books.

Binford, Leigh. 2003. "Migrant Remittances and (Under)Development in Mexico." *Critique of Anthropology* 23(3): 305–36.

Birn, Anne-Emanuelle. 1999. "Federalist Flirtations: The Politics and Execution of Health Services Decentralization for the Uninsured Population in Mexico, 1985–1995." *Journal of Public Health Policy* 20(1): 81–108.

———. 2005. "Healers, Healing, and Child Well-Being: Ideologies, Institutions, and Health in Latin America and the Caribbean." *Latin American Research Review* 40(2): 176–92.

Bledsoe, Caroline, Susana Lerner, and Jane I. Guyer, eds. 2000. *Fertility and the Male Life Cycle in the Era of Fertility Decline.* Oxford: Oxford University Press.

Bleek, Wolf. 1987. "Lying Informants: A Fieldwork Experience from Ghana." *Population and Development Review* 13(2): 314–22.

Bliss, Katherine. 2003a. "Clinical Trials: Paternity, Modernity, and the Politics of Family Planning in Mexico, 1935–1975." Unpublished ms.

———. 2003b. "From Syphilis to Cervical Cancer: Gender, Politics, and Reproductive Health in Mexico, 1903–Present." Unpublished ms.

Bloch, Maurice. 1986. *From Blessing to Violence: History and Ideology in the Circumcision Ritual of the Merina of Madagascar.* Cambridge: Cambridge University Press.

Bordo, Susan. 1993. *Unbearable Weight: Feminism, Western Culture, and the Body.* Berkeley: University of California Press.

———. 1999. *The Male Body.* New York: Farrar, Straus, and Giroux.

Boston Women's Health Book Collective. 1973. *Our Bodies, Ourselves.* New York: Simon and Schuster.

Bourgois, Philippe. 2002. "Anthropology and Epidemiology on Drugs: The Challenges of Cross-Methodological and Theoretical Dialogue." *International Journal of Drug Policy* 13: 259–69.

Bowles, Paul. 1937 [1995]. "Diversions and Excursions, 1937–1940." In *The Reader's Companion to Mexico,* edited by Alan Ryan, 66–78. San Diego, CA: Harcourt.

Brambila, Carlos. 1998. "Mexico's Population Policy and Demographic Dynamics: The Record of Three Decades." In *Do Population Policies Matter? Fertility and Politics in Egypt, India, Kenya, and Mexico,* edited by Anrudh Jain, 157–91. New York: Population Council.

Brandes, Stanley. 1980. *Metaphors of Masculinity: Sex and Status in Andalusian Folklore.* Philadelphia: University of Pennsylvania Press.

———. 2002. *Staying Sober in Mexico City.* Austin: University of Texas Press.

Brennan, Denise. 2004. *What's Love Got to Do with It? Transnational Desires and Sex Tourism in the Dominican Republic.* Durham, NC: Duke University Press.

Briggs, Charles L., and Clara Mantini-Briggs. 2003. *Stories in the Time of Cholera: Racial Profiling during a Medical Nightmare.* Berkeley: University of California Press.

Briggs, Laura. 2002. *Reproducing Empire: Race, Sex, Science, and U.S. Imperialism in Puerto Rico.* Berkeley: University of California Press.

Brod, Harry, and Michael Kaufman, eds. 1994. *Theorizing Masculinities.* Thousand Oaks, CA: Sage.

Bronfman, Mario. 1998. "Mexico and Central America." *International Migration* 36(4): 609–42.

Bronfman, Mario, Ana Amuchástegui, Rosa María Martina, Nelson Minello, Martha Rivas, and Gabriela Rodríguez, eds. 1995. *Sida en México: Migración, adolescencia y género.* Mexico City: Información Profesional Especializada.

Bronfman, Mario N., and Roberto Castro, eds. 1999. *Salud, cambio social y política: Perspectivas desde América Latina.* Mexico City: EDAMEX.

Bronfman, Mario, René Leyva, and Mirka Negroni. 2004. *Movilidad poblacional y VIH/SIDA: Contextos de vulnerabilidad en México y Centroamérica.* Cuernavaca, Mexico: Instituto Nacional de Salud Pública.

Bronfman, Mario N., René Leyva, Mirka J. Negroni, and Celina M. Rueda. 2002. "Mobile Populations and HIV/AIDS in Central America and Mexico: Research for Action." *AIDS* 16 (supp. 3): S42–S49.

Bronfman, Mario, and Sergio López Moreno. 1996. "Perspectives on HIV/AIDS Prevention among Immigrants on the U.S.–Mexico Border." In *AIDS Crossing Borders: The Spread of HIV among Migrant Latinos,* edited by Shiraz I. Mishra, Ross F. Conner, and J. Raul Magaña, 49–76. Boulder, CO: Westview.

Bronfman, Mario, and Nelson Minello. 1995. "Hábitos sexuales de los migrantes temporales mexicanos a los Estados Unidos de América: Prácticas de riesgo para la infección por VIH." In *Sida en México: Migración, adolescencia y género,* edited by Mario Bronfman, et al., 1–89. Mexico City: Información Profesional Especializada.

Browner, Carole H. 1985a. "Plants Used for Reproductive Health in Oaxaca, Mexico." *Economic Botany* 39(4): 482–504.

———. 1985b. "Criteria for Selecting Herbal Remedies." *Ethnology* 24(1): 13–32.

———. 1986a. "The Politics of Reproduction in a Mexican Village." *Signs* 11(4): 710–24.

———. 1986b. "Gender Roles and Social Change: A Mexican Case Study." *Ethnology* 25(2): 89–106.

———. 1991. "Gender Politics in the Distribution of Therapeutic Herbal Knowledge." *Medical Anthropology Quarterly,* n.s., 5(2): 99–132.

———. 2000. "Situating Women's Reproductive Activities." *American Anthropologist* 102(4): 773–88.

Browner, Carole H., and Sondra T. Perdue. 1988. "Women's Secrets: Bases for Reproductive and Social Autonomy in a Mexican Community." *American Ethnologist* 15(1): 84–97.

Browner, Carole H., and Carolyn F. Sargent. 1996. "Anthropology and Studies of Human Reproduction." In *Medical Anthropology: Contemporary Theory and Method,* rev. ed., edited by Carolyn F. Sargent and Thomas M. Johnson, 219–34. Westport, CT: Greenwood Press.

Cabral Soto, Javier, Ángel Flores Alvarado, Ma. Del Carmen Baltazar Rivas, Fabiola García Vargas, Ma. Concepción Orozco Meinecke, and Carlos Brambila Paz. 2000. *Salud sexual y reproductiva en jóvenes indígenas de las principales etnias de México: Hñahñú, Maya, Mixteca, Nahua, Tzeltal, Zapoteca: Enfoque sociodemográfico, antropológico y psicosocial.* Mexico City: Instituto Mexicano del Seguro Social.

Cabrera, Gustavo. 1994. "Demographic Dynamics and Development: The Role of Population Policy in Mexico." In *The New Politics of Population: Conflict and*

Consensus in Family Planning, edited by Jason L. Finkle and C. Alison McIntosh, 105–20 (a supplement to vol. 20 of *Population and Development Review*). New York: Population Council.

Cáceres, Carlos. 1998. "Jóvenes varones en Lima: Dilemas y estrategias en salud sexual." In *Masculinidades y equidad de género en América Latina,* edited by Teresa Valdés and José Olavarría, 158–74. Santiago, Chile: FLACSO/UNFPA.

Caldwell, John, and Pat Caldwell. 1986. *Limiting Population Growth and the Ford Foundation Contribution.* London: Frances Pinter.

Camarena Córdova, Rosa María. 2001. "Educación, medios de comunicación y salud reproductiva." In *Encuentros y desencuentros en la salud reproductiva: Políticas públicas, marcos normativos y actores sociales,* edited by Juan Guillermo Figueroa and Claudio Stern, 137–64. Mexico City: El Colegio de México.

Campbell, Cathy. 1997. "Migrancy, Masculine Identities, and AIDS: The Psychosocial Context of HIV Transmission on the South African Gold Mines." *Social Science & Medicine* 45(2): 273–81.

Campbell, Howard. 2001. *Mexican Memoir: A Personal Account of Anthropology and Radical Politics in Oaxaca.* Westport, CT: Bergin and Garvey.

Carrier, Joseph M. 1995. *De Los Otros: Intimacy and Homosexuality among Mexican Men.* New York: Columbia University Press.

———. 1999. "Reflections on Ethical Problems Encountered in Field Research on Mexican Male Homosexuality: 1968 to Present." *Culture, Health, and Sexuality* 1(3): 207–21.

Carrillo, Héctor. 1999. "Cultural Change, Hybridity, and Male Homosexuality in Mexico." *Culture, Health, and Sexuality* 1(3): 223–38.

———. 2002. *The Night Is Young: Sexuality in Mexico in the Time of AIDS.* Chicago: University of Chicago Press.

———. 2003a. "Another Crack in the Mirror: The Politics of AIDS Prevention in Mexico." In *Sexual and Reproductive Health Promotion in Latino Populations,* edited by M. Idalí Torres and George P. Cernada, 307–29. Amityville, NY: Baywood.

———. 2003b. "Neither *Machos* nor *Maricones:* Masculinity and Emerging Male Homosexual Identities in Mexico." In *Changing Men and Masculinities in Latin America,* edited by Matthew C. Gutmann, 351–69. Durham, NC: Duke University Press.

Castañeda Jiménez, Elena. 2005. "Hipooligoastenoteratozoopermia: Representaciones y prácticas de médicos y parejas pacientes en torno a la infertilidad masculina." Tesis de doctorado, Centro de Investigaciones y Estudios Superiores en Antropología Social, Mexico.

Castillo, Debra A., and Bonnie Delgado. 1999. "Border Lives: Prostitute Women in Tijuana." *Signs* 24(2): 387–423.

Castro, Arachu. 2004. "Contracepting at Childbirth: The Integration of Reproductive Health and Population Policies in Mexico." In *Unhealthy Health Policy: A Critical Anthropological Examination*, edited by Arachu Castro and Mer-
rill Singer, 133–44. Walnut Creek, CA: AltaMira.

Castro, Roberto. 2000. *La vida en la adversidad: El significado de la salud y la reproducción en la pobreza*. Cuernavaca: Universidad Nacional Autónoma de México, Centro Regional de Investigaciones Multidisciplinarias.

———. 2001. " 'When a Man Is with a Woman, It Feels Like Electricity': Subjectivity, Sexuality, and Contraception among Men in Central Mexico." *Culture,
Health, and Sexuality* 3(2): 149–65.

Castro Morales, Patricia. 1998. "Qué razones exponen los hombres que están re-
curriendo a la vasectomía 'sin bisturí' para limitar su fecundidad?" In
Varones, sexualidad y reproducción, edited by Susana Lerner, 341–66. Mexico
City: El Colegio de México.

Chant, Sylvia, with Nikki Craske. 2003. *Gender in Latin America*. New Brunswick,
NJ: Rutgers University Press.

Chant, Sylvia, and Matthew C. Gutmann. 2000. *Mainstreaming Men into Gender
and Development: Debates, Reflections, and Experiences*. Oxford: Oxfam.

Chavez, Leo. 1992. *Shadowed Lives: Undocumented Immigrants in American Society*.
Fort Worth, TX: Harcourt, Brace, Jovanovich.

Chiñas, Beverly. 1983. *The Isthmus Zapotecs: Women's Roles in Cultural Context*.
Prospect Heights, IL: Waveland.

Chodorow, Nancy. 1978. *The Reproduction of Mothering: Psychoanalysis and the So-
ciology of Gender*. Berkeley: University of California Press.

———. 1994. *Femininities, Masculinities, Sexualities: Freud and Beyond*. Lexington:
University of Kentucky Press.

———. 1999. *The Power of Feelings*. New Haven, CT: Yale University Press.

Clarke, Adele E. 1998. *Disciplining Reproduction: Modernity, American Life Sciences, and "The Problem of Sex."* Chicago: University of Chicago Press.

Cohen, Jeffrey, Richard Jones, and Dennis Conway. 2005. "Why Remittances
Shouldn't be Blamed for Rural Underdevelopment in Mexico: A Collective
Response to Leigh Binford." *Critique of Anthropology* 25(1): 87–96.

Cohen, Lawrence. 1995. "The Epistemological Carnival: Meditations on Disci-
plinary Intentionality and Ayurvedic Medicine." In *Knowledge and the Scholarly Medical Traditions*, edited by Don Bates, 320–43. Cambridge: Cambridge
University Press.

Connell, R. W. 1987. *Gender and Power: Society, the Person, and Sexual Politics*.
Stanford, CA: Stanford University Press.

———. 1995. *Masculinities*. Berkeley: University of California Press.

———. 1997. "Sexual Revolution." In *New Sexual Agendas*, edited by Lynne
Segal, 60–76. New York: New York University Press.

————. 2005. "Change among the Gatekeepers: Men, Masculinities, and Gender Equality in the Global Arena." *Signs* 30(3): 1801–25.

Connell, R. W., and G. W. Dowsett. 1992. " 'The Unclean Motion of the Generative Parts': Frameworks in Western Thought on Sexuality." In *Rethinking Sex: Social Theory and Sexuality Research,* edited by R. W. Connell and G. W. Dowsett, 49–75. Philadephia: Temple University Press.

Consejo Nacional de Población. 1997. *Encuesta de comunicación en planificación familiar 1996.* Mexico City: Consejo Nacional de Población.

————. 2003. "Distribución porcentual de las usuarias de métodos anticonceptivos, según tipo de método por entidad federativa, 1997." www.conapo .gob.mx/oocifras/oosalud/Republica/RM042.xls (accessed 5 February 2007).

Cornwall, Andrea A. 2003. "To Be a Man Is More Than a Day's Work: Shifting Ideals of Masculinity in Ado-Odo, Southwestern Nigeria." In *Men and Masculinities in Modern Africa,* edited by Lisa A. Lindsay and Stephan F. Miescher, 230–48. Portsmouth, NH: Heinemann.

Coronil, Fernando. 2001. "Smelling Like a Market." *American Historical Review* 106(1): 119–29.

Corrêa, Sonia. 1994. *Population and Reproductive Rights: Feminist Perspectives from the South.* London: Zed.

Corrêa, Sonia, and Rosalind P. Petchesky. 1994. "Reproductive and Sexual Rights: A Feminist Perspective." In *Population Policies Reconsidered,* edited by Gita Sen, Adrienne Germain, and Lincoln C. Chen, 107–23. Cambridge, MA: Harvard Center for Population and Development Studies.

D'Adesky, Anne-Christine. 2002. "Mexico's Rural HIV Fighters Forced to Improvise Amid Official Neglect." *American Foundation for AIDS Research* 3(6): 4–7.

Daniels, Cynthia R. 2006. *Exposing Men: The Science and Politics of Male Reproduction.* Oxford: Oxford University Press.

De Keijzer, Benno. 1998. "El varón como factor de riesgo." In *Familias y relaciones de género en transformación: Cambios trascendentales en América Latina.* Mexico City: Population Council / EDAMEX.

————. 2001. "Para negociar se necesitan dos: Procesos de interacción en la pareja con énfasis en la crianza: Una aproximación crítica desde lo masculino." In *Elementos para un análisis ético de la reproducción,* edited by Juan Guillermo Figueroa, 259–73. Mexico City: Universidad Nacional Autónoma de México.

Dudgeon, Matthew R., and Marcia C. Inhorn. 2003. "Gender, Masculinity, and Reproduction: Anthropological Perspectives." *International Journal of Men's Health* 2(1): 31–56.

————. 2004. "Men's Influences on Women's Reproductive Health: Medical Anthropological Perspectives." *Social Science & Medicine* 59: 1379–95.

Eager, Paige Whaley. 2004. *Global Population Policy: From Population Control to Reproductive Rights*. Aldershot, U.K.: Ashgate.

EngenderHealth. 2002. *Contraceptive Sterilization: Global Issues and Trends*. New York: EngenderHealth.

Estado de Oaxaca. 2005. "Usos y costumbres." www.gobiernodeoaxaca.gob .mx/web/index.php?option=com_content&task=view&id=123&Itemid=29 (accessed 20 November 2005).

Farmer, Paul. 1992. *AIDS and Accusation: Haiti and the Geography of Blame*. Berkeley: University of California Press.

———. 1994. "AIDS-Talk and the Constitution of Cultural Models." *Social Science & Medicine* 38(6): 801–9.

———. 2003. *Pathologies of Power: Health, Human Rights, and the New War on the Poor*. Berkeley: University of California Press.

Fausto-Sterling, Anne. 2000. *Sexing the Body: Gender Politics and the Construction of Sexuality*. New York: Basic Books.

Figueroa, Juan Guillermo. 1998a. "Algunos elementos para interpretar la presencia de los varones en los procesos de salud reproductiva." *Revista de Cadernos de Saúde Pública* 14, supp. 1: 87–96.

———. 1998b. "Algunas propuestas analíticas para interpretar la presencia de los varones en los procesos de salud reproductiva." In *Masculinidades y equidad de género en América Latina*, edited by Teresa Valdés and José Olavarría, 175–98. Santiago, Chile: FLACSO/UNFPA.

———. 1998c. "Fecundidad en el ciclo de vida masculina: Apuntes sobre algunos temas para discusión." In *Varones, sexualidad y reproducción*, edited by Susana Lerner, 47–55. Mexico City: El Colegio de México.

———. 1999. "Algunos desencuentros al normar servicios sobre salud reproductiva: Un apunte desde la experiencia de las organizaciones no gubernamentales." In *Las organizaciones no gubernamentales mexicanas y la salud reproductiva*, edited by Soledad González Montes, 139–71. Mexico City: El Colegio de México.

———. 2003. "A Gendered Perspective on Men's Reproductive Health." *International Journal of Men's Health* 2(2): 111–30.

Finkler, Kaja. 1994a. *Women in Pain: Gender and Morbidity in Mexico*. Philadelphia: University of Pennsylvania Press.

———. 1994b. *Spiritualist Healers in Mexico: Successes and Failures of Alternative Therapeutics*. Salem, WI: Sheffield.

Ford Foundation. 1991. *Reproductive Health: A Strategy for the 1990s*. A Program Paper of the Ford Foundation. New York: Ford Foundation.

Foster, Robert F. 2003. *W. B. Yeats: A Life*. Oxford: Oxford University Press.

Foucault, Michel. 1963 [1994]. *The Birth of the Clinic: An Archaeology of Medical Perception*. New York: Vintage.

————. 1980. *The History of Sexuality.* Vol. 1, *An Introduction.* Translated by Robert Hurley. New York: Vintage.

Frank, Katherine. 2003. *G-Strings and Sympathy: Strip Club Regulars and Male Desire.* Durham, NC: Duke University Press.

Freud, Sigmund. 1962 [1905]. *Three Essays on the Theory of Sexuality.* New York: Basic Books.

————. 1989 [1918]. "From the History of an Infantile Neurosis ('Wolf Man')." In *The Freud Reader,* edited by Peter Gay, 400–26. New York: W. W. Norton.

Frey, Dr. n.d. *Fecundación y anticoncepción.* Mexico City: Ediciones Lux.

Fuller, Norma. 2001. *Masculinidades: Cambios y permanencias: Varones de Cuzco, Iquitos y Lima.* Lima: Fondo Editorial Pontificia Universidad Católica del Perú.

Galeano, Eduardo. 1982. "Literatura y cultura popular en América Latina: Diez errores o mentiras frecuentes." In *La cultura popular,* edited by Adolfo Colobres, 93–109. Tlahuapan, Puebla, Mexico: Porrúa.

García, Brígida, and Orlandina de Oliveira. 2004. "El ejercicio de la paternidad en el México urbano." In *Imágenes de la familia en el cambio del siglo,* edited by Marina Ariza and Orlandina de Oliveira, 283–317. Mexico City: Universidad Nacional Autónoma de México.

————. 2005. "Fatherhood in Urban Mexico." *Journal of Comparative Family Studies* 36(2): 305–27.

García Helmes, Karla, Owen Chaim Jiménez Coronado, Adriana Hernández Villacaña, Lucero A. Rodríguez Santiago, and Fabiola Rojas Terrazas. n.d. "La influencia en el nivel social, cultural y económico en la toma de decisión para la anticoncepción definitiva en el varón." Oaxaca, Mexico: Universidad Regional del Sureste.

Gardiner, Judith K., ed. 2002. *Masculinity Studies & Feminist Theory: New Directions.* New York: Columbia University Press.

Gereffi, Gary. 1983. *The Pharmaceutical Industry and Dependency in the Third World.* Princeton, NJ: Princeton University Press.

Giddens, Anthony. 1983. *Profiles and Critiques in Social Theory.* Berkeley: University of California Press.

————. 1992. *The Transformation of Intimacy: Sexuality, Love, and Eroticism in Modern Societies.* Stanford, CA: Stanford University Press.

Ginsburg, Faye, and Rayna Rapp, eds. 1995. *Conceiving the New World Order: The Global Politics of Reproduction.* Berkeley: University of California Press.

Givaudan, Martha, Susan Pick, and Carmen Fuertes. 1999. "Los hombres mexicanos frente a la vasectomía." In *Reproducción, salud y sexualidad en América Latina,* edited by Edith Alejandra Pantelides and Sarah Bott, 59–71. Buenos Aires: Editorial Biblos.

Gómez-Dantés, Octavio. 2000. "Health Reform and Policies for the Poor in Mexico." In *Healthcare Reform and Poverty in Latin America*, edited by Peter Lloyd-Sherlock, 128–42. London: Institute of Latin American Studies.

González-López, Gloria. 2005. *Erotic Journeys: Mexican Immigrants and Their Sex Lives*. Berkeley: University of California Press.

González Montes, Soledad. 1999. "Los aportes de las ONG a la salud reproductiva en México." In *Las organizaciones no gubernamentales mexicanas y la salud reproductiva*, edited by Soledad González Montes, 15–51. Mexico City: El Colegio de México.

Green, James. 2000. *Beyond Carnival: Male Homosexuality in Twentieth-Century Brazil*. Chicago: University of Chicago Press.

Greene, Graham. 1951. *The Heart of the Matter*. Garden City, NY: Garden City Books.

Greene, Margaret E., and Ann E. Biddlecom. 2000. "Absent and Problematic Men: Demographic Accounts of Male Reproductive Roles." *Population and Development Review* 26(1): 81–115.

Greene, Shane. 2004. "Culture as Politics, Culture as Property in Pharmaceutical Bioprospecting." *Current Anthropology* 45(2): 211–37.

Greenhalgh, Susan. 1990. "Toward a Political Economy of Fertility: Anthropological Contributions." *Population and Development Review* 16(1): 85–106.

———. 1994. "Controlling Births and Bodies in Village China." *American Ethnologist* 21(1): 3–30.

———. 1996. "The Social Construction of Population Science: An Intellectual, Institutional, and Political History of Twentieth-Century Demography." *Comparative Studies in Society and History* 38(1): 26–66.

Gutmann, Matthew C. 1997. "The Ethnographic (G)Ambit: Women and the Negotiation of Masculinity in Mexico City." *American Ethnologist* 24(4): 833–55.

———. 1999. "Ethnicity, Alcohol, and Acculturation." *Social Science & Medicine* 48(2): 173–84.

———. 2002. *The Romance of Democracy: Compliant Defiance in Contemporary Mexico*. Berkeley: University of California Press.

———. 2003a. "Discarding Manly Dichotomies in Latin America." In *Changing Men and Masculinities in Latin America*, edited by Matthew C. Gutmann, 1–26. Durham, NC: Duke University Press.

———. 2003b. "Iniciación sexual y salud reproductiva entre adolescentes en Oaxaca de Juárez, México." In *Varones adolescentes: Género, identidades y sexualidades en América Latina*, edited by José Olavarría, 153–64. Santiago, Chile: Facultad Latinoamericana de Ciencias Sociales.

———. 2004. "Dystopian Travels in Gringolandia: Engendering Ethnicity among Mexican Migrants to the United States." *Ethnicities* 4(4): 477–500.

———. 2005. "Scoring Men: Vasectomies and the Totemic Illusion of Male Sexuality in Oaxaca." *Culture, Medicine, and Psychiatry* 29(1): 79–101.

———. 2006 [1996]. *The Meanings of Macho: Being a Man in Mexico City.* 10th anniversary ed. Berkeley: University of California Press.

Gutmann, Matthew C., and Mara Viveros Vigoya. 2005. "Masculinities in Latin America." In *Handbook of Studies on Men and Masculinities,* edited by Michael S. Kimmel, Jeff Hearn, and R. W. Connell, 114–28. Thousand Oaks, CA: Sage.

Hart, Angie. 1994. "Missing Masculinity? Prostitutes' Clients in Alicante, Spain." In *Dislocating Masculinity: Comparative Ethnographies,* edited by Andrea Cornwall and Nancy Lindisfarne, 48–65. London: Routledge.

Hartmann, Betsy. 1995. *Reproductive Rights and Wrongs: The Global Politics of Population Control.* Boston: South End Press.

Hayden, Cori. 2006. "Bioprospecting the 'Promise' and Threat of the Market." *NACLA Report* 39(5): 26–31.

Heald, Suzette. 1999. *Manhood and Morality: Sex, Violence, and Ritual in Gisu Society.* New York: Routledge.

Heider, Karl G. 1976. "Dani Sexuality: A Low Energy System." *Man,* n.s., 11: 188–201.

Helzner, Judith. 1996. "Men's Involvement in Family Planning." *Reproductive Heath Matters* 7: 146–54.

Hernández-Díaz, Jorge. 2001. *Reclamos de la identidad: La formación de las organizaciones indígenas en Oaxaca.* Oaxaca: Universidad Autónoma Benito Juárez de Oaxaca.

Higgins, Michael J., and Tanya L. Coen. 2000. *Streets, Bedrooms, and Patios: The Ordinariness of Diversity in Urban Oaxaca: Ethnographic Portraits of the Street Kids, Urban Poor, Transvestites, "Discapacitados," and Other Popular Cultures.* Austin: University of Texas Press.

Hirsch, Jennifer S. 2003. *A Courtship after Marriage: Sexuality and Love in Mexican Transnational Families.* Berkeley: University of California Press.

Hirsch, Jennifer S., and Constance A. Nathanson. 2001. "Some Traditional Methods Are More Modern than Others: Rhythm, Withdrawal, and the Changing Meanings of Sexual Intimacy in Mexican Companionate Marriage." *Culture, Health, and Sexuality* 3(4): 413–28.

Hirsch, Jennifer S., and Holly Wardlow, eds. 2006. *The Anthropology of Romantic Courtship and Companionate Marriage.* Ann Arbor: University of Michigan Press.

Homedes, Núria, and Antonio Ugalde. 2005a. "Las reformas de salud neoliberales en América Latina: Una visión crítica a través de dos estudios de caso." *Revista Panamericana de Salud Pública* 17(3): 210–20.

———. 2005b. "Why Neoliberal Health Reforms Have Failed in Latin America." *Health Policy* 71: 83–96.

Hondagneu-Sotelo, Pierrette, ed. 2003. *Gender and U.S. Migration: Contemporary Trends.* Berkeley: University of California Press.

Huber, Brad R., and Alan R. Sandstrom, eds. 2001a. *Mesoamerican Healers.* Austin: University of Texas Press.

Huber, Brad R., and Alan R. Sandstrom. 2001b. "Recruitment, Training, and Practice of Indigenous Midwives: From the Mexico–United States Border to the Isthmus of Tehuantepec." In *Mesoamerican Healers*, edited by Brad R. Huber and Alan R. Sandstrom, 139–78. Austin: University of Texas Press.

Hurston, Zora Neale. 1990 [1937]. *Their Eyes Were Watching God.* New York: Harper and Row.

Illich, Ivan D. 1969. *Celebration of Awareness: A Call for Institutional Revolution.* Garden City, NY: Doubleday.

Inhorn, Marcia C. 2002. "Sexuality, Masculinity, and Infertility in Egypt: Potent Troubles in the Marital and Medical Encounters." *Journal of Men's Studies* 10(3): 343–59.

———. 2003. " 'The Worms Are Weak': Male Infertility and Patriarchal Paradoxes in Egypt." *Men & Masculinities* 5(3): 236–56.

———. 2004. "Middle Eastern Masculinities in the Age of New Reproductive Technologies: Male Infertility and Stigma in Egypt and Lebanon." *Medical Anthropology Quarterly* 18(2): 162–82.

Inhorn, Marcia C., and Frank Van Balen, eds. 2002. *Infertility around the Globe: New Thinking on Childlessness, Gender, and Reproductive Technologies.* Berkeley: University of California Press.

Instituto Mexicano del Seguro Social. 1998. *Vasectomía sin bisturí: Guia de capacitación.* Mexico City: Instituto Mexicano del Seguro Social, Dirección de Planaficación Familiar.

Instituto Nacional de Estadística y Geografía Informática (INEGI). 2000. *Anuario Estadístico del Estado de Oaxaca, Edición 2000.* Vol. 1. Mexico City: INEGI.

———. 2003. *Mujeres y hombres en México 2003.* Aguascalientes, Ags.: CD-Rom.

International Planned Parenthood Federation. 1979. *Family Planning in Mexico: A Profile of the Development of Policies and Programmes.* London: International Planned Parenthood Federation.

International Union for the Scientific Study of Population. 1998. *Men, Family Formation, and Reproduction.* Buenos Aires: IUSSP/CENEP.

Jordan, Brigitte. 1993 [1978]. *Birth in Four Cultures: A Cross-Cultural Investigation of Childbirth in Yucatan, Holland, Sweden, and the United States.* Prospect Heights, IL: Waveland.

Kahn, Susan Martha. 2000. *Reproducing Jews: A Cultural Account of Assisted Conception in Israel.* Durham, NC: Duke University Press.

Kertzer, David I., and Tom Fricke. 1997. "Toward an Anthropological Demography." In *Anthropological Demography: Toward a New Synthesis*, edited by David I. Kertzer and Tom Fricke, 1–35. Chicago: University of Chicago Press.

Kidder, Tracy. 2004. *Mountains beyond Mountains: The Quest of Dr. Paul Farmer, a Man Who Would Cure the World*. New York: Random House.

Kimmel, Michael S. 1994. "Masculinity as Homophobia: Fear, Shame, and Silence in the Construction of Gender Identity." In *Theorizing Masculinities*, edited by Harry Brod and Michael Kaufman, 119–41. Thousand Oaks, CA: Sage.

———. 2003. "An Unnatural History of Rape." In *Evolution, Gender, and Rape*, edited by Cheryl Brown Travis, 221–33. Cambridge, MA: MIT Press.

Kimmel, Michael S., Jeff Hearn, and R. W. Connell, eds. 2005. *Handbook of Studies on Men & Masculinities*. Thousand Oaks, CA: Sage.

Koss-Chioino, Joan D., Thomas Leatherman, and Christine Greenway, eds. 2003. *Medical Pluralism in the Andes*. London: Routledge.

Kulick, Don. 1998. *Travesti: Sex, Gender, and Culture among Brazilian Transgendered Prostitutes*. Chicago: University of Chicago Press.

Kulick, Don, and Margaret Willson, eds. 1995. *Taboo: Sex, Identity, and Erotic Subjectivity in Anthropological Fieldwork*. New York: Routledge.

Lamas, Marta, ed. 1996. *El género: La construcción cultural de la diferencia sexual*. Mexico City: UNAM/Porrúa.

Lancaster, Roger N. 1992. *Life Is Hard: Machismo, Danger, and the Intimacy of Power in Nicaragua*. Berkeley: University of California Press.

———. 1998. "Sexual Positions: Caveats and Second Thoughts on 'Categories.'" *The Americas* 54(1): 1–16.

———. 2003. *The Trouble with Nature: Sex in Science and Popular Culture*. Berkeley: University of California Press.

Laqueur, Thomas. 1990. *Making Sex: Body and Gender from the Greeks to Freud*. Cambridge, MA: Harvard University Press.

———. 2003. *Solitary Sex: A History of Masturbation*. New York: Zone Books.

Laurell, Asa Cristina. 2001. "Health Reform in Mexico: The Promotion of Inequality." *International Journal of Health Services* 31(2): 291–321.

Leal, Ondina Fachel, ed. 1995. *Corpo y significado: Ensaios de Antropologia Social*. Porto Alegre, Brasil: Editora da Universidade.

———. 1998. "Sexualidad e identidad masculina: Impases y perspectivas de análisis." In *Masculinidades y equidad de género en América Latina*, edited by Teresa Valdés and José Olavarría, 90–105. Santiago, Chile: FLACSO/UNFPA.

Lerner, Susana, ed. 1998. *Varones, sexualidad y reproducción*. Mexico City: El Colegio de México.

Lévi-Strauss, Claude. 1963. *Totemism*. Boston: Beacon Press.

———. 1992 [1955]. *Tristes Tropiques*. New York: Penguin.

Lewis, Oscar. 1952. "Urbanization without Breakdown." *Scientific Monthly* 75: 31–41.

Lewontin, Richard. 1995. "Sex, Lies, and Social Science." *New York Review of Books*, 20 April.

Liguori, Ana Luisa, and Peter Aggleton. 1998. "Aspectos del comercio sexual masculino en la ciudad de México." *Debate feminista* 18: 152–85.

Liguori, Ana Luisa, Miguel González Block, and Peter Aggleton. 1996. "Bisexuality and HIV/AIDS in Mexico." In *Bisexualities and AIDS: International Perspectives*, edited by Peter Aggleton, 76–98. London: Taylor and Francis.

Liguori, Ana Luisa, and Marta Lamas. 2003. "Gender, Sexual Citizenship and HIV/AIDS." *Culture, Health, and Sexuality* 5(1): 87–90.

Lock, Margaret. 2001. "The Tempering of Medical Anthropology: Troubling Natural Categories." *Medical Anthropology Quarterly* 15(4): 478–92.

Lodge, David. 2001. *Thinks—: A Novel.* New York: Penguin.

Lomnitz, Claudio. 2001. *Deep Mexico, Silent Mexico: An Anthropology of Nationalism.* Minneapolis: University of Minnesota Press.

Lopez, Iris. 1998. "An Ethnography of the Medicalization of Puerto Rican Women's Reproduction." In *Pragmatic Women and Body Politics*, edited by Margaret Lock and Patricia A. Kaufert, 240–59. Cambridge: Cambridge University Press.

López Juárez, Alfonso. 2003. "Programa Gente Jóven Mexfam." In *Varones adolescentes: Género, identidades y sexualidades en América Latina*, edited by José Olavarría, 279–83. Santiago, Chile: FLACSO.

Loyo, Gilberto. 1974 [1967]. "The Demographic Problems of Mexico and Latin America." In *The Dynamics of Population Policy in Latin America*, edited by Terry L. McCoy, 183–201. Cambridge, MA: Ballinger Publishing.

Magaña, J. Raúl. 1991. "Sex, Drugs and HIV: An Ethnographic Approach." *Social Science & Medicine* 33(1): 5–9.

Magis-Rodríguez, Carlos, Cecilia Gayet, Mirka Negroni, Rene Leyva, Enrique Bravo-García, Patricia Uribe, and Mario Bronfman. 2004. "Migration and AIDS in Mexico: An Overview Based on Recent Evidence." *Journal of Acquired Immune Deficiency Syndromes* 37: S215–S226.

Markens, Susan, C. H. Browner, and H. Mabel Preloran. 2003. " 'I'm Not the One They're Sticking the Needle Into': Latino Couples, Fetal Diagnosis, and the Discourse of Reproductive Rights." *Gender and Society* 17(3): 462–81.

Markowitz, Fran, and Michael Ashkenazi, eds. 1999. *Sex, Sexuality, and the Anthropologist.* Urbana: University of Illinois Press.

Marks, Lara V. 2001. *Sexual Chemistry: A History of the Contraceptive Pill.* New Haven, CT: Yale University Press.

Márquez, Viviane B. de. 1984. "El proceso social en la formación de políticas: El caso de la planificación familiar en México." *Estudios Sociológicos* 2: 309–33.

Marsiglio, William. 1998. *Procreative Man.* New York: New York University Press.

Marsiglio, William, and Joseph H. Pleck. 2005. "Fatherhood and Masculinities." In *Handbook of Studies on Men and Masculinities*, edited by Michael S. Kimmel, Jeff Hearn, and R. W. Connell, 249–69. Thousand Oaks, CA: Sage.

Marston, Cicely. 2004. "Gendered Communication among Young People in Mexico: Implications for Sexual Health Interventions." *Social Science & Medicine* 59: 445–56.

Martin, Emily. 1987. *The Woman in the Body: A Cultural Analysis of Reproduction.* Boston, MA: Beacon Press.

———. 2003. "What Is 'Rape'?—Toward a Historical, Ethnographic Approach." In *Evolution, Gender, and Rape,* edited by Cheryl Brown Travis, 363–81. Cambridge, MA: MIT Press.

Mascia-Lees, Frances E., and Nancy Johnson Black. 2000. *Gender and Anthropology.* Prospect Heights, IL: Waveland.

Mateos Cándano, Manuel, Rosalba Bueno Lázaro, and Luis Fernando Chávez Murueta. 1968. *Actitud y anticoncepción: Estudio de la actitud de 500 mujeres de un área urbana de la Ciudad de México.* Mexico City: Centro Estudios Reproducción.

Matus, Macario. 1978. "Conceptos sexuales entre los zapotecas de hoy." *Siempre!* no. 859.

McCoy, Terry L. 1974. "A Paradigmatic Analysis of Mexican Population Policy." In *The Dynamics of Population Policy in Latin America,* edited by Terry L. McCoy, 377–408. Cambridge, MA: Ballinger Publishing.

McIntosh, Mary. 1968. "The Homosexual Role." *Social Problems* 16: 182–92.

McKinley, James C. 2005. "A New Law in Tijuana Regulates the Oldest Profession." *New York Times,* 13 December.

McNamara, Robert S. 1974. "The World Bank Perspective on Population Growth." In *The Dynamics of Population Policy in Latin America,* edited by Terry L. McCoy, 107–21. Cambridge, MA: Ballinger Publishing.

———. 1984. "Time Bomb or Myth: The Population Problem." *Foreign Affairs* 62(5): 1107–31.

Mejía, María Consuelo. 2001. "Normas y valores de la Iglesia católica en la sexualidad y la reproducción: Nuevas perspectivas." In *Encuentros y desencuentros en la salud reproductiva: Políticas públicas, marcos normativos y actores sociales,* edited by Juan Guillermo Figueroa and Claudio Stern, 101–21. Mexico City: El Colegio de México.

Mellado, Virginia, Carlos Zolla, and Xochitl Castañeda. 1989. *La atención al embarazo y el parto en el medio rural mexicano.* Mexico City: Centro Interamericano de Estudios de Seguridad Social.

Mercado, Francisco Javier, Catalina A. Denman, Agustín Escobar, Claudia Infante, and Leticia Robles, eds. 1993. *Familia, salud y sociedad: Experiencias de investigación en México.* Guadalajara: Universidad de Guadalajara.

Merrick, Thomas W. 1985. *Recent Fertility Declines in Brazil, Colombia, and Mexico.* Washington, DC: World Bank.

Miano, Marinella. 2002. *Hombre, mujer y muxe' en el Istmo de Tehuantepec.* Mexico City: INAH / Plaza y Valdés.

Mills, Lisa. 2006. "Maternal Health Policy and the Politics of Scale in Mexico." *Social Politics* 13(4): 487–521.

Minello, Nelson. 2002. *La masculinidad al fin del milenio: Una mirada sociológica.* Doctoral thesis, CIESAS–Occidente, Universidad de Guadalajara.

Mishra, Shiraz I., Ross F. Conner, and J. Raul Magaña. 1996a. Preface to *AIDS Crossing Borders: The Spread of HIV among Migrant Latinos,* edited by Shiraz I. Mishra, Ross F. Conner, and J. Raul Magaña, vii. Boulder, CO: Westview.

Mishra, Shiraz I., Ross F. Conner, and J. Raul Magaña. 1996b. "Migrant Workers in the United States: A Profile from the Fields." In *AIDS Crossing Borders: The Spread of HIV among Migrant Latinos,* edited by Shiraz I. Mishra, Ross F. Conner, and J. Raul Magaña, 3–24. Boulder, CO: Westview.

Mistry, Rohinton. 1997. *A Fine Balance.* New York: Vintage.

Monsiváis, Carlos. 1997. *Mexican Postcards.* Edited and translated by John Kraniauskas. London: Verso.

———. 2006. "El mago de San Peterburgo." *El Universal,* 23 July.

———. 2007. "We Are Living in a Time of Pillage." *NACLA Report on the Americas* 40(1): 6–11.

Mora Bravo, Miguel. 1984. *El derecho a la planeación familar: Marco jurídico.* Mexico City: Consejo Nacional de Población.

Morgan, Lynn. 1993. *Community Participation in Health: The Politics of Primary Care in Costa Rica.* Cambridge: Cambridge University Press.

———. 1998. "Latin American Social Medicine and the Politics of Theory." In *Building a New Biocultural Synthesis: Political-Economic Perspectives on Human Biology,* edited by Alan H. Goodman and Thomas L. Leatherman, 407–24. Ann Arbor: University of Michigan Press.

Munroe, Robert L., Ruth H. Munroe, and John W. M. Whiting. 1973. "The Couvade: A Psychological Analysis." *Ethos* 1(1): 30–74.

Murphy, Arthur D., and Alex Stepick. 1991. *Social Inequality in Oaxaca: A History of Resistance and Change.* Philadelphia: Temple University Press.

Nanda, Serena. 1990. *Neither Man nor Woman: The Hijras of India.* Belmont, CA: Wadsworth.

Nigh, Ronald. 2002. "Maya Medicine in the Biological Gaze: Bioprospecting Research as Herbal Fetishism." *Current Anthropology* 43(3): 451–77.

Nugent, David L. 1999. "State and Shadow State in Turn-of-the-Century Peru: Illegal Political Networks and the Problem of State Boundaries." In *States and Illegal Practices,* edited by Josiah Heyman, 63–98. London: Berg.

Núñez Noriega, Guillermo. 1994. *Sexo entre varones: Poder y resistencia en el campo sexual.* Mexico City: UNAM / Porrúa / El Colegio de Sonora.

———. 2001. "Reconociendo los placeres, desconstruyendo las identidades: Antropología, patriarcado y homoerotismos en México." *Desacatos* 6: 15–34.

Olavarría, José. 2002. "Hombres y sexualidades: Naturaleza y cultura (castrar o no castrar)." In *Hombres: Identidad/es y sexualidad/es*, edited by José Olavarría and Enrique Moletto, 13–27. Santiago, Chile: FLACSO.

Olavarría, José, and Enrique Moletto, eds. 2002. *Hombres: Identidad/es y sexualidad/es*. Santiago, Chile: FLACSO.

Olavarría, José, and Rodrigo Parrini, eds. 2000. *Masculinidad/es: Identidad, sexualidad y familia*. Santiago, Chile: FLACSO.

Ortiz Ortega, Adriana, Ana Amuchástegui, and Marta Rivas. 1998. " 'Because They Were Born from Me': Negotiating Women's Rights in Mexico." In *Negotiating Rights: Women's Perspectives across Countries and Cultures*, edited by Rosalind P. Petchesky and Karen Judd, 145–79. London: Zed Books.

Oudshoorn, Nelly. 1994. *Beyond the Natural Body: An Archaeology of Sex Hormones*. New York: Routledge.

———. 2003. *The Male Pill: A Biography of a Technology in the Making*. Durham, NC: Duke University Press.

———. 2004. " 'Astronauts in the Sperm World': The Renegotiation of Masculine Identities in Discourses on Male Contraceptives." *Men & Masculinities* 6(4): 349–67.

Paige, Karen E., and Jeffery M. Paige. 1981. *The Politics of Reproductive Ritual*. Berkeley: University of California Press.

Palma, Yolanda, and Gabriela Rivera. 2000. "La planificación familiar en México." In *Mujer: Sexualidad y salud reproductiva en México*, edited by Ana Langer and Kathryn Tolbert, 153–77. Mexico City: EDAMEX and Population Council.

Pan American Health Organization (PAHO). 1998. *Health in the Americas*. Washington, DC: World Health Organization.

Pan American Health Organization, World Health Organization, Joint United Nations Programme on HIV/AIDS. 2001. *HIV and AIDS in the Americas: An Epidemic with Many Faces*. Washington, DC: Pan American Health Organization.

Parker, Richard. 1999. *Beneath the Equator: Cultures of Desire, Male Homosexuality, and Emerging Gay Communities in Brazil*. New York: Routledge.

———. 2000. "Administering the Epidemic: HIV/AIDS Policy, Models of Development, and International Health." In *Global Health Policy, Local Realities: The Fallacy of the Level Playing Field*, edited by Linda M. Whiteford and Lenore Manderson, 39–55. Boulder, CO: Lynne Rienner Publishers.

———. 2001. "Sexuality, Culture, and Power in HIV/AIDS Research." *Annual Review of Anthropology* 30: 163–79.

———. 2002. "The Global HIV/AIDS Pandemic, Structural Inequalities, and the Politics of International Health." *American Journal of Public Health* 92(3): 343–46.

———. 2003. "Changing Sexualities: Masculinity and Male Homosexuality in Brazil." In *Changing Men and Masculinities in Latin America*, edited by Matthew C. Gutmann, 307–32. Durham, NC: Duke University Press.

Parker, Richard, Regina Maria Barbosa, and Peter Aggleton. 2000. "Framing the Sexual Subject." In *Framing the Sexual Subject: The Politics of Gender, Sexuality, and Power,* edited by Richard Parker, Regina Maria Barbosa, and Peter Aggleton, 1–25. Berkeley: University of California Press.

Parker, Richard, and Carlos Cáceres. 1999. "Alternative Sexualities and Changing Sexual Cultures among Latin American Men." *Culture, Health and Sexuality* 1(3): 201–6.

Patton, Cindy. 1996. *Fatal Advice: How Safe-Sex Education Went Wrong.* Durham, NC: Duke University Press.

Pérez Vázquez, María Teresa. 1999. "El trabajo de las ONG en el campo de la sexualidad y la educacción sexual." In *Las organizaciones no gubernamentales mexicanas y la salud reproductiva,* edited by Soledad González Montes, 53–74. Mexico City: El Colegio de México.

Petchesky, Rosalind P. 1999. "Sexual Rights: Inventing a Concept, Mapping an International Practice." In *Framing the Sexual Subject: The Politics of Gender, Sexuality, and Power,* edited by Richard Parker, Regina Maria Barbosa, and Peter Aggleton, 81–103. Berkeley: University of California Press.

Petchesky, Rosalind P., and Karen Judd, eds. 1998. *Negotiating Reproductive Rights: Women's Perspectives across Countries and Cultures.* London: Zed Books.

Petryna, Adriana, Andrew Lakoff, and Arthur Kleinman, eds. 2006. *Global Pharmaceuticals: Ethics, Markets, Practices.* Durham, NC: Duke University Press.

Pigg, Stacy L. 1995. "Acronyms and Effacement: Traditional Medical Practitioners (TMP) in International Health Development." *Social Science & Medicine* 41(1): 47–68.

Potter, Joseph E. 1999. "The Persistence of Outmoded Contraceptive Regimes: The Cases of Mexico and Brazil." *Population and Development Review* 25(4): 703–39.

Pratt, Mary Louise. 1992. *Imperial Eyes: Travel Writing and Transculturation.* New York: Routledge.

Prieur, Annick. 1998. *Mema's House, Mexico City: On Transvestites, Queens, and Machos.* Chicago: University of Chicago Press.

Proyecto IMSS–PRIME. 2001. *Manual de capacitación en salud reproductiva.* Oaxaca: IMSS.

Rapp, Rayna. 2000. *Testing Women, Testing the Fetus: The Social Impact of Amniocentesis in America.* New York: Routledge.

———. 2001. "Gender, Body, Biomedicine: How Some Feminist Concerns Dragged Reproduction to the Center of Social Theory." *Medical Anthropology Quarterly* 15(4): 466–77.

Redfield, Robert, and Alfonso Villa Rojas. 1971 [1934]. *Chan Kom: A Maya Village.* Chicago: University of Chicago Press.

Rense, Jeff. 2004. "Mexican Migrant Workers HIV Infection Rate 'Alarming.'"

Rense.com. www.rense.com/general59/migrant.htm (accessed 5 February 2007).

Rich, Adrienne. 1993 [1982]. "Compulsory Heterosexuality and Lesbian Existence." In *The Lesbian and Gay Studies Reader*, edited by Henry Abelove, Michèle A. Barale, and David M. Halperin, 227–54. New York: Routledge.

Rival, Laura. 1998. "Androgynous Parents and Guest Children: The Huaorani Couvade." *Journal of the Royal Anthropological Institute* 4: 619–42.

Rivas Vilchis, José Federico, and Raúl Enrique Molina Salazar, eds. n.d. "Políticas farmacéuticas y estudios de actualización de medicamentos en Latinoamérica." n.p.: Organización Mundial de la Salud.

Rodríguez, Gabriela, Esther Corona, and Susan Pick. 2000. "Educación para la sexualidad y la salud reproductiva." In *Mujer: Sexualidad y salud reproductiva en México*, edited by Ana Langer and Kathryn Tolbert, 343–76. Mexico City: EDAMEX and Population Council.

Rosenthal, Joshua P. 2006. "Politics, Culture, and Governance in the Development of Prior Informed Consent in Indigenous Communities." *Current Anthropology* 47(1): 119–42.

Rubin, Gayle. 1975. "The Traffic in Women: Notes on the 'Political Economy' of Sex." In *Toward an Anthropology of Women*, edited by Rayna Reiter, 157–210. New York: Monthly Review.

———. 1999 [1984]. "Thinking Sex: Notes for a Radical Theory of the Politics of Sexuality." In *Culture, Society, and Sexuality: A Reader*, edited by Richard Parker and Peter Aggleton, 143–78. London: UCL Press.

Russell, Andrew, Elisa J. Sobo, and Mary S. Thompson, eds. 2000. *Contraception across Cultures: Technologies, Choices, Constraints*. Oxford: Berg.

Russell, Andrew, and Mary S. Thompson. 2000. "Contraception across Cultures." In *Contraception across Cultures: Technologies, Choices, Constraints*, edited by Andrew Russell, Elisa J. Sobo, and Mary S. Thompson, 3–25. Oxford: Berg.

Ruz, Mario Humberto. 1998. "La semilla del hombre: Notas etnológicas acerca de la sexualidad y reproducción masculinas entre los mayas." In *Varones, sexualidad y reproducción*, edited by Susana Lerner, 193–221. Mexico City: El Colegio de México.

———. 2000. "The Seeds of Man: Ethnological Notes on Male Sexuality and Fecundity among the Maya." In *Fertility and the Male Life-Cycle in the Era of Fertility Decline*, edited by Caroline Bledsoe, Susana Lerner, and Jane I. Guyer, 93–118. Oxford: Oxford University Press.

Sanchez, Melissa A., George F. Lemp, Carlos Magis-Rodríguez, Enrique Bravo-García, Susan Carter, and Juan D. Ruiz. 2004. "The Epidemiology of HIV among Mexican Migrants and Recent Immigrants in California and Mexico." *Journal of Acquired Immune Deficiency Syndromes* 37: S204–S214.

Sankar, Pamela. 2004. "Communication and Miscommunication in Informed Consent to Research." *Medical Anthropology Quarterly* 18(4): 429–46.

Santiago-Irizarry, Vilma. 2001. *Medicalizing Ethnicity: The Construction of Latino Identity in a Psychiatric Setting.* Ithaca, NY: Cornell University Press.

Santow, Gigi. 1993. "*Coitus interruptus* in the Twentieth Century." *Population and Development Review* 19(4): 767–92.

Sapolsky, Robert M. 1997. *The Trouble with Testosterone: And Other Essays on the Biology of the Human Predicament.* New York: Simon and Schuster.

Sargent, Carolyn F., and Caroline B. Brettell, eds. 1996. *Gender and Health: An International Perspective.* Upper Saddle River, NJ: Prentice Hall.

Scheper-Hughes, Nancy. 1990. "Three Propositions for a Critically Applied Medical Anthropology." *Social Science & Medicine* 30(2): 189–97.

———. 1994a. "AIDS and the Social Body." *Social Science & Medicine* 39(7): 991–1004.

———. 1994b. "Embodied Knowledge: Thinking with the Body in Critical Medical Anthropology." In *Assessing Cultural Anthropology,* edited by Robert Borofsky, 229–42. New York: McGraw-Hill.

———. 1997. "Demography without Numbers." In *Anthropological Demography: Toward a New Synthesis,* edited by David I. Kertzer and Tom Fricke, 201–22. Chicago: University of Chicago Press.

Scheper-Hughes, Nancy, and Margaret Lock. 1987. "The Mindful Body: A Prolegomenon to Future Work in Medical Anthropology." *Medical Anthropology Quarterly* 1(1): 6–41.

Schneider, Jane C., and Peter T. Schneider. 1996. *Festival of the Poor: Fertility Decline and the Ideology of Class in Sicily, 1860–1980.* Tucson: University of Arizona Press.

Schoeph, Brooke G. 2001. "International AIDS Research in Anthropology: Taking a Critical Perspective on the Crisis." *Annual Review of Anthropology* 30: 335–61.

Scott, James C. 1998. *Seeing Like a State: How Certain Schemes to Improve the Human Condition Have Failed.* New Haven, CT: Yale University Press.

Secretaría de Salud. 2005. *Panorama epidemiológico del VIH/SIDA e ITS en México.* Consejo Nacional para la Prevención y Control del VIH/SIDA. www.salud .gob.mx/conasida/estadis/2005/dic05/panoramadic05.pdf (accessed 5 February 2007).

Segal, Lynne. 1994. *Straight Sex: Rethinking the Politics of Pleasure.* Berkeley: University of California Press.

———, ed. 1997. *New Sexual Agendas.* New York: New York University Press.

Sepulveda, Jaime. 1992. "Prevention through Information and Education: Experience from Mexico." In *AIDS: Prevention through Education: A World View,* edited by Jaime Sepulveda, Harvey Fineberg, and Jonathan Mann, 127–44. Oxford: Oxford University Press.

Sesia, Paola M., ed. 1992a. *Medicina tradicional, herbolaria y salud comunitaria en Oaxaca.* Oaxaca: CIESAS and Gobierno del Estado de Oaxaca.

———. 1992b. "La obstetricia tradicional en el Istmo de Tehuantepec: Marco conceptual y diferencias con el modelo biomédico." In *Medicina tradicional, herbolaria y salud comunitaria en Oaxaca*, edited by Paola Sesia, 17–54. Oaxaca: CIESAS and Gobierno del Estado de Oaxaca.

———. 1997. " 'Women Come Here on Their Own When They Need To': Prenatal Care, Authoritative Knowledge, and Maternal Health in Oaxaca." In *Childbirth and Authoritative Knowledge: Cross-Cultural Perspectives*, edited by Robbie E. Davis-Floyd and Carolyn F. Sargent, 397–420. Berkeley: University of California Press.

Sobo, Elizabeth J. 1990. "Why Washington Cares." *Progressive* 54(9): 28.

———. 1999. "Cultural Models and HIV / AIDS: New Anthropological Views." *Anthropology & Medicine* 6(1): 5–12.

Soto Laveaga, Gabriela. n.d. "The Pill, Fertile Mexicans, and Memory Lost." Unpublished ms., University of California, Santa Barbara.

Stephen, Lynn. 2002. *¡Zapata Lives! Histories and Cultural Politics in Southern Mexico.* Berkeley: University of California Press.

———. 2005. *Zapotec Women: Gender, Class, and Ethnicity in Globalized Oaxaca.* Durham, NC: Duke University Press.

Stern, Alexandra Minna. 2003. "From Mestizophilia to Biotypology: Racialization and Science in Mexico, 1920–1960." In *Race and Nation in Modern Latin America*, edited by Nancy P. Appelbaum, Anne S. Macpherson, and Karin Alejandra Rosemblatt, 187–210. Chapel Hill: University of North Carolina Press.

Stern, Claudio, Cristina Fuentes-Zurita, Laura Ruth Lozano-Treviño, and Fenneke Reysoo. 2003. "Masculinidad y salud sexual y reproductiva: Un estudio de caso con adolescentes de la Ciudad de México." *Salud Pública de México* 45, supp. 1: S34–S43.

Symonds, Richard, and Michael Carder. 1973. *The United Nations and the Population Question, 1945–70.* New York: McGraw-Hill.

Szasz, Ivonne. 1998a. "Los hombres y la sexualidad: Aportes de la perspectiva feminista y primeros acercamientos a su estudio en México." In *Varones, sexualidad y reproducción*, edited by Susana Lerner, 137–62. Mexico City: El Colegio de México.

———. 1998b. "Masculine Identity and the Meanings of Sexuality: A Review of Research in Mexico." *Reproductive Health Matters* 6(12): 97–104.

Szasz, Ivonne, and Susana Lerner, eds. 1998. *Sexualidades en México: Algunas aproximaciones desde la perspectiva de las ciencias sociales.* Mexico City: El Colegio de México.

Tarlo, Emma. 2003. *Unsettling Memories: Narratives of the Emergency in Delhi.* Berkeley: University of California Press.

Thompson, Mary S. 2000. "Family Planning or Reproductive Health? Interpreting Policy and Providing Family Planning Services in Highland, Chiapas,

Mexico." In *Contraception across Cultures: Technologies, Choices, Constraints,* edited by Andrew Russell, Elisa J. Sobo, and Mary S. Thompson, 221–43. Oxford: Berg.

Townsend, Nicholas W. 2000. "Male Fertility as a Lifetime of Relationships: Contextualizing Men's Biological Reproduction in Botswana." In *Fertility and the Male Life-Cycle in the Era of Fertility Decline,* edited by Caroline Bledsoe, Susana Lerner, and Jane I. Guyer, 343–64. Oxford: Oxford University Press.

———. 2002. *The Package Deal: Marriage, Work, and Fatherhood in Men's Lives.* Philadelphia: Temple University Press.

Travis, Cheryl Brown. 2003. *Evolution, Gender, and Rape.* Cambridge, MA: MIT Press.

Turner, Frederick C. 1974. *Responsible Parenthood: The Politics of Mexico's New Population Policies.* Washington, DC: American Enterprise Institute for Public Policy Research.

United Nations. 2003. *World Contraceptive Use 2003.* www.un.org/esa/population/publications/contraceptive2003/wcu2003.htm (accessed 5 February 2007).

Valdés, Teresa, and José Olavarría, eds. 1997. *Masculinidad/es: Poder y crisis.* Santiago, Chile: Ediciones de la Mujer.

———, eds. 1998. *Masculinidades y equidad de género en América Latina.* Santiago, Chile: FLACSO/UNFPA.

van Balen, Frank, and Marcia C. Inhorn. 2002. "Interpreting Infertility: A View from the Social Sciences." In *Infertility around the Globe: New Thinking on Childlessness, Gender, and Reproductive Technologies,* edited by Marcia C. Inhorn and Frank van Balen, 3–32. Berkeley: University of California Press.

Vance, Carole. 1999 [1991]. "Anthropology Rediscovers Sexuality: A Theoretical Comment." In *Culture, Society and Sexuality: A Reader,* edited by Richard Parker and Peter Aggleton, 39–54. London: UCL Press.

VanWey, Leah K., Catherine M. Tucker, and Eileen Diaz McConnell. 2005. "Community Organization, Migration, and Remittances in Oaxaca." *Latin American Research Review* 40(1): 83–107.

Viveros Vigoya, Mara. 1998a. "Decisiones reproductivas y dinámicas conyugales: El caso de la elección de la esterilización masculina." In *Masculinidades y equidad de género en América Latina,* edited by Teresa Valdés and José Olavarría, 146–57. Santiago, Chile: FLACSO/UNFPA.

———. 1998b. "Quebradores y cumplidores: Biografía diversas de la masculinidad." In *Masculinidades y equidad de género en América Latina,* edited by Teresa Valdés and José Olavarría, 36–55. Santiago, Chile: FLACSO/UNFPA.

———. 2002. *De quebradores y cumplidores: Sobre hombres, masculinidades y relaciones de género en Colombia.* Bogotá: Universidad Nacional de Colombia.

Vogt, Evon Z. 1969. *Zinacantan: A Maya Community in the Highlands of Chiapas.* Cambridge, MA: Harvard University Press.

Welti Chanes, Carlos. 2003. "La Ley General de Población en el contexto internacional." Unpublished ms., Universidad Nacional Autónoma de México.

Whitehead, Stephen M., and Frank J. Barrett, eds. 2001. *The Masculinities Reader.* Cambridge: Polity.

Wilson, Carter. 1995. *Hidden in the Blood: A Personal Investigation of AIDS in the Yucatán.* New York: Columbia University Press.

Wolf, Eric R. 1967. Review of three books by Oscar Lewis. *Current Anthropology* 8(5): 495–96.

World Bank. 1993. *World Development Report 1993: Investing in Health.* New York: Oxford University Press for the World Bank.

Wright, Robert. 1994. *The Moral Animal: Evolutionary Psychology and Everyday Life.* New York: Vintage Books.

Zavala de Cosío, María Eugenia. 1992. *Cambios de fecundidad en México y políticas de población.* Mexico City: El Colegio de México.

Zulawski, Ann. 1999. "New Trends in Studies of Science and Medicine in Latin America." *Latin American Research Review* 34(9): 241–51.

Index

Text:	10/14 Palatino
Display:	Univers Condensed Light 47, Bauer Bodoni
Compositor:	Binghamton Valley Composition, LLC
Printer and Binder:	Maple-Vail Manufacturing Group